Sappho's Sweetbitter S

'To me he seems as fortunate as the gods / this man, who sits opposite you / so close, listening to the sweet sound / of your voice / and your lovely laughter . . . For when I gaze at you, just for a moment / I can no longer speak / for my tongue has snapped, straightaway / a subtle fire runs beneath my flesh.'

The woman-made world described in Sappho's songs has been discussed and analysed for centuries. In her poetry the love of women for other women is lauded, and hymns are sung and pleas addressed to female gods.

The world of Sappho's lyrics at times seems to envisage the dreams of later women. In *Sappho's Sweetbitter Songs*, late twentieth-century theories of feminism, psychoanalysis and literary criticism are applied to Sappho's lyrics for the first time. The study re-creates and examines a voice that sings of the dreams and interactions of women, that tells of the bodies, rhythms and desires of the women of Sappho's circle. At the same time it offers an analysis of sexual difference, comparing the homoerotic lyrics of male poets of that era to those of Sappho.

Lyn Hatherly Wilson has taught Classics at Monash University, Australia. She now lectures in English at James Cook University. She also writes and edits poetry.

Sappho's Sweetbitter Songs

Configurations of female and male in ancient Greek Lyric

Lyn Hatherly Wilson

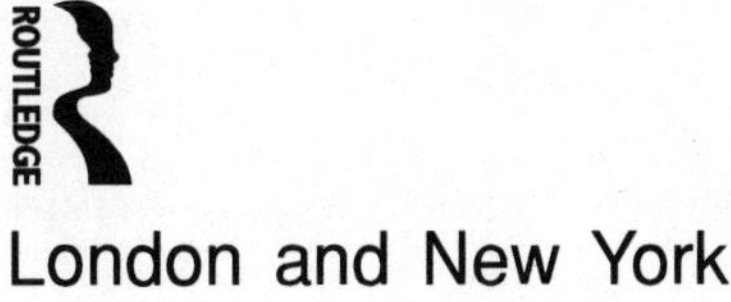

London and New York

First published 1996
by Routledge
11 New Fetter Lane, London EC4P 4EE

Simultaneously published in the USA and Canada
by Routledge
29 West 35th Street, New York, NY 10001

Routledge is an International Thomson Publishing company

Typeset in Sabon by
Florencetype Ltd, Stoodleigh, Devon
Printed and bound in Great Britain by
TJ Press Ltd, Padstow, Cornwall

British Library Cataloguing in Publication Data
A catalogue record for this book is available from the British Library

Library of Congress Cataloguing in Publication Data
Wilson, Lyn Hatherly, 1945–
Sappho's sweetbitter songs: configurations of female and male in ancient Greek lyric / Lyn Hatherly Wilson.
p. cm.
Includes bibliographical references and index.
1. Sappho–Criticism and interpretation. 2. Psychoanalysis and literature–Greece. 3. Feminism and literature–Greece. 4. Gender identity in literature. 5. Women and literature–Greece. 6. Authorship–Sex differences. 7. Sex role in literature.
I. Title.
PA4409.W54 1996
884′.01–dc20 95–37772
CIP

ISBN 0–415–12670–3 (hbk)
ISBN 0–415–12671–1 (pbk)

To my companions, my mother, sister, daughters, and the friends who encircle me with support and love.

Contents

Acknowledgements

I would like to acknowledge, with gratitude, the excellent advice given to me by Gerald Fitzgerald, Susan MacAlister and Peter Toohey. Special thanks also to Kerin Barry, Paula Carr, Joanne Gower, and Greg Gardiner, for the valuable time and expertise they contributed towards this project. And to my father, Will Hatherly, for his continued support. To J. J. Winkler, I offer thanks, posthumously, for the inspiration I received from his work on Sappho.

Introduction

More than two and a half millennia ago, a woman, Sappho of Lesbos, composed and sang songs telling of the prayers and rites, the eroticism and the dreams of women. The lyric songs she composed were well-crafted and emotionally evocative, sufficiently so to ensure their preservation through the centuries, and Sappho's renown throughout much of the ancient world. The world she inhabited, or at least the world represented in her songs, was a community of women, a musically oriented environment that appears detached, separate from 'public arenas'. She was one of the first women authors of recorded western culture[1] and her songs tell of the worship of female gods and the idealisation of beauty and erotic love. Fragmentary as these songs now are, they appear to have been constructed in a manner that was woman-centred, to give expression to a woman's desires and specificity. One of my desires is to map this woman-made world, to engage in an analysis of the imagistic and symbolic constructs contained within a distinctive poetic territory. In the process I would like to direct my/your gaze at another, more positive view of womankind, a counterbalance to offset the negative images that prevail in later western culture.

My investigation centres on sexual difference. It features a comparison of Sappho's songs or poems[2] with relevant examples of the lyric poetry[3] of other, male, authors composing songs between the seventh and fifth centuries BC. Some questions are prompted by the nature of my investigation. Did differences (and similarities) exist between the poetic constructs of a woman and those of men who were composing lyrics in a specific cultural and historical space? Have there been moments in the history of western civilisation when cultural conditions, such as segregation of the sexes, could provoke changes in the construction of sex/gender[4] differences? These questions site my discussion at the centre of current debates and dilemmas regarding male/female difference and the politically perilous process of comparativism.[5] Rather than proceeding in a way that could, as Rhode (1984: 6) suggests, 'inevitably, if inadvertently, flatten analysis', I hope that the comparative processes engaged upon, the questions raised by/in this work will in fact expand the range of enquiry. The intersection of a unique site of difference – the world of Sappho of Lesbos – with the proliferation of theories, on sex/gender difference and discourse, currently engaging a late twentieth-century western culture, is opportune and exciting. The period focused on, the seventh to fifth century BC and the place, ancient Greece, present a distinctive set of cultural characteristics, eminently suitable for an analysis of poetic representation and difference. Socially, linguistically, intellectually and artistically, the developments which took place during this period were dynamic and intriguing. I believe that in this differently divided context – a socio-cultural environment oriented towards oral rather than literate texts – there was space for the co-existence of two separate but interactive lyric traditions, one concerned with the desires and pre-occupations of women, another that was configured in relation to the predilections of men. This was a poetically oriented environment which initiated the first written lyrics of our culture and continued through the divergent strains of an extraordinary tradition.

In the course of my discussion, I look to the theories of women who are reconceptualising female specificity in the late twentieth century in Europe to elucidate Sappho's songs. Images of circles: of women, of singers, of songs, of recurring love, resonate through this analysis of a woman's voice and constructs. To these circles I would add another circle, one that unites Sappho's circle, or at least her songs about the circle, with women now. Although I am all too aware of the unfathomable interstice that separates 'then' from 'now', of the bulk of patriarchy dividing Sappho's world from the desires of later women, I dream of two time/spaces in western culture where women could formulate a woman-centred framework.

There are problems which attend every attempted analysis of ancient literature, particularly archaic manuscripts such as those of Sappho of Lesbos. One difficulty is the fragmentary state of the papyri, and the knowledge that although the collection we possess is slowly increasing, it comprises a small and not necessarily representative selection of a once munificent tradition. Parker (1993: 311) calls the text of Sappho a 'palimpsest', a precious collection of songs and fragments thickly overwritten with the comments of scholarly generations, in which 'the language is difficult, the society obscure'. The records that told of Sappho's existence, that attested perhaps to some individual and discursive coherence, sometime in that 'other' space called ancient Greece, are also in tatters. All we have are reports of statuary, coins and renown, the gossipy bits of news and/or legend provided by later, but relatively antique, commentators. And, of course, the information contained in her songs. These lyrical fragments have provided a fruitful basis for a great number of analyses of a historical, sociological and/or literary nature. To resurrect Sappho's life and her social context on the basis of her fragmentary songs has been the method employed by a 'time-honoured' tradition of scholarship which assumed that some exact and referential interface could be posited between a woman's life and her artistic constructions. The personal (I/you) voices that sing out of ancient lyrics encourage such ventures, and the positing of relationships and 'realities' which extend beyond the interactions implied in fragile texts that were/are essentially poetic. The links between the world re-constructed in Sappho's lyrics and some non-discursive 'reality', however, are necessarily destabilised and arbitrary. Parker (1993: 309) states that 'we know nothing about Sappho'. Taking into consideration the culturally specific and poetically oriented nature of songs which were constructed not for the transmission of biographical details but within the conventions of a particular genre, it seems that we must rely upon hypothesis – the suggestions of others and our own surmises – when discussing the life of Sappho.

Differences, between the lyric representations of Sappho and the male poets of her time, between me, a poet, but one constructed within the twentieth century and a poet constructed within and composing songs in the seventh to sixth century BC, are continually foregrounded by my discussion. Like duBois (1988: 18), 'I look with my feminist desire, as a fragmented, historically produced, subject-in-question, at the Greeks as others who can decenter our mythologies of sexual difference'. From the libraries of Hellenistic Greece to this time and place, commentators and scholars of various denominations have examined the extant texts of ancient Greece in search of a great variety of truths. The disparities in the results (including translations) which arise when male or female scholars from diverse backgrounds apply themselves to the same corpus of ancient authorship are, as duBois (1988: 26) has discovered, intriguing, and I allocate space to their investigation. Through the passage of time the signs or signifiers of 'then' have become detached from whatever they signify 'now', while the authority and coherence of the past have been destabilised and defiled. In this postmodernistic context, signifier has been officially detached from signified and authority and its claims have been undermined. 'Now' our attitudes and approaches to 'then' should also be distinctive. Within a deconstructed universe, should there be, ideally, space for the co-existence of different cultures, or even sexes, for the acceptance of a pluralistic condition which Owens (1983: 57) believes 'reduces us to being an other among others'? In this context some terms have also assumed a whole new range of meaning, and since I will be including the theories of some of the practitioners of these ideas, the differences in difference or *différance*[6] appear relevant.

Since its beginnings, classical studies has been a male-dominated field. More recently, a generation of women scholars has thought and written about the ancient world and their work reveals alternative and often distinctive perspectives. With the aura of privilege that their cultural allocation affords them, the male subjects of western culture have often represented and spoken for female, subjects-in-question, while the masculine subject has been constructed as sexually neutral and universal. The perspective evident behind the texts of the commentators who have contributed the bulk of traditional classical analyses confirms this orientation. It is resolutely male-centred, and set within the specifics of historical, cultural moments. Adapting this theoretical basis to a more woman-centred investigation is problematic. It has been suggested (by Arthur 1984: 47–52) that the logocentric, patriarchal structures which haunt the women of our culture were inaugurated in ancient Greece. Whether or not this assumption is entirely plausible, it provides an additional incentive for an analysis of sex/gender difference in the poetic representations of that anterior context. Some of the conditions pertaining to this alternative space and time appear to be particularly, culturally and linguistically, significant.

The world of Sappho of Lesbos has been nominated[7] as the site of a linguistic revolution, a movement between orality and literacy that disrupted the history of human communication. In archaic Greece, by all reports, texts were still formulated in accordance with oral modes and conventions, with the mnemonic sound patterns, the fluidity and flexibility characteristic of spoken rather than written language.[8] The poetic constructs of this time – the metrical, rhythmic units Sappho used to construct her lyrics, the music which accompanied and features intrinsically in them – appear to differ from later poetic constructions. Also of relevance is genre, the classification of kinds of antique poetic discourse, an activity which was formalised in the third century by a group of Hellenistic librarians and textualists who collected and collated the creations of past centuries and initiated a classical discipline. In the late twentieth century, the critical/theoretical frameworks employed in the analysis of representations of antiquity have expanded enormously under the impact of other 'disciplines': psychoanalytic, semiotic, linguistic, and feminist concepts and strategies.

At one time in ancient Greece, all thoughts worth recording, whether philosophical, scientific, religious or poetic, were constructed in dactylic hexameters. For librarians/textualists of the Hellenistic age the criteria which determined the allocation of poetic material into generic categories still centred on its metrical constituents. The categories which resulted from this retrospective classification – discrete categories for epic and lyric compositions, with lyric also separated into elegiac, iambic, melic (monodic) and melic (choral) strains – have, as Kirkwood affirms, been accepted and applied throughout the history of classical literature.[9] The genre of lyric poetry supposedly emerged in the seventh century BC as the vehicle of a new, individualistic form of expression (compared to the dignified style of epic songs). Kirkwood (1974: 2) reiterates two conventional definitions of Greek lyric poetry: one 'includes everything that is not epic . . . or dramatic', the other 'narrower use of the term describes what was in Greek of the classical period called *melos*, or "melic" poetry'. He goes on to nominate Archilochus as 'the first voice of the poetry of the individual man' (Kirkwood 1974: 23). Russo's (1974: 711) view on this subject is somewhat divergent. He expresses doubt about whether Archilochus was actually 'a pivot of change', and if in fact we can 'deny the likelihood of two separate genres, epic and lyric, each with its own traditions, developing side by side'.

Russo's remarks raise other questions concerning the nature of an oral lyric tradition, the question, for example, of whether the poets who contributed to it were both male and female. It seems possible that there were times when a definably female culture was sufficiently established to generate songs and genres which suited women's personal and cultural roles, and centred on the female gods they worshipped. It seems inconceivable that women would never have created songs to sing while they worked or grieved or worshipped their gods or celebrated/agonised over the important events of a woman's life: the advent of sexual maturity, love, weddings and the first sexual experience, or the birth or death of a child. And that these songs would not have been organised, however privately and informally, into generic categories which related to these events and/or occasions and altered subtly with the mutations of other cultural constructs. In seventeenth-century England where Aphra Behn was reintroducing a female specificity into literature, Greer (1988: 11–12) considers there were some genres that were considered to be 'always, everywhere female': 'poetic instructions from a dying mother to the child she cannot rear' or 'poems accepting child loss'.

Presumably women of every culture commemorate the joys and losses of female existence with poetry or songs, creations which may be less formalised or less public, some of which are constructed in memorable rhythms and genres that are often dismissed as popular or folk-culture. Fragments of such songs linger, singing mysteriously of women's desires and experiences in genres that cannot be easily fitted into male schemata. Lyric poetry, a broad and flexible genre with characteristics such as brevity, euphony and an emotional and personal emphasis, is a category that manages to assimilate these woman-made songs. Friedrich (1978: 110) makes the point that women on Lesbos in Sappho's lifetime and earlier had relatively high status in a community in which poetry was a significant aspect of daily life. He thinks that 'Lesbos may have been the most distinguished in what . . . was an early pan-Hellenic "woman's culture" of colloquial poetry whose brilliance is hinted at in our evidence'. In this 'woman's culture', suggested by a passage from Homer (*Iliad* 9.128–30), Lesbian women are praised for their beauty and skill. The traces of a flourishing poetic tradition which included

Sappho and is implicated in her songs appear to have included some specifically female genres. It seems to have been constructed by female creators, and transmitted by women's voices through the centuries. It tells of a private world that interacted with a larger circle of male/public generic and other constructs. While such a private tradition appears to have included some female genres, it also incorporated elements of male poetry, tropes, metres, themes, etc., and used them in a manner that highlights differences and similarities.

The split between the *polis* or public sector, where male poetic pronouncements are formulated and audited, and the *oikos* or women's territory to which that public sector appears to stand in direct opposition, is well-defined in Greek literature. Discussing Sappho's appropriation of Homeric characteristics, Winkler (1981: 68–9) proposes that since 'men's culture is truly public, displayed as the governing norm of social interaction "in the streets," it is accessible to women as well as men', so 'women are in the position of knowing two cultures where men know only one'. If there are, as Winkler suggests, two somewhat disparate cultures existing simultaneously in ancient Greece, are there also two lyric traditions? Traditions which are to some extent separate and distinct but which correspond with each other through the usual processes of imitation and innovation in the common context of lyric poetry. In this way Sappho could extract base elements, metrical units, themes or phrases from epic and reuse them, or a later poet such as Anacreon could select one of Sappho's songs and create his own version of an erotic/religious scenario, albeit differently. Lyric poetry appears to act as an interface between antique public/private territories that share some genres, and some interests.[10]

Questions of difference, between constructs of the late twentieth century and those of ancient Greece, between conceptual categories such as gender and sex, between the poetic representations of Sappho and those of the male poets of antiquity, are issues I focus upon. Gender is a term which refers to the construction, representation, identification and classification of masculine and feminine characteristics. If we agree with de Lauretis (1987: 5), then 'gender is not sex . . . but the representation of each individual in terms of a particular social relation which pre-exists the individual in terms of a particular *conceptual* and rigid (structural) opposition of two biological sexes'. This statement does not exclude the possibility, however, that there are links between these characteristics and the biological sex of male or female subjects, that biological sex is implicated in the cultural determination of the appropriate gender identity.[11] The term 'gender' was used only to denote grammatical gender categories in inflected languages such as ancient Greek, or more arbitrary 'natural' classifications in uninflected tongues. The significance and conceptual value of 'gender', and the use of this term as an analytical or critical concept has increased dramatically over the past few decades. Due to the interest shown by feminists and the influx of psychological, sociological and critical theories, the notion of 'gender' carries considerable theoretical weight. 'Gender' is pervasive, it is represented and/or manipulated in a majority of the texts which constitute our cultural heritage. But the distinction, or lack of it, between gender and sexual difference has remained, as Gatens demonstrates, a complex and contentious issue. This is an issue which is not adequately resolved by the idea that sex is a biological category while gender is a social one, since this typically bipolar construction appears to imply a division, somewhat arbitrarily, into two entirely discrete categories.[12] Throughout my discussion sex and gender are both treated as constructs which are tainted with historical and cultural specificity, which cannot be accessed without mediation or exist independently as biological entities.

Gender now operates as one of the systems of signification which enable identification and assessment in this particular framework. Like other human-made systems or structures (genre for example), it is organised on a hierarchical basis; some gender categories or characteristics tend to be valued above others. In contemporary society, and also in antiquity, masculine behaviour enacted by a male subject is perceived differently, valorised inordinately. Even in discourses where the symbolic body is substituted for the anatomical, the male symbol, the phallus, remains the transcendental signifier. But how do these sex/gender inequities, or the late twentieth-century frameworks which examine and comment upon them, relate to lyric poetry in Greece in the seventh to the fifth century BC?

If women thought or spoke out in a feministic manner in antiquity, then their statements have not lasted. There are no overt traces of them in the extant lyric songs where women such as Sappho are represented as speakers or singers, who address themes that could be designated as woman-centred. These songs do not appear to be politically motivated, or to give voice to women's oppression. The female protagonists of dramatic works – Aristophanic caricatures such as Lysistrata or Praxagora, Aeschylus' striking portrayal of Clytaemnestra, Sophocles' Antigone, and many of the heroines of Euripidean drama – do sometimes speak of common female interests,[13] and behave like liberated women (or possibly alternative men). At times the mythical basis of these works, epic poetry, also uses and confuses the sexual stereotypes which appear to be part of some intrinsic theoretical framework. Although these representations provide evidence of the conscious knowledge and manipulation of gender characteristics in the ancient world, the Greeks of that time seemingly have no conception of 'gender' as we understand it.

Conversely, sexual difference was discussed often, and even in the seventh century BC it is constructed into a socio-cultural matrix. Lloyd (1966: 90) comments on 'a stylistic trait which is common throughout early Greek literature from Homer onwards', the use of 'polar expressions', couplets such as mortals and immortals; men and women. In a broader context Cornford (1957: 65) tells us that 'the prototype of all opposition or contrariety is the contrariety of sex'. There is a tendency in a great many societies throughout the ages to classify not only sex, but all kinds of phenomena in this way, in oppositional pairs. This tendency appears to be one of the patterns which humans continually fall into, a natural ordering mechanism converting experiential phenomena into a linguistic framework. Although in ancient Greece male authors fall into these constructions, Sappho's treatment of the conventional bipolar oppositions that represent the joy/angst of love and life reveals some alternative trends. Lloyd notes (1966: 28) that 'Greek writers seem to have a special fondness for coupling terms in this way', and he cites the Pythagoreans, Plato, Aristotle, and some others, as examples. The male poets of antiquity also demonstrate a decided fondness for this construct.

One of the most fundamental, frequently recurring dualisms is the male/female dyad.[14] Aristotle's (*Metaphysics* 101 1b 18ff) statement that 'it is true of contrary terms as a whole, that one of each pair is a positive term, the other a (mere) privation', is particularly relevant when applied to this pair. Aristotle (*Generation of Animals* 737a 27ff) considered 'the female to be like a deformed male', and later Freud asserted that women were nothing more than castrated men, and that it was the presence or absence of the phallus that signified the primary distinction between the sexes, the phallus that was the marker of subjectivity and sexuality.[15] So actually and symbolically, whether the differentiation is concerned with sexual, gender or psycho-sexual difference, the female has been assigned a negative position while the male has taken up a privileged, positive position. The question of whether this dichotomous construct (among others) was inaugurated in ancient Greece, at some earlier stage, either before or soon after the first written texts appeared, is one which I feel should be considered. Two and a half millennia after the Pythagoreans compiled their list of essential polarities, Cixous and Clément (1986: 63–4) write: 'thought has always worked through opposition . . . through dual, hierarchical oppositions . . . [is it a] fact that Logocentricism subjects thought – all concepts, codes and values – to a binary system, related to "the" couple, man/woman?'

Apart from the man/woman dyad, there are other pairs of binary oppositions which are used frequently and exert considerable influence on theories of representation and sexual difference. In Platonic dialogues there are arguments in which pairs of different kinds (eg. being/not-being, one/many) operate as mutually exclusive and exhaustive alternatives. Greek philosophers (and scientists and physicians) often attempted to contain the universe with dichotomous pairs such as: earth/water, atoms/void, love/strife, etc. By now they are accepted as 'natural'. The distinction which Plato effected between his immanent, immutable ideals and the imperfect complexity of the world to which they distantly relate – the split which privileges a metaphysical world over the more ephemeral territory of bodies and experience – has had long-lasting consequences. Women are implicated in the representation or reconstruction of physical/emotional existence. Some relatively modern philosophers (ie. Simmel and Schopenhauer) have proposed that women are not capable of rational thought or reason, that, from a position outside the subject–object dyad which determines identity and rationality they merely intuit knowledge and/or exist within an immediate, present time–space or the 'reality' of experiential existence.[16] Men apparently conceive glorious ideas, or produce perfect, metaphysical worlds, while women – bestial, irrational creatures – conceive and produce only the next generation. The man/woman, mind/body, reason/emotion, symbolic/reality oppositions which relegated women to a position of irrational, purely physiological inferiority, still flourish.[17] Perhaps the Greeks initiated the process, but the male subjects of late twentieth-century western culture continue to construct, or maintain, a symbolic order which excludes or devalues the 'other' sex, womankind, in logocentric systems that rely on a logic of identity based on the exclusion and binary polarisation of difference.

One of the basic concepts of psychoanalytic theory is the distinction made between this form of psycho-sexuality – which is distinct from and more complex than mere genitality and/or biological drives – and more physiological notions of sexuality. In the terms of this psycho-sexual concept, female subjects take up a position in a Freudian/Lacanian framework that renders them symbolically non-phallic and therefore unequal. In an extended psychoanalytic partnership which could perhaps be compared to the philosophical association of Plato and Aristotle, Lacan has attempted to explicate and advance certain aspects of the work of Freud. Rather than analysing how men and women do or should live as sexually differentiated beings, Lacan has concentrated on elucidating the question of how the human subject is constructed. The theory which evolved from these efforts – augmented by Saussurean linguistic precepts and the idea that the unconscious is itself a sign-system, one which is mediated by language – affirmed that humans are born into language and that it is within the terms of language that the human subject is constructed. Within the dictates of this theory, historically produced binarism is merely one component of a larger symbolic framework mediated by the linguistic system. In this framework, the symbolic phallus changes but it does, as far as Lacanian theory is concerned, appear to remain pre-eminent.[18]

Or does it? Page duBois reminds us that in Lacanian thought, the phallus, that arbitrary over-rated symbol of logocentricism and the patriarchal order, becomes a commodity, a linguistic term, one which is transferable and is therefore not necessarily the property of one sex or one class. While it remains 'a bit of binarism', 'a new form of the old metaphysical justification of gender hierarchy', duBois (1988: 15) feels that we can now see not only 'the ideological basis, the metaphysical overvaluation of the signifier of male supremacy', but also 'the historical specificity of psychoanalysis as a discourse'. By revealing that this form of discourse, like all others, relies on language techniques and by overtly acknowledging the linguistic elements in psychoanalytic contexts, Lacan made these contexts, and the structuralist concepts which they articulate, more acceptable and accessible to feminist theorists. The concept of linguistic determinism, the notion that as human subjects we are constructed by/into a language which determines perception and thus reality,[19] also appears arbitrary, another male metaphysical creation that has been amalgamated into some store of accepted wisdom. Linked to this concept is the belief that political control is founded and maintained primarily by linguistic means, which men have appropriated and exploited in order to maintain power over women. Lacan posits the perpetual and ahistorical nature of such concepts, but the question of whether they are in fact anchored to a particular historical and cultural specificity must be considered. And with it an obvious corollary: were the women of ancient Greece positioned within an analogous framework and/or subordinated by a similarly deterministic combination of political/linguistic control?

In his discussion of the public/private split in an ancient Greek context, Winkler (1981: 68–77) proposes a model in which the larger circle of male territory encloses a smaller, internally discrete, but externally mobile, sector of women's territory. Presumably these two socio-sexual sectors are each bounded by the phallocentric codes, the language and symbols of the male circle, by the 'law-of-the-father'. But the female inhabitants of the 'other' more private circle possess, in the terms of Winkler's model, some advantages, since women, as a necessarily bilingual minority, have access to the literature of both worlds, to the publicly displayed products of male culture as well as knowledge of the more mysterious constructs of the private female sphere. Men, on the other hand, have no desire to learn the language of the minority group, and thus know only of the linguistic products of the public sphere. Therefore women are able to cultivate a form of 'double-consciousness', a perspective which is woman-centred but takes on some aspects of the male world. Winkler demonstrates this by isolating the differences which a Sapphic perspective produces in some typically epic passages. Through the interaction of male texts with this double/female-consciousness, a subtle metamorphosis is initiated, altering the significance and structure of the original discourse. Other commentators also remark upon the transformations which result.[20] Whether or not this transformational process is consciously subversive, as Winkler suggests, or is merely the result of a clash between male-centred constructions and a female subject, remains to be seen. The codes and constructs of the public world are dislocated and reconstructed into new forms by Sappho's treatment.

In relation to Winkler's model, I suggest that this bilingual, but to some extent separate world, and the female consciousness generated within it, could construct a symbolic world that is formulated on more female, collective lines. Culturally, the conditions pertaining to this time appear uniquely suited to the production of a form of female specificity. The women who appear in Sappho's songs seem to have lived within a predominantly female environment where even love was female-to-female or homoerotic. Constructed within this environment, the poetic texts which are extant create or re-present a world according to a female perspective, in order to transmit and maintain a woman-centred culture. Outside this community, in the public sphere, looms a phallocentric symbolic context that is perhaps similar to the symbolic world posited by Lacan, a social and signifying order that was founded on paternal authority. The interactions between these two cultural/symbolic entities are uncertain, but it seems probable that the territories involved were differently formulated and were more sexually segregated than twentieth-century western socio-cultural contexts. If a Sapphic symbolic world existed in the dim context of archaic consciousness, however, it can only be inferred through the traces that linger in her poetry, the reiteration of particular images, the frequent references to female gatherings and experiences. While an all-embracing Lacanian-type structure appears to dominate the order of law, language and exchange in both ancient and modern societies despite the differences separating these two sites of western culture.

In the twentieth century, Lacan can posit the existence of a symbolic world that is revealed in the discourse of the unconscious, that is linguistically based and allots every subject, male or female, a position in a phallocentric framework. In the seventh century BC myth provided an outlet for the repressed and/or conscious needs of each member of a community and was an expression of collective unconscious that incorporated the dreams and fantasies of past cultures.[21] Drawing selectively upon these myths, adding the murmurs of women's culture sung by women to women through the ages, Sappho constructed a symbolic world that articulated and reformulated the dreams, fears, desires and rites of a female community. In Sappho's world men, rather than women, were represented as 'other' and erotic interaction was a vital factor, adding to the sensuality that reverberated throughout and was translated into the patterning of poetic discourse, into rhythms, metaphors and images.

For our culture, Sappho's songs represent not the immanent dreams and desires of a community, or the form of oral storage facility that Havelock (1986: 90) believed was essential for the transmission of information, but aesthetically pleasing, historically intriguing, poetic artefacts. Some features of the world contained within these songs reinforce twentieth-century ideas of the 'feminine',[22] since they refer to characteristics that have been traditionally associated with women. The emotional emphasis, the physical exchanges in many of the dreamlike scenes Sappho constructs, the flowers and metaphorically female fruits, small birds, music, perfume, headbands and clothes that cluster within Sapphic songs, conform to a single, stereotypical column of a twentieth-century list of dual, hierarchised oppositions. This intersection, of the constructs of two specific, but disparate cultural frameworks, sets up a comparison which is, I believe, misleading. The world constructed by/into Sappho's lyrics is distinctive. The socio-poetic world represented by Sappho appears to be a place where female subjects – gods, mythic figures and mortals – were attributed positive qualities. Unlike twentieth-century western culture, where no specificity is accorded to the female. As far as a Sapphic system of values can be inferred, these women and the qualities associated with them, particularly love, beauty and close relationships, were all-important. The same attributes are, of course, devalued in later, more logocentrically structured contexts, perhaps because they are associated with the feminine. Poetic and symbolic dimensions, as Plato's philosophical constructions indicate, tend to be idealised, composed of a few significant elements that relate ambivalently to their counterparts in the world of imperfect experience.

Sappho's world presents us with a site of difference, a place where distinctive, if stereotypically 'feminine', values can attain prominence, where the interactions between female subjects, both mortal and immortal, appear to differ from the exchanges of a later, pervasively phallocentric universe. Here women direct their gaze not at a desired object – as male participants of a modern scopic economy appear to gaze – in a detached and objective manner,[23] but face-to-face in an attitude of mutuality not unlike the ideal form of lesbian activity described by de Beauvoir (1975: 465) in *The Second Sex*. The tactics of the public world – represented by poetic modes of social control and stigmatism such as praise and blame, or rhetorical or philosophical tropes – also appear in Sappho's broken songs, but their representation seems distinctive. Frequently the mode of discourse reveals a 'delicate divergency' (Spacks 1975: 5), subtle dislocations and new significances that distinguish it from the utterances of the male poets. Despite the apparent woman-centredness of Sappho's songs there has never been an identifiably female tradition of expression or a formalised language in western culture, so women have instead appropriated or subverted elements of a discourse that Irigaray (1985: 149) calls 'the master discourse: the one that prescribes, in the last analysis, the organisation of language, the one that lays down the law to others'. In her own representations Irigaray proceeds duplicitously or double-mindedly, using textual strategies to mimic and in that way destabilise the paradigmatic constructs of male authors. Like some other twentieth-century women writers, she also furthers the process and attempts to write in a way which is consciously woman-centred.

Irigaray and other French feminists work against a Lacanian background where the marker of sexual difference, of lack or presence, is the phallus. It is presumed that a subject is socially, linguistically and libidinally positioned on one side of a conceptual universe. Within this symbolic order, women and their representations are fixed linguistically and culturally (since language corresponds with reality) by sign, image and meaning into a negative position. The textual techniques and strategies these feminists employ, both creatively and critically, to question relations between language/representation and subjectivity owe some debt to the writings of Derrida. By utilising Derrida's deconstructive strategies, strategies which challenge logocentricism and the framework of binary oppositions operating therein, French feminists have formulated reading techniques designed to undermine the metaphysical basis of a culture which they consider to be logocentric and phallocentric in orientation.[24] I am less concerned with their critical techniques than with their efforts to isolate or formulate language which is in some way/s woman-centred, and attempts to exceed or bypass the formidable laws and patterns of logocentric thought. Irigaray, Cixous and Kristeva use metaphors of women's bodies, and write about symbolic, imaginary worlds which are anti-logocentric, specifically female. Since their representations inform the theoretical framework I inhabit, I would like to project their theories about women's language on to the poetic representations of a woman singing in a differently constructed world at the other edge of a circle of western culture: Sappho of Lesbos.

In the orally/poetically centred context of antiquity, both male and female poets (and other authors) constructed their works in accordance with, or on the basis of, a wide range of established forms. One of the most popular of these forms was ring-composition. Irigaray's texts are also deliberately circular. Beginning and ending indefinitely, resonating with ambiguities, they afford multiple interpretations. In this way they match the plurality of Irigaray's (1986: 64) symbolic representation of the female sex, the two lips which are always touching, joining, but with 'neither subject nor object'. In the current cultural context, Irigaray believes that woman is indefinable, but using the future conditional tense she posits a world where there is space for a definition of women. In this space women's 'style' or 'writing' would be diffusive, but unified: 'simultaneity is its "proper aspect" . . . it is always fluid . . . its style resists and explodes every firmly established form, figure, idea or concept' (Irigaray 1986: 64). Unlike male discourse which is singular, logical and restrictive, alien to the 'other' sex, this discourse is ideally pluralistic and polysematic. It is also potentially capable of articulating a woman's thoughts, her imaginary worlds, and her desires.

Have women's representations of desire changed perceptibly over the time span of western culture, throughout the passage of historically specific but interfaced conceptual frameworks? Were they substantially different, or at least less submerged or repressed, two and a half millennia ago, when the first written texts of our culture were being produced? It seems that 'sexuality' then differed substantially from 'sexuality' now, in the heterosexually oriented and divided world of the twentieth century, a cultural framework which the editors of *Before Sexuality* label 'sex-centred'. Many of the contributors to *Before Sexuality* make the point that 'sexual meanings and practices in the ancient Greek world were constituted differently from our own'.[25] One major difference is the predominantly homoerotic nature of the sexual interaction represented in the songs of the Greek lyric poets. Representations of female desire are relatively rare in this homoerotic lyric territory, but Sappho frequently composed songs about the desire of women. Whether or not the women of ancient Greece could express their identity and desire in a manner that could be defined as woman-centred is uncertain. In the twentieth century, Irigaray believes this expression is not possible.[26]

Working within, rather than against a Lacanian theoretical background, Kristeva conceptualises (sexual) pleasure or *jouissance*[27] in her textual practices. Lacan considers that 'there is a jouissance . . . a jouissance of the body which is, if the expression be allowed, beyond the phallus' (Lacan 1975: 65) and each of these feminists makes use of this expression of excess in her own fashion. In my analysis of female desire, I explore the possibility that Sappho exceeded this phallic threshold. The 'semiotic' impulses Kristeva (1976: 64) conceptualises are particularly dominant when 'the semiotic explodes in an excessive, uncontrolled *jouissance* of madness . . . of the "holiness" of transgressive ecstasy . . . and of poetry'. At such times they are capable of contradicting, undermining the symbolic and its systems of signification and control.

Cixous's work, her effusive attempts to 'write the body', and to encourage other women to write about themselves, and their 'sexuality', appears to resonate with an erotic/sensual emphasis similar to that which reverberates through Sappho's songs. Like Irigaray's poetically ambivalent celebrations of sexual difference, these writings announce the plurality, fluidity and diffusiveness which is ideally manifested in feminine language. Breathless, trembling, writing and voice 'entwined and interwoven . . . Her discourse, even when "theoretical" or political, is never simple or linear or "objectivised", universalised' (Cixous 1981: 92). Despite her spirited rhetoric, however, Cixous (1981: 105) also believes that women remain trapped in symbolic silence, as they have been since the 'Dawn of phallocentricism' in ancient Greece (before or after the seventh century BC?), awaiting 'the invention of a *new, insurgent* writing' (Cixous 1981: 97). To displace or subvert (since a feminine text cannot be more than subversive) this apparently incontrovertible order, and the hierarchical oppositions on which it is based, Cixous (1988: 18) urges women to 'try as quickly as possible to abandon these binary distinctions which never make any sense'. Oppressive patriarchal schemes such as these should be replaced with 'multiple, heterogeneous *difference*' (Cixous 1981: 105), and should be destabilised by allowing neither pole (man/woman, conscious/unconscious, etc.) to assume positive characteristics, to become the centre of presence.

A male subverter of signifying practices, Derrida, has supplied, through his own textual practices, strategies which effectively mine gaps and irregularities present within the 'text of patriarchy', and both Cixous and Irigaray use these strategies deconstructively to question the logical, grammatical structures of male discourse. One of the textual strategies favoured by Cixous is Derrida's disordering, distancing notion of *différance*. *Différance* is a neologism coined by Derrida which, to quote Norris (1986: 32), 'cannot be reduced to any single, self-identical meaning'. Its function is to produce within the texts or signifiers to which it is applied a similar, pluralistic state, an apparently endless displacement of meaning, and to initiate a differential excess which 'shakes' totalitarian systems such as binary oppositions or structuralism.[28]

Difference, in its diverse forms, is my primary focus. The difference between spoken and written discourse, or the techniques intrinsic to oral poetry and those involved in the making of later and more literate poetic constructs. Differences between those metrical systems, and themes, chosen or initiated by the male poets of antiquity, and those which Sappho elected to use, appear equally relevant. Also of consequence are the frameworks of early antiquity and those distinctive constructs which formulate the attitudes of twentieth-century commentators. Cixous (1988: 14) proposes that poetry provides a link of some sort with the unconscious, that 'it is in poetic writing that something of the mystery and continuity of life can appear, through grammatical subversion, through a certain liberty taken inside language, with regard to the law of gender'. It would also appear appropriate to question this proposal. The manifest difference/s between symbolic/imaginary worlds created by a woman (as representations of female specificity) and those created and published by men feature as another interesting phenomenon. The divergent attitudes to, and assessment of, the poetic output of men and that of women also deserve space. These issues are contextualised within an analysis of the lyric songs of Sappho. Perhaps within the fragmentary texts of a woman who composed and sang lyrics in the ancient world, and some of the male poets who were working in the same genre, reside differences and/or similarities which may facilitate an approach to some conclusions about the construction of poetic/sexual difference in this anterior space.

Other, more formal matters, such as the translations I refer to, should be mentioned at this stage. In the main, translations of Sappho's songs are my own. I use Campbell's relatively unaugmented and unadorned translations in *Greek Lyric*, to assist me at times towards a basic Greek/English rendition to which I could then apply my poetic skills. One of my desires was to produce a correct and suitably attractive version of the texts, a version that also complemented my comments about Sappho's lyrics.

The poetic partnership between Sappho and myself, attenuated as it is – the common ground which I, as a woman and a poet feel that I share with Sappho – should perhaps also be elucidated more fully. To date, all my major academic projects have focused on women, both modern and ancient, and have involved analyses of the poetic constructs of these women. I also write and publish poetry, often about the experiences and specificity of women, edit a poetry journal, assist other people with the intricacies of poetic composition, formally in workshops, and less formally at other times, judge poetry competitions and address groups of women writers and artists. Despite this poetic orientation, I do not compose or sing songs which celebrate and/or tell of rituals that involve an association of women, or articulate praise or prayers addressed to a female god. I do feel, however, that some link exists between myself and Sappho, a tenuous, woman-oriented connection that furthers my own discussion and analysis of her songs, and that in some way/s bridges the space that separates 'then' from 'now'.

The order of the following chapters is not sequential and, although at times the discussion undertaken in one chapter does lead into the material covered in the next, the chapters are relatively autonomous and are relatable more to the chapter headings than to an all-embracing structure. These headings do, however, encompass subjects or themes which I consider are significant to the general context of Sappho's songs and to my interpretation of those songs.

I begin with some discussion of Aphrodite, the female god of love, the god who appears, and is appealed to, most often in Sappho's songs. An analysis of textual relationships and sexual comparisons leads into some discussion of a mortal/immortal relationship which appears uncommonly, and unlogocentrically, close.

In chapter two, songs of love follow on from this view of Aphrodite, and her son Eros, the gods who were thought to initiate and/or manipulate erotic affairs in ancient Greece. Sappho's version of Aphrodite, and of love, is consistently female and revisionist, and her mode of expression points up a contrast with similar homoerotic episodes in male lyric songs. The form of erotic desire that is represented in Sappho's lyrics, the woman-to-woman love that has shocked/fascinated later scholars, is intriguingly distinctive. So in chapter three I proceed to investigate the specifics of a woman's desire and her response to, and treatment of, the site of sexuality, the body. Chapter four looks at another related and significant female matter, the contentious subject of virginity, and its representation in Sapphic songs. Beauty, of women, song and 'nature', is one of the central issues in Sappho's songs, and in chapter five I examine the unusual perspective revealed by her songs and the difference in gazes exchanged between women, as opposed to those directed by a male subject at a female object. The focus of religious, erotic and ritualistic interactions, the group of women that is often referred to as Sappho's circle, and the specifics of inter-relations between women, is the topic of the next chapter. This subject leads, in chapter seven, into more detailed discussion of the memorable and timeless rituals enacted within the circle, of the cyclic nature of 'woman's time'. In chapter eight I analyse Sappho's representations of the ritual which sometimes ends this female-oriented existence – weddings – which feature extraordinarily beautiful brides. These weddings are semi-public affairs, signifying as they do a transition between female and male territories, and Sappho's epithalamia and other songs appear also to feature in both these territories, competing with the poetic products of both public and private worlds, products which earned lasting renown for their creators. The two penultimate chapters deal with such matters as fame, poetic traditions, and a form of honour which is definably female. The concluding chapter examines the symbolic constructs which feature and recur most often in Sappho's songs, as well as in the preceding chapters. Again I engage in a process which compares these constructs and the world which they themselves construct, with other, later, symbols and symbolic worlds. My desire, however, is not just to compare, but to map, to re-present the woman-made world of Sappho of Lesbos.

Chapter 1

Aphrodite

Representations of the gods appear so frequently in Sappho's extant songs that it has been suggested that this community of women was dedicated to a religious cult.[1] Amongst invocations to the Graces, Muses, Hera and occasional references to male gods such as Hermes, one god figures most often and most significantly. Aphrodite, god of erotic love, craft and persuasion, is effectively reconstructed by Sappho's poetry into a figure with poetic, symbolic, even visual dimensions. In this many-sided format Aphrodite or Cypris features in a larger symbolic framework intrinsic in Sappho's poetry. This framework also centres on Aphrodisian characteristics: beauty, love and associated symbols such as the flowers that decorate her worshippers. Although it draws upon some constituents and mythic/poetic constructions of the public arena, this world and this representation of Aphrodite seem to be distinctively Sapphic and pervasively woman-centred. In Greek antiquity, hymns worshipping the gods and reports of their words and deeds were still formulated in the metres of an oral tradition. By then religious institutions were one of the few arenas in which women could act with some autonomy.

Was there a time when the status of female divinities of the Greek pantheon and their antecedents in Old Europe, Sumer and Egypt was more prestigious than it appears in later and more male-centred constructions?[2] Did Aphrodite have her beginnings in such a time and evolve as a deity created, to some extent, for and by women? Some of the female gods of other, geographically and culturally contiguous regions, the Sumerian Inanna, the many Semitic Ishtars and Ishtar-type figures and the Phoenician Astarte for example, share many of the characteristics and symbols associated with Aphrodite: eroticism, fertility, astrality, goldenness, flowers, fruits, birds and water.[3] The worship of a powerful female god of love indicates/incites conspicuous differences in cultural and religious practices and attitudes; approval of female eroticism for example, or veneration of the symbols and stereotypes associated with that god and the women who dedicate themselves to her. Friedrich (1978: 103) has noted that many of the traditional, and Sapphically endowed, Aphrodisian characteristics fit perfectly, if stereotypically, into a 'feminine' gender scheme. I would add that, at least in a Sapphic framework, their value is paramount. Friedrich (1978: 110) also mentions the prominence of a tradition of women's poetry that flourished in archaic Lesbos and is evidenced by Sappho's songs. That evidence, the extant songs of Sappho, focuses on and re-creates this god suitably, beautifully, endowing her with poetic immortality, and with an accessible, erotic and powerful persona.

Sappho's prayer to Aphrodite, her only complete extant song, features an unusual combination of traditional form and idiosyncratic treatment. Genre-wise it is irregular; Kirkwood (1974: 111) cites it as the one 'example we have in monodic lyric of the cletic hymn'. This is only one aspect of its difference, its generic, genderic unaccountability. Sappho 1 features a woman's voice singing songs or prayers usually heard in a public arena, using the language of rhetoric and cult, but telling of past and present erotic experience, and of her close relationship with an immortal. Kirkwood (1974: 111) considers that 'the tone and the matter of fr. 1 are alien to worship'. In my opinion Greek religion is replete not with the dogma and creed we are accustomed to, but with mythical episodes glorifying and demonstrating the power of gods and their interactions with humankind. Sappho's prayer fits this criterion, just as its form duplicates the traditional sequence. It is a hymn which demands, confirms religious faith, but this poetic dedication, and the artistic techniques which model it, are constructed on woman-centred lines. Certainly there are few songs from male poets which resemble this dramatic, confessional, hymnal articulation of a singular version of eros. The scenario gives an impression of a prayer from suppliant to god, and the dialogue between these apparently unequal participants, one assured, empowered, the other ostensibly humble, reinforces this illusion.

Constructed in Sapphic stanzas, a metrical pattern which falls away on the final line of each stanza and is particularly satisfying to the ear, this song uses all Sappho's euphonic tactics. Aurally and orally it flows musically (almost sensually), into gentle patterns, into distinct and thematically appropriate sequences of sound. Were its metrical and rhythmic components chosen by Sappho from a range of traditional Lesbian genres to fit a woman-oriented occasion because they were appropriate for the representation of female experience? Or did she adapt existing patterns, reshape them into what appears to be a distinctive mode of expression? Sappho apparently chose her consonants carefully, and considered which vowels would interact best in repetitive combinations that achieve the alliterative and musical effect she desired. It is noticeable that hard consonants such as β were eschewed, while liquids and vowels incorporating α and ο sounds proliferate, adding to the fluid movement, the mellifluousness of a distinctive mode of composition. Other oral features – repetition, rhyme and assonance – also contribute favourably to both the sense and sound of this erotic/cletic hymn. Whether by design or unconscious borrowing, the song also seems aurally and mythically reminiscent of Homeric verse. Another characteristic of oral poetry, a feature of its mnemonic design, is the manner in which rhythmic sequences, epithets and formulaic phrasing can be transferred from one context to another. It was customary for Greek poets to reuse these segments, along with the themes of oral verse and, in the process, to redefine them in line with contemporary trends. Arguably, Sappho 1, as a synthesis of old and new, a blend of male language and female creativity – the female appropriation and conversion of some elements of male culture – represents a remarkable illustration of this process.

The language of the first stanza, the invocation that forms the first stage of a traditional tripartite structure, is formal and elaborate, textually analogous to invocations from epics and hymns made by men.

ποικιλόθρον' ἀθανάτ' Αφρόδιτα,
παῖ Δίος δολόπλοκε, λίσσομαί σε,
μή μ' ἄσαισι μηδ' ὀνίαισι δάμνα,
4 πότνια, θῦμον,

Throned in intricate splendour, deathless Aphrodite
child of Zeus, charm-fashioner, I entreat you,
do not, with grief and bitterness,
4 subdue my spirit, Mistress,

Men are more likely to address their pleas to male gods, as when Achilles solicits Zeus (*Iliad* 16.233–48), for the purpose of immortal intervention in a human battle. Sappho is composing within the frame of lyric, not epic, conventions, but Winkler (1981: 67) feels that she is 'articulating her own experience in traditional (male) terms'. He also suggests that 'Sappho's use of Homeric passages is a way of allowing us, even encouraging us, to approach her consciousness as a woman and poet reading Homer.' It seems to me that her creation of cult-type epithets, 'ποικιλόθρον' (1.1) and 'δολόπλοκε' (1.2), presents an illustration of this conjunction of male/female cultures. They are words which – in a careful reproduction of the correct phraseology – identify one particular mythological construct of Aphrodite. This divinity appeared to provide a focus for the Sapphic community. Her characteristic attributes and persona accorded with those of the author as well as relating to the singer's present predicament. Just as Zeus was the god of thunder, an awesome symbol of male hierarchical power, Aphrodite was the female symbol or force (the male symbol more frequently represented in male poetry was Eros) who incited/controlled erotic emotion.

The epithets used to describe her in Sappho 1 are not only idiosyncratic, a departure from traditional titles, they are also slightly duplicitous or ambiguous, each weaving double images of craft, intricacy and subtlety, an example perhaps of Sappho's many-mindedness.[4] Burnett translates them as 'blossom-clad' and 'snare-weaving', Page considers that they mean 'richly-enthroned' and 'weaver of wiles', differences which are reflected in each commentator's interpretation. Whether this Sapphic version of Aphrodite was in fact 'a richly devious divinity' (Burnett 1983: 249) or traditionally empowered as would be expected in an ordinary 'imitation of that type of ritual prayer' (Page 1955: 16) is significant. There is no doubt however, that for the singer, whose spirit is reported to have been subdued, once again, by the 'grief and bitterness' (1.3) of love, Aphrodite was the appropriate god to alleviate her suffering. Aphrodite was also represented as being the cause of these pangs, and the signs of distress which contribute to the persistent note of urgency that enlivens the song.

In his prayer to Zeus (*Iliad* 16.233–48), Achilles, as brave and proud as any epic hero, does not plead, nor does he mention his fear or torment, he merely articulates his present request. He also speaks in a solemn manner which appears typically direct and masculine, a fit tone for a procedure which Bowra (1961: 200) surmises 'we might expect in a religion which allowed a considerable element of contract in the relations of gods and men'. Contracts between gods and women, if Sappho's prayer can be considered an example, are clearly different, more flexible, personal negotiations, to be discussed and then resolved to the satisfaction of all parties. Surprisingly, though apparently in accordance with the adversary relationships depicted in male lyrics, where omnipotent gods such as Zeus oppress powerless humans or an unwilling beloved is subjugated by a masterful lover, Sappho uses the verb 'δάμνα' – to tame, subdue, overpower (1.3) – to describe Aphrodite's influence.

Although Aphrodite's power is acknowledged, it becomes obvious that she may choose not to exercise it. Uncertainty is a vital aspect of this prayer, it is necessarily conditional: you are capable of subduing me, but if I enact a particular ritual correctly, skilfully, then perhaps, as on other similar occasions, you might aid rather than oppress me. Only faith can assure certainty in the illusory ambience that Sappho delineates. Men can be certain of the hierarchical nature of mortal/immortal interaction – a system which reproduces relations of dominance and submission, of kings/subjects, masters/slaves – and of myths constructed to explain and order the universe. Sappho, as a female myth-maker, appears deliberately to question, to subvert this order by her treatment and representation of the relationship between Aphrodite and the singer. After juxtaposing Aphrodite's strength with the singer's vulnerability, she then undermines not only this dichotomous structure but also a number of other conventional oppositions.

In the second stanza, after the singer asks Aphrodite to come to her, Sappho begins her version of the next stage of a cletic hymn, a persuasive delineation of the god's past deeds and epiphanies.

ἀλλὰ τυίδ᾽ ἔλθ᾽, αἴ ποτα κἀτέρωτα
τὰς ἔμας αὖδας ἀίοισα πήλοι
ἔκλυες, πάτρος δὲ δόμον λίποισα
8 χρύσιον ἦλθες

But come here to me, if ever before now
from far away you heard me calling
and descended, leaving your father's
8 house of gold,

Achilles, briefly (in a single line), reminds Zeus of the time he honoured him by greatly harming the Achaean army; Sappho lingers over five stanzas decoratively relating not only the assistance Aphrodite has given this lover in the past, but details of the sight and sound of her epiphanies. In this way she adds a sensual, almost tangible, dimension to an experience already touched with symbolic, ritualistic significance. Despite the economy of his depiction, Homer makes a clear distinction between Zeus' former intervention on behalf of Achilles and this present request, taking time to nominate the prior foe, and differentiate between the distant environment of this god and Achilles' earthly surroundings. Sappho dissolves such oppositions, conjoining this occasion with innumerable past requests, collapsing the illusion of separate instances; and bringing Aphrodite down from her father's house to a mortal setting, to face-to-face, verbal interaction with the lover/singer. Homer's Zeus is not described in sufficient imagistic detail to provoke a visual dimension, and he is not expected to descend to Achilles' level to honour him, he can smite Achilles' enemies with a thunderbolt from a heavenly realm.[5] Other gods enter the thick of human combat – even Aphrodite ventures to rescue her beloved son Aeneas (*Iliad* 5.331–428) – and is sent wounded and shrieking back to Olympus,[6] but throughout this and other epic representations, Zeus remains aloof. Despite distinctions between epic and lyric there are similarities between these two invocations. The hymnal form imposes specific restrictions upon each poet and each responds by providing the correct details, conforming to a particular sequence. The results, however, are discernibly different.

Not content with simply relating Aphrodite's manifestation in a past epiphany, Sappho moves into narrative mode to fill out that miraculous event, to embroider her offering imagistically. So that the portrait of Aphrodite as a glorious but beneficent deity becomes almost tangible.

ἄρμ’ ὐπασδεύξαισα· κάλοι δέ σ’ ἆγον
ὤκεες στροῦθοι περὶ γᾶς μελαίνας
πύκνα δίννεντες πτέρ’ ἀπ’ ὠράνωἴθε-
12 ρος διὰ μέσσω,

αἶψα δ’ ἐξίκοντο· σὺ δ’, ὦ μάκαιρα,
μειδιαίσαισ’ ἀθαντῳ προσώπῳ

ἤρε' ὄττι δηὖτε πέπονθα κὤττι
16 δηὖτε κάλημμι,

κὤττι μοι μάλιστα θέλω γένεσθαι
18 μαινόλᾳ θυμῳ·

coming with chariot yoked; beautiful
swift sparrows leading you down to black earth
the pulse of countless fluttering wingbeats trembling
12 through mid-air,

swiftly then they came; and you, blessed lady,
smiling at me out of your immortal beauty
asked what was afflicting me this time,
16 why I was calling, this time,

what above all else I wished to befall
18 my maddened heart.

The emotional impulse in this section contrasts with less passionate sequences in male poetry and highlights the woman-centred scheme of values operating behind the song. The episode also produces a visual image, proof for the faithful, utilising details which are graphically precise, but infinitely general, since they are drawn from the host of mythical characteristics which define this immortal. It is also allusive, redeploying descriptive techniques often used in Homeric epics and hymns, although Sappho's choice of detail is again idiosyncratic, prompting the question of the degree of conscious subversive intent. Is Sappho, as Winkler proposes (1981: 61), deliberately reversing some aspects of the situation delineated, phallocentrically, by Homer in *Iliad* 5, and therefore 'adopting multiple points of view in a single poem'? Or is she undercutting traditional male symbols by allowing them to be juxtaposed with apparently inappropriate images? Aphrodite, who is Homerically *amachos*, is equipped in Sappho's prayer with a chariot, fostering male images of war. As it descends to the black earth, however, this divine equipage is seen to be drawn by sparrows, diminutive creatures who were, appropriately perhaps, associated with fecundity, and confirm Aphrodite's ornithic aspect,[7] but fall short when compared to teams of snorting stallions (eg. Zeus' team in *Iliad* 8.41–6 or Nestor's 'fast-footed horses', *Iliad* 8.116–29). The description of sparrows swiftly slipping through mid-air, their wings whirring – actions which are conveyed through soft syllabic patterns: 'ὤκεες στροῦθοι περὶ γᾶς μελαίνας / πύκνα δίννεντες πτέρ' ἀπ' ὠράνωἴθε- / ρος διὰ μέσσω' (1.10–12) – is, however, extremely attractive. Is it in any sense also 'feminine'? Aphrodite arrives and, in line with her traditional reputation as the goddess of smiles, smiles at the singer.

After the lengthy formalities of the previous four stanzas and the renewed urgency of the lover's need, stressed by the repetition of 'this time', ('δηὖτε' 1.15, 16 and 17),[8] Aphrodite's appearance is magical, almost startling. It is a manifestation which must remind the audience of Aphrodite's persuasive trickery, of the attributes most needed by the singer. Without doubt it is also dramatically expedient, creating as it does, with the god's epiphany and the dialogue between her and the lover, a sensation of immediacy and intimacy. It becomes evident as the song develops that the problematic human relationship represented here is the latest of many, hence the slur of fickleness which this song has attracted. Along with the attitude that as these affairs are transient they must also be entirely light-hearted, and therefore represented ironically or playfully. Arguably, erotic emotion is not singular but pluralistic – grave and playful, agonising and delightful – and Sappho's representations of it foreground its multiple aspects. Poetically, these short-lived relationships are not dissimilar to affairs represented by the male poets who are not censored for their sexual inconstancy. And the reiteration of 'δηὖτε' (as a word combining now and then) appears to signify not changeability, but a continuum that incorporates similar past, present and future erotic situations.

When Aphrodite speaks she addresses the lover as Sappho, conjoining singer, lover and creator and increasing the impression of a personal statement.

. . . . τίνα δηὖτε πείθω
ἄψ σ' ἄγην ἐς ϝὰν φιλότατα; τίς σ', ὦ
Ψάπφ', ἀδικήει;

'. . . Who am I to persuade this time,
who should I lead back to your love, who is it
Sappho, that hurts you?'

It is a statement which confirms some commentators' belief that women's poetry flows straight from the heart. As Stigers (1979: 465) reminds us, however,

> one must keep in mind that the 'I' of the poem is not necessarily the 'I' of the poet at all . . . The original emotions themselves must have their stimulus in the poet's experience, but the process of clarifying them requires the poet to refine, transform, extrapolate experience imaginatively, perhaps beyond recognition.

Since I am in agreement with Stigers, I can only add that this song is an artistic production, not a true confession. The self-awareness implied by the identification does change the mood however, introducing a note of detachment. The singer has talked of her 'μαινόλᾳ θυμῳ' (1.18), a heart which, in the first stanza, she begged Aphrodite not to oppress. Aphrodite, in a disconcertingly intimate manner (like an intuitive confidante or mother-figure), suggests that her distress is caused by an unresponsive beloved and asks who is wronging her this time, who is refusing to partake of an experience that Stigers (1981: 51) describes as: the 'loveliness and joy, of contact with the divine, of (the) heightened self-awareness', concomitant with love and its symbol/goddess. In this passage, as Bowra (1961: 203–4) notes, there is a lack of 'the absorbing self-importance which makes for solemnity'. He considers that 'the whole episode is at a level of affectionate understanding'. It is true that although Aphrodite retains her divine status, the relationship between mortal and deity is shown to be unusually close, like epic relationships between immortal lovers and human beloveds which endow glory on the human participants and their offspring. In this instance however, it is more familiar and equitable, resembling an ideal woman to woman affiliation.[9] Sappho has much in common with Aphrodite. Aphrodite has the power to subdue all beings, but Sappho has the power to invoke her presence, and in their conversation each contributes part of the story, using similar language.

In the next stanza this mutuality is extended to include the two human protagonists in a speech resembling an incantation or a spell, as it evokes a sense of mystery that seems congruent with a world inhabited by gods, poets and lovers.

> καὶ γὰρ αἰ φεύγει, ταχέως διώξει·
> αἰ δὲ δῶρα μὴ δέκετ', ἀλλὰ δώσει·
> αἰ δὲ μὴ φίλει, ταχέως φιλήσει
> 24 κωὔκ ἐθέλοισα·

For if she flees, soon she will pursue;
if she does not accept gifts now, she will give them;
and if she does not love, soon she will desire
even against her will.

Aphrodite, or perhaps Sappho, dispenses comfort, since this list effectively dissolves the erotic inequities between the two human protagonists and reverses the situation. The language in this stanza, integrated as it is with repetition and assonance, divided/stressed by end rhymes and rendered impatient with the reiteration of 'ταχέως' (1.23), compounds the impression of a miraculous co-ordination, an inversion which causes both parties to be equally infected. Oppositions are, in this manner, integrated rather than contrasted. Of course the whole process is illogical and beyond rational explanation, but aurally and emotionally it soothes and provides comfort. Women have traditionally been associated with esoteric practices, and with a form of reasoning which is not logocentric.[10] This prayer is constructed in ways which clash with the codes inherent in the male hymns and narratives that provide an allusive background.

The final stanza (the last stage of a cletic hymn, the entreaty) brings us back from the generality of a remembered past event to the present of the song – now, this time – with a plea that is textually and emotionally reminiscent of the singer's initial invocation.

ἔλθε μοι καὶ νῦν, χαλέπαν δὲ λῦσον
ἐκ μερίμναν, ὄσσα δέ μοι τέλεσσαι
θῦμος ἰμέρρει, τέλεσον· σὺ δ' αὔτα
σύμμαχος ἔσσο·

Come to me once again, set me free from bitterness
and concern, accomplish all that my heart
most desires to be accomplished, and you yourself
be my co-fighter.

The dreamlike aura is dissipated by this development, but the poetic sequence is satisfyingly circular, as other Sapphic songs no doubt would be if we had access to the complete text. Ring composition was one of the most frequently used structures of Greek antiquity, and the repetitions, the patterns of sound and sense that echo and connect throughout this song place it within this category. In this stanza however, despite the reiteration of some of the key words of the first stanza, such as 'θῦμος', 'ἔλθε', and the repeated suggestion of longing and cruel anxiety, it is clear there has been a gentle progression. The resolution afforded by Aphrodite in that previous epiphany still echoes in the minds of her audience, assuring them that this petition will also be answered. The concluding image reinforces this impression. Sappho, in her roles of singer, poet, lover, has a further request, she wants Aphrodite herself 'ἔσσο' (1.28) to be her fellow fighter and she uses a martial expression – 'σύμμαχος', (1.28) to express that desire. An expression which, considering the recent demonstration of the equality of the human lovers, appears incongruous. It suggests a potential union between lover and god, one which is not dissimilar to that of Zeus and Achilles or Diomedes and Athene; but it also appears to postulate an adversary relationship between lover and beloved. Achilles' concise entreaty in *Iliad* 16, which also stresses the difference between past and present with 'καὶ νῦν', seems a less complicated reiteration.

Does Sappho's final petition include a reversion to erotic angst, in contrast to the ideal situation portrayed in the passage describing Aphrodite's epiphany? Does it refer defiantly to Aphrodite's manifold talents, insisting that her ability as a warrior is as great as her expertise in seductive wiles? This expression again draws a comparison between an ideal female relationship and the relations of dominance and submission which are an integral part of a male environment where words such as 'σύμμαχος' (1.28) and the relationships they represent, flourish and overpower. In antiquity Dionysius of Halicarnassus (*Demosthenes* 40 [v. 214ss. Usener and Radermacher]) praised Sappho's craft in this prayer, her ability to combine words and sounds with the result that 'the verbal beauty and the charm of the writing lie in the cohesion and smoothness of the joinery'. Her ability to integrate a range of potentially disparate issues and mortal/immortal participants in a single song just as smoothly and cohesively suggests the kind of multiplicity that is at times associated with womankind. Perhaps her poetic skill also enabled her to include several interpretations, increasing the complexity, while retaining a sense of wholeness, like some poststructuralist representations which deliberately resonate with ambiguities, or play polysemously with a number of meanings.

The only song by a male author which can be compared with this complex religious/erotic song is an invocation by a later Ionian poet (well known in 536/5 BC), Anacreon of Teos. The two songs are, however, noticeably different. The dissimilarities foreground anomalies between two representations of the most renowned love poets of the ancient Greek world, and in the attitudes to religion and eros constructed into their songs. Despite superficial divergencies, the sex of the protagonists, male in this case, female in Sappho 1, and some structural disparity, the scenario of Anacreon's song (fr. 357) is thematically similar. Both songs represent a plea to a god for intercession in an unfulfilled, homoerotic affair and it seems possible that Anacreon knew of Sappho's prayer and based his song on it, although the situation and the time when Anacreon sang his song are far removed from a Sapphic milieu. Anacreon's song was almost certainly meant for a courtly, possibly a sympotic occasion, for the amusement of a predominantly male audience.

Anacreon's love song densely and ironically compresses a wealth of tradition and emotion into a minimum of lines and reduces it to a single view which climaxes in an elegant joke. This single view is somewhat broadened by the number of gods invoked within the song. Like Sappho, Anacreon goes through a shorter, if more conventional sequence, addressing Dionysus and his immortal playmates with suitable epithets, then requesting his presence and stating the lover's case. Unlike Aphrodite, Dionysus – the one god who is directly addressed – does not make an appearance in the mortal context inhabited by the singer. Anacreon places him, with Eros, Aphrodite and some Nymphs, in a distant, immortal sphere, and although like the Sappho-singer his singer begs him to come, Dionysus remains tucked away out of sight in the background. If some contract was entered into between god and man then once again it was on a basis of male solidarity, in accordance with the hierarchical social strata often constructed into male lyric poetry, between a powerless mortal and a superior god who inhabited 'the lofty mountain peaks' ('ὀρέων κορυφάς' 357.5). The lack of actual godly presence and the absence of dialogue makes this song a straightforward announcement of desire, a plea for immortal intervention in a love affair in which the human participants remain as conspicuously separate as the petitioner and his god. Several other disparities distinguish this song from Sappho's prayer: the deft economy of Anacreon's language; the constant, lighter tone (which tends to neutralise the representation of personal torment and make love merely a game played by both mortals and immortals:

'συμπαίζουσιν' 357.4); the more detached perspective of a lover who seems to view Kleoboulus as an object; and the logical, less circular, sequence of thought: address, description, followed by a plea that is left hanging, unanswered.

Viewing each of these decorative songs we, as audience and/or readers, gaze at an antique representation of a request for godly intervention in erotic situations which are, in a number of ways, disparate. In their dramatic technique, in the assumption of masks, the practice of illusion, these poets also differ, not in complexity, for in this they are equivalent, but in tone and intent. Sappho, by naming herself, by representing emotion and religious belief, using dialogue that mimics normal speech and interaction, appears to discard the mask, to present a close imitation of 'lived experience'. Some commentators are struck by the artlessness of this poet, her ability to report the intensity of her own desires. The possibility that Sappho 1 was just as consciously and skilfully constructed as Anacreon's plea appears less acceptable. But Sappho's prayer seems in fact to be superlatively idealistic, a multi-dimensional product of artifice. Conversely, Anacreon, from a more detached and anonymous perspective behind the mask, appears to announce the artificiality of his prayer as he boldly proffers decorative images and epithets, not it seems as offerings for the gods, but as a richly ornamented gift for Kleobulus. Is sexual or gender difference an issue here? Concepts such as 'feminine' and 'masculine' cannot be easily comprehended when they are extracted from their original context, the field of representation and/or significance in which they were initially constructed and to which they relate, but skill, wittiness, and detachment have traditionally been considered 'masculine' attributes more likely to be found in the work of male authors than in the heartfelt 'feminine' outpourings of female poets.

There is one other fragment (288) of Ibycus, a contemporary of Anacreon who also spent some time at the court of Polycrates, which captures something of the sensuality, the hymnal quality of Sappho 1. It is again erotically directed at a beloved of the same sex, but the role of the immortals in this petition seems distinctive. Ibycus infers that the Graces, Seasons, Aphrodite and Persuasion have nurtured the beloved, Euryalus. Just as Sappho's prestige is enhanced by her association with, her likeness to, Aphrodite, the connection between these gods and personifications and Euryalus confers special favour upon him, so that the song seems more a poetic compliment than a hymn. Rather than appealing to his group of deities for assistance, Ibycus simply bestows upon them descriptions or epithets of sensuous beauty and projects these qualities on to Euryalus. It is a deft process and light, irreligious, court-oriented as it is, Ibycus' fragment seems as gracefully artificial as Anacreon 357. Sappho's representation of her relationship with and her belief in one female god, her emotionalism, her combination of remembered and present incidents, her unusual treatment of traditional elements, are all factors that set her song apart from those composed by two poets from differently constructed socio-poetic contexts.

Sappho 2 is also a prayer, one which takes the form of a 'κλητίκος ὕμνος' and again centres around an invocation to Aphrodite and the relationship of this god with Sappho's community of women. Unfortunately, the fragment is less complete, making it difficult to discern its original form or purpose.

δεῦρύ μ' ἐκ Κρήτας ἐπ[ὶ τόνδ]ε ναῦον
ἄγνον, ὄππ[ạ τοι] χάριεν μὲν ἄλσος
μαλί[αν], βῶμοι δὲ τεθυμιάμε-
νοι [λι]βανώτω̣·

ἐν δ' ὔδωρ ψῦχρον κελάδει δι' ὔσδων
μαλίνων, βρόδοισι δὲ παῖς ὀ χῶρος
ἐσκίαστ', αἰθυσσομένων δὲ φύλλων
κῶμα κατέρρει·

ἐν δὲ λείμων ἰππόβοτος τέθαλεν
ἠρίνοισιν ἄνθεσιν, αἰ δ' ἄηται
μέλλιχα πνέιοσιν [
[ ]

ἔνθα δὴ σὺ .... έλοισα Κύπρι
χρυσίαισιν ἐν κυλίκεσσιν ἄβρως
ὀμμεμείχμενον θαλίαισι νέκταρ
οἰνοχόαισον·

Come here to me from Crete, to [this] sacred
temple. Here is your graceful grove
of apple-trees, and altars smoking
with incense

in here cold water murmurs through branches
of apple, and roses overshadow every part of

this place, and from quick-shivering leaves falls
8 a sleep of enchantment

in here also swells a meadow, grazing for horses
it blossoms with spring flowers, and the winds
11 breathe sweetly . . . [
[ ]

In this place. . . . Cypris, take up
the golden cups and pour into them, delicately
nectar that is intermingled
16 with our festivities.

This plea is also structured on conventional lines, but this time the section between invocations is dominated by a detailed description, not of the god or her epiphany, but of the human environment to which her presence is requested. Constructed in Sapphic stanzas, it contains some of her most melodious lines, in rhythms which are almost mesmeric. If, as Bagg (1964: 49) suggests, 'the rhythms and laws of sexual tension underlie several of Sappho's poems', then this song is stilled by a quietude of waiting, or pressing sensuality. Once more we are confronted with a mingling of the erotic and religious, an assimilation which is noticeably different from the love song/prayer portrayed in Sappho 1, but which still appears problematic for some scholars. Page (1955: 42) is prompted to remark that such songs must be 'records of personal experience, designed to be heard rather by mortals than gods, to be judged by the standards not of priesthood but of poetry'. Must erotic emotion and religious ritual, or priesthood and poetry necessarily be constructed into a scheme of oppositional pairs? Particularly as Sappho's song was composed during an era in which the accepted medium of all religious and hymnal material was poetic. This song purports to deal with communal festivity, not personal experience. The petitioner places herself in the background and there is no sense of the private anguish which disturbed Sappho's first prayer. Neither the singer nor her companions are identified and she sings of her desire, not for another mortal, but for the presence and participation of an immortal in a eucharistic ritual. Again that immortal is Aphrodite and again the traditional characteristics focused on by Sappho are suitable and significant. These characteristics are different, however, as is the manner of evocation; the diversity of Sappho's invocations to

Aphrodite is a further indication of her many-mindedness. Although this singer also requests an epiphany – persuasively, as befits a petition to the god of persuasion – her invocation is simply worded, reasonably bare of formulaic epithets and patronymics. There also appear to be fewer Homeric echoes in this hymn, and while some features of this garden might resemble the landscapes inhabited by gods during moments of erotic activity, the description and co-ordination of sacred/natural elements seem typically Sapphic.

In form and intention however, this hymn appears similar to Alcaeus' invocation to the Dioscuri (fr. 34), a song also constructed in Sapphic stanzas, composed in colloquial language, and likewise incomplete. Both singers address their chosen god/s familiarly, nominating the place they are to leave – in each case an earthly locality dedicated to their worship – and asking these divinities to 'come to me', ('δεῦρύ μ',' Sappho 2.1). Both of these Lesbian poets match Kirkwood's (1974: 86) description of Alcaeus 34 and achieve a striking 'combination of tradition and originality'. The gods and their epiphanies appear distinctive, however, as do the methods of poetic enticement. The tasks which these divinities are to perform, as well as the human environments they are to invigorate with their presence are accordingly disparate (since each of these contexts concurs with their traditional characteristics), adding to a range of differences which again parallel 'feminine/masculine' oppositions. Just as Sappho's Aphrodite exhibits characteristics which appear to befit a 'feminine' scheme, the gods represented by Alcaeus are endowed with 'masculine' talents: Castor, who is known as a tamer of horses, and physically fit Polydeuces, are divine horsemen, impetuous saviours of men who roam the earth performing athletic feats, delivering mortals from danger at sea or 'chilling' ('ζακρυόεντος' 34.8) death. In his song, whether referring to a politically allegorical 'ship of state' or an actual vessel, Alcaeus portrays a black ship which is swamped by dark storms and night, until it is rescued by the light[11] which is a relatively unconventional attribute of these brilliant twins. His images, particularly the oppressive power of dark storms, clash with Sappho's murmuring streams and quiet garden. The binary contrasts he draws, of mortal/immortal, strong/weak, sky/sea, dark/bright, are potent and effectively cohere the three stanzas which remain. Alcaeus also employs Homerisms such as 'broad earth' ('εὔρηαν χ[θόνα]' 34.5) and 'well-benched ships' ('εὐσδ[ύγ]ων νάων' 34.9) which not only add a further epic dimension, but also endow solemnity on a hymn which is already said to possess 'a serene dignity', and to be elevated by the ingenious, 'picturesque manifestation' (Page 1955: 266–7) of St Elmo's fire. The vivid movement of flaring light and leaping bodies that vitalises his prayer, and the contrasts inherent in it, seems also to introduce a natural/godly phenomenon that excites male imagination. Perhaps it is easier to relate to this form of ingenuity than to the unconventional religious/erotic combinations constructed into Sappho 2 – a garden, for instance, that is serenely, sensually attractive, but woman-centred in its orientation.

A description of the garden takes up a large portion of the remaining four stanzas of Sappho's second prayer. Beginning and ending as it does with requests to Aphrodite, this hymn seems again to retain a satisfying circularity, unlike the apparently logical progression of events in Alcaeus' prayer. It is also cohesive. Each section, every metrical and environmental component, and the relation of these components to the deity who is asked to officiate, contributes to a conjunction of 'natural' and traditional detail, of mortal/immortal interaction. Alcaeus constructed his hymn around a scheme of sharp, conventional oppositions and the contrasts clash effectively. There are no such dichotomous comparisons in Sappho's landscape. Mortal/immortal, natural/sacred and traditional/symbolic elements are merged into a pluralistic entity. This song, and the garden it gracefully delineates, are created to glorify a goddess or tempt her down to earth. To that end, conventionally but innovatively, it produces what Burnett (1983: 263) calls a 'portrait in which the goddess's best-known attributes and parts are rendered as bits of landscape . . . Gardens, apples, perfumes, roses, field-flowers and horses all serve to remind Aphrodite of herself, as she is worshipped in her various cults.'

The locality of Sappho's garden, the time of day when the ritual took place, are unspecified, and while the season seems to be springtime with the blossoming, potential fruitfulness typical of that season, it could as easily be late summer when apples ripen and trees spread shade. This external landscape also closes around itself, becomes an internalised and suitably protected territory, with the repetition of 'ἐν' at the beginning of the final three stanzas. Page (1955: 40) insists that 'the place is real, not imaginary'; McEvilley (1972: 328) seems equally certain that 'Sappho's geography is of the imagination'. Surely though, this landscape is both real and imaginary, with elements that might be drawn from a store of mythological information and co-ordinated by Sappho's imagination, but also have a visual, tangible dimension. Through their links to Aphrodisian attributes the sacred/botanical/ imaginative elements of the garden are endowed with traditional associations, and they each have a place in a metaphorical network of sexual images which allude to, or represent parts of, the female body. Rose bushes and apple trees cluster at the secret, shaded centre of this garden and while, in an antique vocabulary of sexual metaphors, *mêlon* equates to various clitoral objects, roses have often been linked euphemistically to female genitalia. Just outside this inner circle, flower-strewn, uncut meadows flourish, meadows which form a barrier between the garden and the outside world. Within Sappho's 'ἰππόβοτος' meadow, horses graze, calmly, they are one of the images connected with Aphrodite, but they can also be compared with the divine horses which are tamed, then ridden rapidly around the world by the Dioscuri in Alcaeus' hymn. More generally, as symbols of speed, mastery and prestige in male competitive arenas and battlefields, such glorious creatures possess a tremendously 'masculine' aspect.

Other components of Sappho's garden are also endowed with tangible characteristics. As she draws her word picture, paratactically, loosely, with *de*-clauses and few grammatical breaks, the images proliferate, develop into a visual representation. Other senses are also involved – smell, hearing, touch, even taste with the mention of the nectar that is mixed like wine with festivities and women – and the imagery flows in sensual undercurrents. The sensuousness is as physical as it is verbal and metaphorical. The air, the water, the patterns of light and shade, are constantly moving in this glade, causing these images to integrate, to unite and then disengage. As Burnett (1983: 264) notes, 'substance here tends to give way to insubstantiality'. 'Cold water murmurs through branches of apple' (2.5–6), 'roses overshadow every part of this place' (2.6–7) (flowers which have changed from colour to shade), and not only does incense spread from altars; from shimmering leaves, sleep falls ('κῶμα' 2.8), a deep sleep of enchantment which is presumably capable of infiltrating, altering any and all mortals gathered at the grove's arcane centre. Once more we are poetically transported to a realm of mystical power, into the influence of an erotic god who is capable of subduing all creatures, and a poet who can subsume normal oppositions in her representations.

Composing some fifty years after Sappho, Ibycus produced a song (fr. 286) containing a description of a garden which bears some resemblance to Sappho's erotic grove. In Ibycus' garden, in a flourish of spring there are quince trees (another species of *mêlon*), flowing rivers, and 'vine-blossoms growing luxuriantly beneath the protection of shady vine-branches' ('οἰνανθίδες / αὐξόμεναι σκιεροῖσι ὑφ' ἔρνεσιν / οἰναρέοις θαλέθοισιν' 286.4–6). This place is described as 'the undefiled garden of the Virgins' ('Παρθένων κᾶπος ἀκήρατος' 286.3–4). With its flowing rivers and fruitful vines and trees, the scene manifests a relatively vigorous ambience, but the peace and potential fecundity of Ibycus' paradisiacal representation are not all that different to the atmosphere evoked in Sappho 2. Suddenly however, half-way through this short song, love enters upon the scene and irrevocably disrupts the serenity, showing it to be a temporary, contrived state, one side of yet another male scheme of binary oppositions. The switch is dramatically effective and is skilfully interwoven into the metaphoric background of the song, but the imagery which accompanies this metamorphosis is full of violence and disorder, of the madness which often attacks victims of eros. In Sappho 1 the singer also experiences 'μαινόλᾳ θύμῳ' (1.18) but her distress is temporary and self-contained, and the decorative, comforting images of Aphrodite provide a positive counterbalance. Love is recognised as being agonisingly double-sided, but within the framework of Sappho 1 and other Sapphic contexts, sweet and bitter are confused and conjoined so that while the duplicity of eros is recognised, a relatively painless resolution is effected. In Ibycus 286, a love that saturates every image of the song appears to be either potential or virginal, in which state it is controlled, seasonal and tranquilly beautiful; or uncontrollable, unseasonable and punitive, a malicious onslaught.

The Cyprian, Aphrodite, is held responsible for some, if not all of these assaults, and her representation, like the presentation of the negative forces she apparently unleashes, is perceptibly different from Sappho's divine creation. As is the relationship between this version of Aphrodite, and the singer/lover: two adversaries caught up in an age-old battle that results in mortal debilitation. In fr. 286, as part of a male creation the god is associated not only with the madness that is a conventional

Aphrodisian attribute, but also with blazing north winds, dark storms and lightning bolts. (A scenario which appears similar to Alcaeus fr. 34, except there men are rescued by male gods, here a female god torments a male subject.) These malevolent blasts are portrayed shortly, powerfully, by epithets which are then condensed into a minimal metrical space. Ibycus' technique, and the contrasts contained therein, are compelling, but single-minded, and the song ends with one of its few personal references, an image of the human heart which is shaken from the roots by this actual/metaphorical battering. In spite of its effectiveness, the deliberate juxtapositioning makes this second set of images appear to be as poetically convenient, as detached and metaphorically oriented as the initial sequence.

But is this song phallocentric, male-centred in either its orientation or construction? In Sappho 2 smoke rises, breezes blow, water murmurs and sleep falls from shimmering leaves, but can these sensuous sounds and sights, and the technique which coheres them, be considered emblematic of some female or 'feminine' mode of discourse? It can only be stated that the comparison of these dreamlike movements with flowing rivers, blasting winds, rushing lightning and violently shaken hearts promotes awareness of difference, of the historically specific and conventional 'feminine/masculine' schemes which appear to be constructed into these songs. Considering that both poets are singing of the power of Aphrodite, however, the dissimilarity is startling.

At the centre of Sappho's grove, where smoking altars stand beneath apple trees and rose bushes, Aphrodite is requested, in the final invocation which unites the song structurally, to take golden cups and fill them delicately with nectar. In this way intermingling festivities, nectar and presumably both mortal and immortal celebrants. These celebrants are unnamed, undefined, as non-specific as the landscape they inhabit. Sappho implies their presence by mentioning cups and festivities. This earthly garden has become a symbol of Aphrodite and her presence dominates in the last remaining stanza. Whatever the purpose of the ritual, whoever its participants, this image concludes a process of integration that has occurred throughout the song. It is a process which amalgamates these celebrants and joins them with scenic elements that are associated with Aphrodite and integrated, piece by piece, in the previous stanzas. Mortal and immortal protagonists are again conjoined, and the combination of magical substances – the drink of the gods and enchanted sleep – seems to add a concluding touch. Sappho's treatment of Aphrodite is again idiosyncratic, but it is also positive and traditionally correct. Her use of generic and metrical elements is equally precise. Despite this superficial conformity however, the resulting prayer with its coherent structure, its combination of symbolism, eroticism, enchantment and ritual, appears unique. Not just because it delineates an esoteric female festival, but because Sappho evokes that event skilfully, foregrounding its woman-centred ambience, using creative tactics which diverge from the techniques that construct other, more conventional, hymns.

The final tiny fragment (fr. 140a) that is directly addressed to Aphrodite is also concerned with a negative aspect of love and again centres on a male figure, Adonis, the beautiful young lover of Aphrodite.

> κατθνάσκει, Κυθέρη', ἄβρος Ἄδωνις· τί κε θεῖμεν;
> καττύπτεσθε, κοραι, καὶ κατερείκεσθε κίθωνας·

> He is dying, Cytherea, delicate Adonis is dying. What are we to do?
> Beat your breasts, girls, and tear your clothes.

Linked mythically to the natural world that is featured often in Sappho's songs, this semi-divinity was a vegetation-deity, said to be born from the myrtle-tree which became his emblem, and like other beautiful, ephemeral, beings he died every autumn and was reborn in the spring. Once again, by singing of the mythical union of Aphrodite and Adonis, Sappho destabilises the dichotomous construct usually inserted between gods and mortals. She seems to favour these stories of love, of god/mortal unions, and of erotic female empowerment.[12] This fragment also incorporates the earliest attested mention of the Adonis cult in Greek literature and is interesting in the way it links to a form of ritual activity that continues in ancient Greece and suggests the presence of a female counter-culture. In Aristophanes' *Lysistrata* (lines 387–96), and other representations, women are reported as shouting 'Beat your breasts for Adonis' at a women's festival called the Adonia during which, according to Winkler (1990: 188–91), women gathered on rooftops and 'indulged in hilarious obscenity' in 'an acceptable, if loud and riotous, women's rite'. Sappho composed other songs on this subject; (frr. 168 and 211) and fr. 211b(ii) tell of Aphrodite's burial of Adonis in a lettuce-bed, another link with the Athenian Adonian celebrants who prepared gardens of lettuce and fennel in terracotta pots and then allowed the green shoots to wither and die. Since the anaphrodisiac properties of lettuce were well known in ancient Greece (Winkler 1990: 204), it seems that it is impotence as much as death that is mourned here, and the weakness of this young divinity is contrasted with the perpetual power and fertility of female gods and women. It is also women who are most involved in rituals of death and regeneration. These women are mourning with/for Aphrodite, grieving the loss of her lover. As in Sappho 1 the singer or singers (the sense of community strong in fr. 140a) turn to this god for guidance, and her answer, since once again she replies directly within the hymnal form, reminds them that some natural occurrences are inevitable and that pain can only be alleviated by ritual and song.

This remnant of a cult song is one of the representations that support the proposition that the Sapphic community had a religious focus, that it was devoted to the worship of Aphrodite. Songs that comment self-consciously on song, ritual instructions that were originally part of a ritual, are typical Sapphic occurrences. We are once again witnesses to an incident that is poetically articulated, and centres on a ritual enacted entirely by female personae. The uncomplicated but unusual cult form it takes resounds with the oral rhythms and social dynamics of an earlier age. The cultic activity depicted in fr. 140a appears to continue to find expression in Greek women's lives, but it seems possible that some of Sappho's songs, to Aphrodite, or on topics such as virginity and marriage, also incorporated traces from an earlier 'woman's culture' (Friedrich 1978: 110). So that rather than mimicking or subverting male forms Sappho simply repeated these female themes poetically, fitting them into a corpus of songs that centred on the dreams and experiences, the rites and symbols, of women.

Chapter 2

Songs of love

The songs that Sappho sings most often and with greatest intensity focus on the subject of love. They tell of the love of the singer for her family, of love between brides and grooms, or the women of Sappho's community, or desire for one particular member of the group. In the songs representing these passionate or tender relationships Aphrodite frequently plays a part, assisting or interceding between characters. As a result, the diverse characteristics that attend this god, which Friedrich (1978: 1) feels are combined into 'a meaning that interconnects female sexuality, tenderness, procreation, subjectivity, and other complexes of symbols', are projected on to these songs and the relationships they represent and/or construct. There is one form of love, however, that is most frequently associated with both Aphrodite and Sappho: erotic, or more specifically, homoerotic, desire.[1] Male and female lyric poets are united in Campbell's (1983: 26–7) statement on this theme, the comment that love in the context of Greek lyric poetry 'is sexual, usually, homosexual desire, a temporary admixture of admiration and lust caused by Eros or his mother Aphrodite'. Admiration and lust appear to be oppositional to other more traditionally 'feminine' qualities such as the 'tenderness' and 'subjectivity' that Friedrich gives prominence to in his commentary, but love is one of the few subjects that intrigued both the male and female lyric poets of ancient Greece. Some similarity is also ensured by the fact that the generic constructions used to display these erotic re-creations are derived from a common store. Since the love/desire represented in antiquity is itself disturbing and disordering, the language of these female/male representations could be expected to be equally destabilising. It is also likely to be 'fluid, decentred, multiple', so that 'every discourse of desire is therefore simultaneously a critique of language' (Kauffman 1986: 32).

The extent to which the signifying mechanisms encoded within the 'alternative' world constructed in Sappho's songs can be equated with signs and concepts of love considered 'natural' by the commentators of later, differently constructed contexts, preempts some questions. Our ignorance of the social manifestation of this erotic interplay is manifold,[2] and awareness of the concepts of love which prevail in our own framework, concepts which have been labelled 'sex-centred',[3] can only accentuate the disparity between ancient and modern cultures. Sappho's erotic representations describe/define a love which seems alien to the ideals of our cultural context. Evidence which could corroborate or expand upon these poetic reports is not readily available. The world in which they were constructed – and related constructs within that world, such as masculinity and femininity – are distant and inaccessible, but Sappho's songs of love do give us the opportunity to examine a woman's representation of desire and to map out, more adequately and empoweringly, traces of a tradition of female creativity. Frequently however, critical responses to the representations of love contained in Sappho's lyrics seem to ignore the poetic qualities and falter over the subject of Sappho's 'homosexuality'.[4] The orientation of later western society is towards an ideal relationship involving the male/female couple. Within this particular milieu it is generally accepted that we are constructed according to the precept, articulated in this instance by Rossi (1976: 139), that 'biologically men have only one innate orientation – a sexual one that draws them to women, – while women have two innate orientations, sexual toward men and reproductive toward their young'. Within the seductive artificiality of their attractive settings however, in modes that are not dissimilar to the homoerotic songs of male poets, Sappho's songs sing 'romantically', joyously, of love shared only by women.

In the terms of a late twentieth-century 'sex-centred' culture, wherein sexuality and the individual psyche are constructed into a symbolic entity that legitimises male presence, woman's desire is said to be unrepresentable, even though it is endlessly discussed. If it was possible for woman's desire to be represented, then Irigaray (1985: 25) believes that this form of 'desire would not be expected to speak the same language as man's'. It is feasible that the creations of a woman who was constructed within an apparently female context, who was representing not the 'disinterested'[5] desire of a man for a woman but the desire of one woman for another, would manifest some distinctive characteristics. In the dichotomous frameworks underlying both ancient and modern western cultures, woman is associated with emotion, passivity, and disorder – man with reason, action and the power to control and define female sexuality, to create a dominant representation of love. In her analysis of the *Heroides* and other derivative representations, Kauffman (1986: 314) discusses the manner in which Ovid re-presents the stories of a range of past authors (including Sappho), mixing the categories of genre and gender and in this way demonstrating 'that the literary construction of gender is always artificial, that one can never unveil the essence of masculinity or femininity. Instead all one exposes are other *representations*.' Whether or not a concept such as the 'essence of masculinity or femininity' is any more immutable than the myths that Ovid and other ancient authors freely re-create, it seems that the distinction between another dichotomous pair – gender and sex – is currently being shown to be equally arbitrary and 'artificial' (Threadgold *et al.* 1990: 25). Trapped though they are between the tensions inherent in a broad range of polarised pairs, of 'language on the one hand and extralinguistic reality on the other; between nature and culture; between "biological sex" and the endless social and political markers of difference' (Laqueur 1990: 11–12); sex and gender both appear as conceptual entities which are continually reconstructed and mediated by cultural practices.

Sappho's representations of erotic love and its female symbol, Aphrodite – culturally and linguistically grounded as they are – appear to some extent to construct an actively sexual, female speaking subject. At times her representations are also capable of subverting the binary-type schemata that splits human subjects, their contexts and characteristics dimorphically and inequitably. Working within the constrictions of a Lacanian framework Kristeva posits a form of excess: when a 'woman experiences a *jouissance beyond the phallus*' (Grosz 1990: 139). *Jouissance* is a term defining sexual pleasure and the disorder traditionally associated with women. It is said to be the means by which a socio-symbolic order can be cracked, split open, 'changing vocabulary, syntax, the word itself' (Kristeva 1984: 80). Kristeva also asserts that its transgressive, libidinal impulses are strongest within poetry. Is it possible that the poetic constructs of a woman of the seventh to sixth century BC, and her attempts, within the limitations of a lyric genre, to define female desire and identity, had the potential to disturb or transgress the socio-symbolic order?

In this section I examine the fragments of Sappho's love songs, working with the assumption that these representations articulate one version of the indefinable: the love/desire of women for women. Wittig's (1992: 47) comments on the exclusion/freedom of 'lesbians here and now in society' appear relevant to the women Sappho sings of, since they also are situated 'philosophically (politically) beyond the categories of sex. Practically they have run away from their class (the class of women), even if only partially and precariously.' The homoerotic and other interactions reported by Sappho's songs also foreground a conventionally 'feminine' aspect – the manner in which personal relationships are focused upon – a practice Friedrich (1978: 108–9) identifies as her 'constant preoccupation with the private, individual relations that sociologists call "primary" – those between friends, relatives, lovers, or small groups'. The environment in which these songs were created – our knowledge of which is gained mainly through poetic descriptions – appears separate, female, centred on poetry, beauty and the worship of Aphrodite. It also seems to have interacted with the public world in complex and (to us) enigmatic ways. Was this a way of presenting the female persona as an erotic subject? Perhaps as a complement to the homoerotic relations portrayed in male songs, or as the representation of an ideal woman-to-woman love? In this woman-centred context, desire assumes multifarious guises as Sappho strives to adequately represent a private, perhaps inexpressible, physical/emotional/divine force.

In one of these erotic scenarios, Sappho 16, the singer sings the praises of love, and Helen and Anaktoria, extravagantly, but convincingly. Craftily formulated, this song again combines public and private worlds, since it is both personal and detached, ostensibly suitable for the declaration of philosophical propositions, but tempered by a woman-centred point of view, by the Sappho-singer's choice of what is best. This voice/viewpoint considers the superlative qualities of soldiers and fine weapons, then compares this splendour to the importance of love and beauty. The juxtapositioning is vital and provocative. More than any other Sapphic song, these several stanzas of a reasonably complete song foreground and challenge male values, giving further indication of

Sappho's 'double-consciousness' (Winkler 1981: 69), her ability to juxtapose male/female constructions. It is also an intense declaration of love and about love; as well as an exposition of the processes of memory; and a philosophical discussion, one which incorporates a rhetorical argument. On a base of public, male forms and techniques, Sappho again constructs an inimitable representation, a private love song that doubles as a rhetorical device. Not surprisingly there are no extant male songs which can be exactly equated with Sappho 16. The comparisons I make must be partial therefore, strands teased from another of her complex webs and placed against similar segments of male representation.

Sappho begins her poem concisely, using a form of demonstration called a priamel, an offshoot of the riddling games enjoyed by convivial players, in which wittiness or erudition was proven by the ability to introduce an unexpected, but not illogical, category into a hierarchically organised sequence.

ο]ἰ μὲν ἰππήων στρότον οἰ δὲ πέσδων
οἰ δὲ νάων φαῖσ' ἐπ[ὶ] γᾶν μέλαι[ν]αν
ἔ]μμεναι κάλλιστον, ἔγω δὲ κῆν' ὄτ-
4 τω τις ἔραται·

πά]γχυ δ' εὔμαρες σύνετον πόησαι
π]άντι τ[ο]ῦτ', ἀ γὰρ πόλυ περσκέθοισα
κάλλος [ἀνθ]ρώπων 'Ελένα [τὸ]ν ἄνδρα
8 τὸν [πανάρ]ιστον

καλλ[ίποι]σ' ἔβα 'ς Τροίαν πλέοι [σα
κωὐδ[ὲ πα]ῖδος οὐδὲ φίλων το[κ]ήων
πά[μπαν] ἐμνάσθη, ἀλλὰ παράγαγ' αὔταν
12]σαν

]αμπτον γὰρ [
]. . . . κούφως τ[ ]οησ[.]ν
. .]με νῦν 'Ανακτορί[ας ὀ]νέμναι-
16 σ' οὐ] παρεοίσας÷

τᾶ]ς κε βολλοίμαν ἔρατόν τε βᾶμα
κἀμάρυχμα λάμπρον ἴδην προσώπω
ἢ τὰ Λύδων ἄρματα κἀν ὄπλοισι
20 πεσδομ]άχεντας÷

] . μεν οὐ δύνατον γένεσθαι
22] . ν ἀνθρωπ[. . . π]εδέχην δ' ἄρασθαι

Some men say a spread of cavalry, some of infantry,
others of ships, is the most beautiful thing
on the black earth, but I say
it is whoever one loves.

It is quite easy to make this understood
by everyone, for she who transcended
all humankind in beauty, Helen, left
the [noblest] husband of all

and went sailing off to Troy
with no thought [at all] for her child
or her beloved parents, but led away
. . .]

]. . . . for. . . . [
]. . . . lightly. . . . [ ]
[she] has reminded me now of Anaktoria
who is not here

I wish, most of all, that I could gaze upon
her graceful walk and the brightness of her face,
this I desire more than the gleam of Lydian chariots
and heavily armed footsoldiers.

]. . . it is not possible that this should happen
]. . . . humankind . . . but pray to share

Having squeezed three 'masculine' preferences – cavalry, foot soldiers, the navy, and a Homeric echo 'γᾶν μέλαι[ν]αν' (16.2) – into a single Sapphic stanza, Sappho introduces her choice: 'whoever a person loves', in the shorter line which emphatically ends the stanza. In many ways her use of this device achieves a result not unlike that of other priamels: Pindar's *Olympian Ode* 1 or Tyrtaeus fr. 12 or possibly Theognis, lines 255–6 in which it is also asserted that love is the most delightful thing. Are there differences? Sequentially they are reasonably similar, a series of different items which are compared to a final element that is rendered supreme by its position and the expansion of detail. Pindar compares water and gold with the Olympic Games, Theognis chooses love over justice and health and Tyrtaeus stresses the superiority of 'warlike strength' over athletic prowess, speed, beauty, wealth, persuasiveness or fame. Like Sappho's trio of war symbols, these comparative elements derive from the public arena.

Are they more internally diverse than the choices submitted by Sappho? The warlike items she lists are united variously: by their relevance to war, to myth, to the male perspective which glories in such heroic sights and by their link with Helen, the mythical figure who provides proof of Sappho's opening statement. Both female and male sets conclude with an element that is interestingly disparate. In Sappho's song, however, even this initial disparity seems to be integrated by the action of the following stanzas.

As an unexpected comparison, her choice, like that of Pindar, Theognis and Tyrtaeus, is expansive and rhetorically effective; but this appears to be an unusually (for Sappho) abstract statement about love. The impulse towards generality, contrived by the reiteration of 'some men' ('οἰ'), and the placement of indefinite forms such as 'τις', tends only to emphasise its abstractness. In this way it resembles Mimnermus 1, a song which begins dramatically by posing the question: 'What is life, and what is joy, without golden Aphrodite?' ('τίς δὲ βίος, τί δὲ τερπνὸν ἄτερ χρυσῆς 'Αφροδίτης;'). Mimnermus goes on to prove his point by compiling a list of oppositions – life/death; youth/old age; joy/sadness and hate/love – which dwindle sorrowfully away. Elegiacs, the metre of Mimnermus' song, were used at this time for poetry of a reflective nature, and the singer's tone is appropriately sombre. The Sapphic voice is much less solemn, leaving her readers with some doubts about whether mimicking or playing with conventional tropes is not a game enjoyed by a female poet. Apart from a difference of form and tone, other disparities are evident: Mimnermus' statement, like the statements of other male poets discussed in this section, apparently applies to all men, so it seems impersonal. And love is pleasant, but not supreme; for this singer, youth is the loveliest and the best. Theognis, also composing in elegiacs, expresses a similar sentiment: 'love of boys is a pleasant thing' ('παιδοφιλεῖν δέ τι τερπνόν' 1345). The inference is, that for men, love, associated as usual with the flower of youth, is pleasant and enjoyable, but not all-important; compared to more serious matters, old age or possibly armies and fleets, it is inconsequential.

In fr. 5 Sappho includes some ethical questions; in the second and third stanzas of fr. 16 she again expounds a moral view, but the position she takes seems less conventional. What results is a song that appears to defend every woman's right to love and act autonomously. In the second stanza, as mythical proof of her initial statement, Sappho introduces Helen, the woman who surpassed all humankind in beauty and who relinquished her noble husband and all thought of her child and her dear parents, for love. (The positive descriptions of husband and parents only serve to accentuate the even more positive qualities of love.) While the singer announces the perfect clarity of this proposition, it seems to be, as Winkler (1981: 72) suggests, 'a charming parody of logical argumentation', a slightly crooked and 'womanly' sequence of logic. It involves an emotional and poetic leap which suddenly shifts the focus to a glorious female protagonist and, with this strategy, overrides more logocentric distinctions. The shift does have some advantages, however; Burnett (1983: 287) feels that 'her choice clearly discriminates *erôs* from three kinds of *philia* or, considered in another way, it places unsanctioned desire above three forms of sanctioned tenderness'.

There is some disagreement (fuelled by the lacunae in the fourth stanza) about whether Sappho condoned, applauded or condemned Helen's actions, or whether Helen was a free agent or was 'led away' (16.11) by Aphrodite. Within the action of the song however, where Helen is used as a positive symbol, with her love, like that of the singer, presumably also described as 'κάλλιστον' (16.3), the impression is that Sappho approves of Helen's disproportionate desire (an emotion that does appear to exceed the bounds of male moral structures). This impression is corroborated by the fact that for once the destructive results of that desire are omitted. The catalogues of ships and soldiers which were involved in the annihilation of Troy link neatly with those mentioned in the first and last stanzas of Sappho 16. In the majority of ancient contexts Helen appears in the traditionally 'feminine' guise of a beautiful but dangerous symbol uniting war and love. In this song she also reverses a social order wherein men actively exchange or leave passive women, leaving ('ἔβα' [16.9] an aorist which stresses the static nature of those left behind), moving away (the movement is illustrated with participles) from such conventional figures as husband, children and parents, towards the man she loves. DuBois (1984: 102) hails her as an 'actant in her own life, the subject of choice, exemplary in her desiring'.

Alcaeus, who composed at least two songs on the subject of Helen, reveals a very different perspective. Textually, Sappho 16 and Alcaeus 42 are not unalike, composed as they are in Sapphic stanzas and unified by apparently circular structures. They both use Helen as a central mythical illustration, in language which is ostensibly natural and unaffected; although both poets expand their brief descriptions by using key images or symbols. The resemblance ends there. Alcaeus, despite his references to love and marriage, demonstrates poetically that Helen's love is adulterous and destructive. Within his song he seems to be maintaining, reproducing the tenets, the socio-moralistic constructions of a contemporary arena that exists beyond the Mycenaean world of epic. The alternative example he introduces – of Thetis the ideal maiden – might also be mythically idiosyncratic,[6] but it resounds with traditional morality and makes Helen's version of eros appear unacceptable. Behind the myth is a personal, if gnomic, statement, but this song, like Mimnermus' elegiac message, appears to be a generalised pronouncement, or perhaps a warning, directed at all men.

Alcaeus 283 is a more passionate mythological adaptation with the same moralistic message, and there are sufficient thematic parallels with Sappho 16 to suggest some conscious connection between these two songs and/or poets. Their technique/s, the manner in which they use a single well-weighted image such as 'child' or 'chariots' or a bed with 'a rich coverlet' ('εὔστρωτον [λ]έχος' Alcaeus 283.8) to suggest a wealth of meaning is similarly effective. Burnett (1983: 187) remarks on the complexity of Alcaeus' song, calling attention to the way in which it creates 'two separate devices (a device for lust and a device for death), making them as different as possible while it yet sets them side by side and insists that they are the mirroring parts of a single design'. This technique, the juxtapositioning and contrasting of two oppositional states, and the pessimistic perspective, seems reminiscent of Mimnermus 1. Despite the superficial similarity of Alcaeus 283 to Sappho 16, and the echoes of Helen's emotional absorption, of her husband and child, and the chariots and soldiers which now lie 'in the dust' ('ἐν κονίαισι' 283.15), the differences between these songs are manifold. Kirkwood (1974: 106) comments that 'in Alcaeus's poems the myth is self-contained, and the meaning depends on the moral point that the poet exemplifies in the myth. Sappho's poem combines the contemporary world with the mythical world of Helen and the Trojan War.' It also amalgamates two male creations, an epic and a form of demonstration, to enhance and broaden a more personal statement.

As Helen moves towards the object of her desire, so too does the song progress towards what duBois (1984: 96) calls its 'phenomenological center', the incarnation of the singer's desire, the final epitome of love and beauty. With Anaktoria's appearance in the fourth stanza of Sappho 16, all semblance of similarity to Alcaeus 283 evaporates. When Aphrodite appears in Sappho 1, the epiphany is startling and dramatic, poetically dynamic. Sappho's introduction of Anaktoria, or at least the verbal incarnation of the singer's memory of/longing for Anaktoria, at the same point in fr. 16 is also surprising and again alters the course, the expected sequence of her song. In this way it acts as a decentring mechanism. The two female protagonists, Helen and Anaktoria, both confute the expectations of conventional listener/readers. From the beginning this song has stated its more private nature by the emphasis on the validity and uniqueness of personal choice. In the second and third stanzas this choice is shown, with the example of Helen, to be not only personal but erotic. Now, with remembrance of Anaktoria, the shift from a public – Sappho's use of a popular form of demonstration and the universalising quality of legend – to a manifestly subjective viewpoint is complete. And the impact, aided by the resemblance of Anaktoria's graceful walk and bright face to footsoldiers and the sheen of chariots and sails, sifts backwards, fluidly merging qualities and superlatives so that Anaktoria emerges ultimately as a symbol or personification of all that is most beautiful and desirable. The final lines consolidate this impression, and as they confirm the superiority of intense, internalised, emotion over objectivised armies, the singer proves both her proposition and her love.

The question of whether or not Sappho's proposition about love – its poetic exposition and the strategies used to verify it – provide in some way a representation of an identifiably female form of desire, lingers on. In fr. 16 Sappho uses the same device as numerous male poets, and a mythical basis that is common knowledge to exemplify her theme but her representation appears finally to be quite different. Certainly her rhetorical strategy is selective and distinctive. The movement from a proposition which insists that love is supremely important, to an episode of paradigmatic myth which proves not only this proposition (albeit crookedly) but other associated premises, before focusing on a contemporary emblem of love, does seem an unusual mode of construction. In the first lines the ideas and emotions are confined within the limitations of a specific construction, then there is a gradual broadening that expands on a personal affirmation until it surpasses conventional tropes. Finally, a philosophical statement is transformed into a passionate declaration of love. The song develops, swells, until it reaches maturity, climactically. As well as her 'womanly' reasoning, Sappho's technique, her lyrical compression, seems oblique. This is a singular method of containing diverse ('masculine/feminine') themes within a song, and expanding on them without upsetting the balance of construction. It clashes with the relative single-mindedness of male songs such as Tyrtaeus' exposition (fr. 12) of a heroic code. The principal personae of Sappho 16 are also, fittingly, not only female, they all appear as extraordinary representatives of that sex.

The manner in which Sappho appears to divide the world in two according to a personal version of a recognisable scheme of male and female values and then explicitly juxtapose those values, does seem to replicate a bipolar mode of construction. Within the song she juxtaposes traditional oppositions such as male/female, war/love, objects/emotions, public/private, and incorporates them in an effective scheme. By lauding those elements traditionally linked with the 'feminine' – love, beauty, and the physical incarnation of whomever rather than whatever one loves – does Sappho establish a distinctive voice that sings softly behind this and other songs? The propositions she presents in fr. 16 are sufficiently unorthodox to contrast with representations such as Alcaeus 283 that mirror a more conventional viewpoint. As in her prayer to Aphrodite, such male/female oppositions appear not only to be subsumed within the logic of the song, but also, to some extent, internally integrated. By taking a philosophical stance, using a device from the public world, Sappho engages that world, just as Helen, by transgressing the active/passive split which makes women objects of male exchange, exceeds and confuses the traditional roles of men and women. Objects such as the accoutrements of war, and emotions such as love, also appear to be split, irreconcilably. But love, as Sappho demonstrates, revolves around the sight or memory of objects, or more specifically, a girl's face or her walk, images which are not unlike the sheen or movement of chariots and armed footsoldiers. In this way disparate, even oppositional elements are craftily integrated, put to the purpose of proving a 'womanly' proposition.

While many other songs from Sappho's first book are about love, some are sufficiently lacunose to make analysis difficult. The fragment I consider next (fr. 22) is sadly broken. Again it tells of the love of women for other women and proffers an illustration of the mechanics of female desire. In fr.22, after two stanzas of which only a few complete words remain, Abanthis, the lover of this song, is bidden by a third party to sing of her beloved, Gongyla.

. . . . κ]έλομαι σ' ἀ[είδην
Γο]γγύλαν [Ἄβ]ανθι λάβοισαν ἀ . [
πᾶ]κτιν, ἆς σε δηὖτε πόθος τ . [
12 ἀμφιπόταται

τὰν κάλαν· ἀ γὰρ κατάγωγις αὔτα[ς σ'
ἐπτόαισ' ἴδοισαν, ἐγὼ δὲ χαίρω·
καί γὰρ αὔτα δήπο[τ'] ἐμέμφ[ετ' ἄγνα
16 Κ]υπρογέν[ηα,

ὡς ἄραμα[ι
τοῦτο τῶ[πος
19 β]όλλομα[ι

. . . . I bid you, [Ab]anthis, to sing
of Gongyla, taking up [your] harp
while once again desire
12 flies around you

the lovely one, for the swirl of her dress
excited you as you gazed, and I rejoice.
For once the holy C]yprian
16 blamed me . . .

So I pray
this [word]. . . .
19 I wish . . .

Once more we are presented with a triangular situation in which the protagonist who is singer/commentator defines and controls the relationships involved; another representation where a female voice sings of love, describing an erotic interaction between two women. Desire, that darkly powerful, but irresistible emotion, 'flies around' (22.12) Abanthis once again ('δηὖτε') like a dress swirling tantalisingly, the dress which excited, attracted, the gaze of this lover. The placement of 'ἀμφιπόταται', on the final five-syllable line of this stanza achieves another close conjunction of metre and meaning as well as conjoining Abanthis' desire with the movement of Gongyla's dress. This moment seems not to be singular, but to be part of a repeated pattern of attraction and reaction that occurs and is celebrated by singer and community. Sappho has co-ordinated her images so that they are each multiplied and yet united. Even the description 'the lovely one' (22.13) at the beginning of the fourth stanza is dislocated, as if it could apply to any of the women or perhaps love itself. And while the transience of this particular relationship is implied by the use of 'δηὖτε', the stability of the community and its approval of *erôs* are made apparent by the tone of the song and the interactions of the three protagonists. The final surviving verses of this song – fragmentary as they are – confirm this impression. Here the singer rejoices at the affair, recalls another instance when the holy Cyprian blamed her for praying, and compares the women of her community with Aphrodite with the suggestion that they approbate love even more than the god of desire.

The lovers of frr. 16 and 22 are excited by the remembrance of certain aspects of a beloved's appearance, a scenario which is re-enacted, but with extraordinary difference, in Sappho 31. This song, one of the better-known love songs of western culture, appears at least partially to be a disquisition on the effects of erotic love.

φαίνεταί μοι κῆνος ἴσος θέοισιν
ἔμμεν' ὤνηρ, ὄττις ἐνάντιός τοι
ἰσδάνει καὶ πλάσιον ἆδυ φωνεί-
4 σας ὐπακούει

καὶ γελαίσας ἰμέροεν, τό μ' ἦ μὰν
καρδίαν ἐν στήθεσιν ἐπτόαισεν·
ὠς γὰρ ἔς σ' ἴδω βρόχε', ὤς με φώναι-
8 σ' οὐδ' ἒν ἔτ' εἴκει,

ἀλλὰ κὰμ μὲν γλῶσσά < μ' > ἔαγε, λέπτον
δ' αὔτικα χρῷ πῦρ ὐπαδεδρόμηκεν,
ὀππάτεσσι δ' οὐδ' ἒν ὄρημμ', ἐπιρρόμ-
12 βεισι δ' ἄκουαι,

κὰδ δέ μ' ἴδρως κακχέεται, τρόμος δὲ
παῖσαν ἄγρει, χλωροτέρα δὲ ποίας
ἔμμι, τεθνάκην δ' ὀλίγω 'πιδεύης
16 φαίνομ' ἔμ' αὔτ[α̣·

17 ἀλλὰ πὰν τόλματον, ἐπεὶ † καὶ πένητα †

To me he seems as fortunate as the gods,
this man, who sits opposite you,
so close, listening to the sweet sound
4 of your voice

and your lovely laughter. Truly, for me
that sound sets the heart trembling in my breast.
For when I gaze at you, just for a moment
8 I can no longer speak,

for < my > tongue has snapped, straightaway
a subtle fire runs beneath my flesh, my eyes
can see nothing, there is a fury of whirring
12 in my ears,

and sweat pours from me, trembling
harries every part of me, I am greener than grass
and little short of dying, or so
16 it seems to me.

17 But all can be endured, since even a pauper

The original function of the song is indeterminate, and arguments about its interpretation, translation, complexity, and its relationship with the 'lived experience' of the poet, have occupied scholars for several centuries. Most of these commentators agree, directly or indirectly, on the stereotypically 'feminine' basis of this song: the description of uncontrolled, physical/emotional symptoms; the 'natural' reaction of a woman maddened with jealousy by the sight of her beloved sitting, talking and laughing, with a man. Despite its 'feminine' ascription the emotional content of this representation seems sufficiently powerful to transgress most socio-literary orders and violent enough to match the pain and passion of any epic hero. To a greater degree than any other Sapphic song, the personal and cultural biases of each scholarly generation[7] are evident in the variant interpretations and translations of fr. 31. Perhaps the unusual (for Sappho) inclusion of a male protagonist complicates this erotic issue, setting up a competitive situation which, aided by the usual autobiographical assumptions, seems somehow to result in Sappho being labelled a masculine lesbian. Beyond these heterosexual suppositions, within a community where it seems that the love of one woman for another provided a reason for communal celebration and godly approbation, Sappho composed her song, telling of the intense reactions incited in a lover by the sight of her beloved, of the symptoms of an apparently female brand of desire.

Sappho 31 begins with two statements which are significant. First, the seemingness (31.1) which confers a dreamlike and indefinite spirit upon the pronouncements which follow. There is no tangible sense of time or place, not even the soft couches and fragrant gardens which decorate other Sapphic songs, only voices, glances, human interaction, with emotion filling the gaps. The characters who act out this surrealistic drama seem equally insubstantial, the man who is only godlike, the beloved, whose beauty is inferred by her relationship with this more than mortal man and the growing torment of the singer-lover. The reference to the godlike nature of this man endows him with quasi-divine qualities: so he is mysterious and powerful. In the female-oriented context of the Sapphic community he seems alien. The proliferation of androcentric comments that the presence of this man, and his subsequent disappearance, inspires are revelatory and gender-specific, but too diverse to consider closely. Instead I examine three premises which recur most often.

First there are the commentators[8] who consider that since a man is present in a Sapphic scenario, it must be a wedding-song. A not unlikely proposition, remembering the fortunateness of this man and the beauty of his companion, but one must discount a substantial portion of the remaining action to justify it. Page (1955: 33) asserts that 'there was never such a wedding-song in the history of society; and there should never have been such a theory in the history of scholarship'. At an earlier stage of his own interpretation, however, Page (1955: 28) states that: 'we shall not be content with any explanation of the poem which gives no satisfactory account of his presence and his prominence in it'. What possible motive could Sappho have had for introducing this all-important male protagonist and then discarding him? Surely if a man is initially placed in a superior position to female personae then he must continue to dominate the action. It seems inconceivable that the author could have intended to use him only as a foil, an anonymous third party in her erotic drama. Page (1955: 30) goes on to offer further proof of this man's vital role: 'to maintain that Sappho feels no jealousy of the man would be to ignore the certain response of human nature to a situation of the type described, and to deprive the introduction of the man, and his relation to the girl, of all significance. On this point, at least, there is little room for doubt.' Devereux (1970: 23) certainly feels there is none, although he considers that Sappho, as a masculine lesbian 'will experience anxiety rather than ordinary jealousy'. And that in an excess of penis envy 'she may both envy and inordinately admire ("godlike") her fortunate ("properly equipped") male rival'.

One literary element reused by Sappho is that disturbing Homeric echo 'ἴσος θέοισιν' (31.1). This echo presents a further example of what Winkler calls Sappho's 'double consciousness'. Perhaps by involving a man in a love scene between two women she is again exhibiting her many-mindedness. The borrowed glory and Homerisms which ennoble the man who sits awkwardly in the centre of a modern debate dissipate in the second line however, as he is reduced in linguistic status to an indefinite pronoun. Seated in close proximity to the beloved girl and recipient of 'the sweet sound of her voice' and 'lovely laughter' (31.3–5), he does form one corner of yet another triangle, 'the geometrical figure formed by their perception of one another, and the gaps in that perception' (Carson 1986: 14). In this way he plays an essential role, 'for where eros is lack' Carson (1986: 13–16) considers that 'its activation calls for three structural components – lover, beloved and that which comes between them'. Is that all this man is? Other commentators have proffered various explanations for his inclusion, suggesting that he was: a rhetorical device; a man honoured with immortality because of his ability to withstand the ambivalent proximity of the beloved, in contrast to the singer; the object of a *makarismos* (Winkler 1981: 73) or a female contribution to one of the stock philosophical debates of Sappho's time. Each commentator promotes a single, distinctive, and not improbable proposition. Considering Sappho's many-mindedness, her use of what appears to be a peculiarly 'womanly' and pluralistic brand of reasoning, perhaps a combination of several of these interpretations is possible. As Carson (1986: 15) affirms: 'the register of normality is missing from Sappho's poem'.

In the second stanza the emphasis moves from this happy, conventional couple to the third, intangibly distanced point of the triangle, the lover/singer. The dreamlike atmosphere Sappho has created is ruffled by the effect that love, and the voice and laughter of the beloved, has upon this vulnerable female protagonist, and by her initial reaction, the agitation of her heart in her breast.[9] Marcovich (1972: 23) believes that line seven, which begins with 'ὥς γὰρ ἔς σ' ἴδω', instigates a further alteration in the proceedings, and that this is the beginning of a recurrent action. Again, as in frr. 1 and 22, there is the suggestion of repeated erotic action. In fr. 31 the inference is that every time the lover gazes at the beloved the effect is equally devastating. This gaze, which is contrasted in the song with the close contact ('ἐνάντιός' refers to a proximity which can be either intimate or hostile) of the man and the beloved, could be classified as objective, even 'masculine', with one qualification or complication: the singer's excessive reaction. This reaction transfigures the dynamics of the viewer/viewed relationship so that it becomes more subjective and therefore more conventionally 'feminine'. The beloved, the object of the singer's gaze, is infinitely more powerful and detached than the woman who gazes at her. The lover/singer's response is physically, emotionally extraordinary, it gives the impression of a consuming passion and reminds us once more of the priority, the significance, *erôs* assumes in Sappho's songs. The portrayal of this passion – the effect the presence of the beloved has upon the lover/singer – takes up the remainder of the song. And in spite of the insubstantiality of protagonists who are never clearly delineated, this imaginative portrayal has a strong physical dimension.

When she hears the voice of a loved girl, this singer's heart is agitated disturbingly, when she gazes at her beloved, it becomes impossible for her to speak. Irigarary (1978: 50) separates sight from its objective with her statement that 'more than other senses, the eye objectifies and masters. It sets at a distance, maintains the distance. In our culture, the predominance of the look over smell, taste, touch, hearing has brought an impoverishment of bodily relations.' Sappho appears to dissolve this visual/sensual separation, to merge sight and the gaze of the lover/singer with other senses such as the power of speech. In another typically Sapphic manoeuvre, a mirroring effect which subtly contrasts oppositional states and coheres the action, the same word – 'φωνεί-σας', 'φώναι-σ'' – placed in an identical stanzaic position (end of third, beginning of fourth line in the first and second stanzas), is used for the speech of the beloved and the loss of speech of the lover. Distanced as they are by the action of the song the two female protagonists are united by one of the verbal echoes of the song, by sounds that add a sensual dimension to lyrics that were intended to be sung, to be experienced musically and rhythmically, rather than accessed from a page.

In the third and fourth stanzas however, syntactical complexities are overtaken by a catalogue of symptoms constructed paratactically and linked with 'δέ' (which occurs seven times). Often Sappho formulates her thoughts in this manner, adding piece by piece, lingering on each detail, cohering the whole loosely without recourse to hierarchical-type ordering that must distinguish best from worst. Wills (1967: 189), who notes Sappho's fondness for these 'vivid lists', each of which 'is contained within a temporal and causal framework that uses complex transitions to prepare one for the "naive" listing', considers that this technique is one of the means by which Sappho manages to temper her 'passionate moods and moments' with 'historical control'. Her ability to merge emotion with artistic control is much remarked upon, particularly in regard to Sappho 31.

Homer was also prone to compiling catalogues and Homeric echoes resonate through Sappho's list. According to Page (1955: 29) 'two only among her symptoms have no counterpart in Homer' and 'it is to be observed that neither of these recurs in later poetry'. But Homer's catalogues tell of ships, warriors and armament while his physiological episodes vivify the fear and pain experienced by men struggling against each other in the extremities of war, not love. Hierarchically, of course, one of these categories is considered glorious, valued unequivocally, the other is devalorised in a male scheme of things, no matter how evocative the representation. By choosing seven formulaic models, Sappho correlates the agony of battle with the agony of love and suggests 'double-consciously' that the pain her lover feels is equivalent to that felt by these warriors – that she is also terrified, physically disabled and anguished. In epic, however, similar afflictions tend to occur singly, divided by passages of description and identification. In fr. 31 they are consolidated, presented together in awesome combination so that the final effect is almost unbearable. Perhaps it is made bearable only by another form of double-sidedness, the almost clinical detachment of the singer/sufferer as she delineates the intensity of her symptoms. Longinus (*On the Sublime*, ix.15–x and x.3) praised Sappho's selection and co-ordination of physiological reactions, the manner in which she managed, almost simultaneously, to include and to draw together soul, body, hearing, tongue, sight, colour, as well as merging contradictory sensations and drawing upon a whole confluence of emotions.

Two extant fragments (84 and 103) of a male and reputedly 'masculine' poet, Archilochus of Paros, also combine the agony of love and/or battle. Campbell (1983: 5) remarks that these fragments 'attempt for the first time to express how it feels to be the victim of erotic desire', and comments on the Homeric emphasis that Archilochus translates into an erotic context. Apart from the metre of these songs, which couple hexameters tersely with short iambic lines, images such as 'κατ' ἀχλὺν ὀμμάτων ἔχευεν' (191.2), the mist which often covers the eyes of dying warriors, evoke a particularly epic version of *erôs*. It is an effective co-ordination of apparently disparate images, genres and contexts, one which again transfers known elements (the injuries of war) into a different, but not inappropriate, zone. The extant fragments of Archilochus' love songs are shorter than Sappho 31, but the descriptions of pain and desire, and the way they are borrowed from epic contexts, are not dissimilar. The symptoms listed by Archilochus are comprehensive and physical, and while they are not as comprehensive, or as devastating, as those depicted in Sappho 31, their effect upon the lover seems analogous. Kirkwood (1974: 41) considers that 'in all of them there is the same suggestion: the emotion is an unwanted force from without, or a disease that afflicts the poet'. Certainly it seems that Archilochus' depiction of love is predominantly negative. The lover is represented as a victim, and in these fragments he is pierced, overwhelmed, dispirited and blinded by *erôs* and/or the gods. An unfortunate fate for any proud warrior. Even the verb 'ἐλυσθεὶς' (191.1), which depicts love curled up beneath the heart, has unpleasant connotations, reminding one of the demeaning position that Odysseus (*Odyssey* 9.433) and Priam (*Iliad* 24.510) were forced to assume.

Carson (1986: 148) compiles an exhaustive list of the weapons of Eros, the 'nets, arrows, fire, hammers, hurricanes, fevers, boxing gloves or bits and bridles' he uses in making his assault, a list which suggests a victor/victim mode of *erôs*. Only one item, 'fevers' features in Sappho's erotic scenarios. The image of *erôs* evolving from male representations seems to be abhorrent and unwelcome, distinct from the more positive perspective implied by the final line of Sappho 31 and evident in other songs. There are other significant differences. This man-made erotic force is usually external to the singer, while in Sappho's songs emotion is internalised and appears to be even more devastating. And whereas the role of the beloved in Sappho 31 is contextually and erotically dynamic, within Archilochus' fragments there is no perception of a beloved. This is an adversary relationship in which a battle takes place between the singer and Eros, one which is presumably instigated and won by Eros. There are no soft glances, voices, or even rivals, merely two combatants locked into a face to face, life or death struggle, where one protagonist is unfairly advantaged and both are definably 'male'. The resemblance to a battlefield in Archilochus' scenarios is indisputable, but there appears to be a process of assimilation or superimposition, a connection of two disparate contexts which, rather than substantially expanding either the militant or the erotic zone, reduces both zones to complementary arenas in which battle is glorious but life-endangering, while engaging with love is simply dangerous.

As Sappho's lover/singer gazes at her beloved she burns, sweats and trembles, so that a whole range of abnormal states is merged into one moment. One of the non-Homeric additions Sappho made to the list in fr. 31, 'the subtle fire which runs beneath her flesh' (31.9–10), itself a collusion of metaphor and experience, of internal/external factors: blood and warmth, skin and colour, contrives to produce this impression. The lover is also deprived of speech, sight, hearing and skin colour, so her symptoms appear to be predominantly physiological. This physiological emphasis appears, at least superficially, to fit into a conventional 'feminine' categorisation: foregrounding the body, not the mind, valuing emotion above reason and the internal, private world above the external public world. In fr. 31, however, although Sappho builds her portrayal piece by piece, there is concord between each element so that what results is an almost indivisible composite, not a scheme of balanced, antithetical states. In the last lines of the fourth stanza the debilitation of the singer is complete, she seems 'to be little short of dying' (31.17). The reiteration of 'seems' at this stage connects the end with the beginning and shifts back from the physiological extremity of the preceding lines to the dreamlike atmosphere of the first stanza. Segal (1974: 146–7) draws our attention to 'the interaction of meter with sound-patterns, sentence structure, and meaning . . . the carefully built up patterns of alliteration and assonance' which accentuate the rhythm in stanzas three and four, the drumming δ beat of lines 10 and 13, and the vowel sounds which reinforce the repetitive effect of recurring conjunctions and short clauses. Other sensual factors, such as speech and hearing (the whirring in the ears is also a Sapphic innovation) have been recurrent motifs in this song, but the drumming beat of the music and the heart pounding in the singers' breast must slow. In the calm after the storm, 'all can be endured' (31.17), and love and life in the Sapphic community must presumably go on.

The sensuality and the cohesiveness of this disquisition on the effects of *erôs* appear to be difficult to match. Sappho 31 is the product of a relatively unmapped lyric tradition, of a unique female creator, of a single oral/literate moment in time. As is evident from the representations of Archilochus and Mimnermus, however, men also sang of the ambivalent effects of *erôs*. Burnett (1983: 235) considers that the enigmatic male character in Sappho's song 'owes a great deal to the ubiquitous figure who allows so many love-songs, both ancient and modern, to argue that anyone who can resist you must be made of stone'. To the extent that he serves in this capacity, his double can be recognised in one of Pindar's songs (123S). Like Sappho 31, Pindar's song also has three (male) protagonists: lover, beloved and a man who is undefined and surprisingly unaffected by the beloved's radiance. It also contains passages describing the effect/s of a single glance from this young man (in this case the protagonist who gazes is detached/active/powerful); and the language appears to be equally rich and varied. Pindar's lyric poetry was produced predominantly for the public arena, and even this personal gesture appears definably grand in both intention and treatment.

Pindar's song opens with a general statement about love's flowers and youth before it moves on to introduce one of the major protagonists – the man who can meet Theoxenus' glance and remain unmoved – a man who seems analogous to the godlike man in Sappho 31. With the evocative description of his steely heart and ambivalent sexuality however, this man's anonymity assumes an immense difference – he is not enigmatic, but generic

– a stereotype that would be readily recognised by Pindar's audience. The suggestive images which enliven this description – 'swell with passion' ('πόθῳ κυμαίνεται' 123.5), a black heart 'forged from iron or adamant' ('ἐξ ἀδάμαντος / ἤ σιδάρου κεχάλκευται' 123.5–6) – do appear to be 'masculine' in orientation and relatively overt, in comparison with the sensuousness which is gently suggested in the first lines of Sappho 31, with the use of words such as 'ἰμέροεν' (31.5), combining a sense of loveliness with desire. Not content with relating his more invulnerable characteristics, Pindar then goes on to denigrate this man, to use the song as a public forum. He is accused of forsaking the worship of Aphrodite for that of wealth, and it is also stated that 'with woman-like courage, (he) rushes along cool[10] paths' ('γυναικείῳ θράσει / ψυχὰν φορεῖται πᾶσαν ὁδὸν' 123.8–9). It seems that chastity is commendable only in women and youthful objects, not male lovers, and the 'woman-like' slur sets the poem in an arena where traditional male values are the status quo. Pindar, it seems, is setting up a scheme of oppositional states that contrasts the frigidity of this man with the warmth of the singer and centres on cold/hot images.

Was Sappho engaging in a similar process when she contrasted the singer's distress with the godlike man's invulnerability? In my opinion there are several differences. While Sappho's descriptions are agonised and specific, Pindar uses a single conventional, and not unpleasant analogy to portray his love. Within the context of the song, his scheme of comparisons and the tradition from which this analogy emanated, it fits admirably, but it seems to have little connection with the physical or emotional state of his lover/singer. Unlike Sappho 31, which contrives, with the succinct physicality of Sappho's representation, to make its audience apprehend the suffering of the lover, the tone and treatment of Pindar's song generate awareness only of the competency of the poet and his desire to compliment a young man. Or any young man, since the singer melts whenever ('εὖτ' ἂν') he looks at 'the fresh skin of boys' ('παίδων νεόγυιον' 123.11–12). This is a gaze which reveals itself to be detached and objective. Rather than concentrating on Theoxenus' attractions or the effect which these have upon him, the lover appears to be announcing, in contrast to his cooler rival, his own sexual vigour, his capacity for voluptuousness. A capacity which is obviously quite acceptable, even approbatory, in this context. Burnett (1983: 235) considers that 'probably Pindar is only pretending to sing a love-song in these fastidiously suggestive lines', and the impersonality of his erotic pronouncements implies that this is the case. The last lines add to the substantiality of this song, giving the audience names and places, even the name of Theoxenus' father. Filling in a paternal background, and locating it in a temporal, geographical environment, Pindar's song differs from the insubstantiality often found in Sappho's songs.

There is one small portion of erotic Sapphic verse (fr. 48), that appears to reproduce Pindar's hot/cold binary patterning.

> ἦλθες, ἔγω δέ σ' ἐμαιόμαν,
> ὂν δ' ἔψυξας ἔμαν φρένα καιομέναν πόθῳ.

> You came, and I was longing for you,
> you cooled my heart, it was burning with desire.

In this scrap of a love story a heart which was previously burning with longing is satisfied, cooled by the presence of the beloved. That presence, conveyed simply, but with immediacy by 'ἦλθες', and the satisfaction it affords, seems to provoke an unusual erotic situation. Carson (1986: 10) points out that 'the Greek word *eros* denotes "want," "lack," "desire for that which is missing." The lover wants what he does not have. It is by definition impossible for him to have what he wants if, as soon as it is had, it is no longer wanting.' The intense drives associated with desire must remain unsatisfied or else become non-erotic. In Sapphic songs such as frr. 31 and 16, Pindar 123S, and in the majority of male love lyrics, this paradoxical situation and the unresolved tensions that accompany it energise a great number of scenarios. But in the few lines that remain of Sappho 48 (and perhaps its fragmentary state misrepresents the poet's original intention) lack is satisfied, the disparate poles of absence and presence meet and merge with a metaphoric hiss that seems to dissolve oppositions and run counter to psychoanalytic theories. It also appears to provide a 'womanly' and subversive solution to an unbearable paradox. In the way this scrap of a poem revolves around the comparison of conventional oppositional states: then/now; hot/cold; as well as lack/satiety, however, it seems just as schematic and phallocentric as Pindar 123S or Alcaeus 283. Some differences are evident. Its minuteness is a definitive factor, but it seems that the conjunction of antithetical states is very close – the time span separating them is almost imperceptible, the burning, cooling sensations which sensually, metaphorically, represent longing and satisfaction are experienced simultaneously – so that the impression received is one of cohesion or at least ambivalence and a logical sequence of events is reduced to a single incalculable moment.[11] Page (1955: 110) comments on Sappho's 'simplicity of thought', her 'delicacy in expression', two characteristics which are apparent in fr. 48. This simplicity and delicacy are deceptively powerful, Sappho has the ability to confine an emotional event into very few words. The fragment, the relationship, end with the satisfaction of desire, but the word itself, 'πόθῳ', sits at the end of the line and leaves the desire it defines hanging, waiting for the next erotic moment.

The final love song analysed in this chapter, in which the divine agent is not Aphrodite but Eros, is more innovative and paradoxical.

> Ἔρος, δηὖτέ μ' ὀ λυσιμέλης δόνει,
> γλυκύπικρον ἀμάχανον ὄρπετον
>
> Once again Eros the limb-loosener makes me tremble,
> the sweetbitter, irresistible creature.
>
> (fr. 130)

This representation of Eros, in a sensuous, bestial image of a creeping, subversive being who conventionally loosens limbs, who steals up 'like a creature' to wreak his 'γλυκύπικρον'[12] force once again on a defenceless victim, resembles Whitmont's (1987: 130) definition of 'an aggressive hunter', and matches some of the male lyric poets' descriptions of a violent persecutor. Is Sappho delving into mainstream constructs once more, double-mindedly mimicking forms and creating a representation that bridges male and female socio-poetical territories? An ironical echo sounds through Sappho's description of Eros. This irresistible creature who loosens limbs and sets the singer trembling appears inescapable but not so frightening. Sappho's singular representation and the double-faceted epithet that seems to epitomise erotic love actually works to integrate the two paradoxical, but simultaneous, sweet and bitter, aspects of love. Carson (1986: 4) asserts that 'Eros is an enemy. Its bitterness must be the taste of enmity. That would be hate.' A statement that befits the enmity represented in some male socio-political contexts where two aggressive beings fight to the death. Within the word, 'γλυκύπικρον' and in many Sapphic representations, however, *erôs* is also sweet, sweet enough perhaps to counteract even the bitter enmity of rejection or unfulfilled love. Arguably, with this further example of simultaneity, of the merger of oppositional descriptions such as sweet/bitter – which relate graphically to the pleasurable/painful nature of love – and the unusual features of her description of Eros, Sappho manages once again to present an erotic depiction which exceeds other, more binary, constructions.

In her love songs Sappho manipulates and expands upon a discourse of desire intrinsic to lyric poetry, representing episodes of love between women that centre on a combination of pleasure and angst, that are almost unbearable but must and 'can be endured' (31.17). With the extremity and simultaneity of these representations she does appear to critique language, to the extent that she transgresses or exceeds some of the patterns and modes normally constructing/constructed into lyric poetry. The lovers Sappho constructs also act within the aegis and with the approval of a female god, gazing at, desiring and sometimes merging with beloveds who are erotically empowered. Sappho uses the same language, the same forms as the male lyric poets, but she sings most often of desire between women, a love which Irigaray considers could be 'the matrix which can generate change' (Whitford 1991: 48). Constructed mnemonically into rhythmic and metrical patterns and sequences the archaic genre of erotic lyric poetry is itself fluid, multiple and open to reformulation. Sappho, it seems, remains within these linguistic patterns, but disturbs other orders. In songs designed to explore and express the eroticism of women, she tells of a distinctive, female, form of desire.

Chapter 3

A woman's desire

The editors of *Before Sexuality* open their discussion with Henderson's comprehensive definition of sexuality: 'Sexuality is that complex of reactions, interpretations, definitions, prohibitions, and norms that is created and maintained by a given culture in response to the fact of the two biological sexes' (Henderson 1988: 1250). The concept 'sexuality' is constructed within, and relatable specifically to, twentieth-century western culture, a context in which it has been used variously to signify gender (in respect of male, female or neuter status), erotic orientation, and sexual experience. As these commentators acknowledge, it is culturally specific and ultimately incapable of defining the sexual status, orientation, and experience of the inhabitants of an 'other' culture such as ancient Greece. Comprehensive as the definition in *Before Sexuality* is, with the reference to 'the two biological sexes' it brings into focus the heterosexual pair, the binary model that represents the sexual norm of later western culture, and is thus imperfectly applicable to the form of sexuality consistently reconstructed from Sappho's representations. According to the specifications of this model, the representations of woman-to-woman relationships that have fascinated and shocked scholars over the centuries are deviant, immoral, and worse, non-creative – at least in the sense of reproducing the species. Sappho's rhythmic songs are poetic artefacts created within the conventions of a genre rather than reports of sexual interactions, prohibitions, norms, etc. constructed in the ancient world. Poetic and homoerotic as they are, they do fit within the broad category of 'a cultural poetics of desire', and construct sexual meanings and describe/effect 'the formation of sexual identities' (Halperin, Winkler and Zeitlin 1990: 4). One of the major projects of *Before*

Sexuality is the exploration of different modes of sexual discourse and behaviours, and this is a project I continue with my discussion of the form/s of 'sexuality' represented in Sappho's lyrics. Concepts of sexuality in their multiple senses, as well as representations of that site of sexuality, the body, shift and change with time. Laqueur (1990: 16) stresses the culturally specific nature of such concepts: 'sex, like being human, is contextual', it cannot be detached from 'its discursive, socially determined milieu' and 'the private, enclosed, stable body that seems to lie at the basis of modern notions of sexual difference is also the product of particular, historical, cultural moments'.

The sexual experience that can be inferred or reconstructed from the fragments of Sappho's songs, as well as from references to the body, foregrounds the instability and historical specificity of later constructions. It is distinctive, offering variant models of 'sexuality', definitions and attitudes. The significance accorded what is essentially a modern sign,[1] a term in currency only since the nineteenth century, has increased greatly over the last hundred years. One influential factor has been the development of psychoanalytic theory and its sex-centred definitions of identity and difference. This discipline claims a universal and ahistorical status for its discourses. How relevant are these discourses to archaic or ancient Greece? In a work concerned with exploring 'representations of the female body in psychoanalytic work and in ancient Greek literature, ritual, and artistic "texts"', duBois (1988: 1–3) asserts 'that the psychoanalytic model of phallocentricism and castration is inadequate for describing the ancient Greek's views about gender difference and about male and female bodies'. Psychoanalytic theory and method can vary, and some practitioners – Klein, Horney and Jones, for example – have attempted to shift the focus from the law of the father to female sexuality and the mother/child relationship. The theories of Freud and Lacan do prioritise the castration complex, and are as phallocentric as the world they reproduce and legitimise in discourses which appropriate the privilege usually accorded to scientific commentaries. Freud was convinced that no human being could become a subject outside the division into two sexes, but other categories seem also to have concerned and divided the subjects of ancient Greece: god/mortal, old/young, Greek/barbarian, dominator/dominated, master/slave, etc. appear more relevant to antique society than a fundamental dichotomy of male/female, phallic/non-phallic, subjects. The segregation of men and women into public or private arenas was more overt, but the construction of sexual identity and meaning, at least before the time of Plato,[2] was differently coded, politicised and represented.

In the marginalised, homoerotic world of the Sapphic community, 'sexuality', as represented in Sappho's songs, appears even more divergent. Outside this community, in a public and more 'heterosexually' ordered world, women's sexual activity was controlled by a plethora of means and mores, some evidence of which can be seen in the poetry of Semonides, Alcaeus and Archilochus. Within the relative isolation of Sappho's community, women interacted only with other women. Did Sappho initiate these women into the *glukupikron* rituals of erotic love? Some commentators have attempted to rationalise her homoerotic inclinations by describing Sappho as 'a kind of female pederast',[3] a woman who loved younger women and within the relationship, educated her beloved in a way that was socially acceptable. The parallel is not entirely unfeasible, although the evidence Lardinois cites – the presence of male pederasts on Lesbos and a single word 'ἀΐτιας' which Alcman (fr. 34) uses to refer to darling girls instead of the usual darling boys (Lardinois 1989: 27) – seems inconclusive. But the use of a male model to explain a relationship between women suggests a further projection of public male culture on to the more mysterious female world. Is this just another instance of men attempting to control female sexuality by theories or representations which emanate from a phallocentric perspective?

Many commentators struggle with the idea that whatever sexual activity occurred within the Sapphic community, it was apparently accepted by the larger community who allowed their womenfolk to gather in what is perceived – particularly by nineteenth-century scholars – to be a den of iniquity where unnatural or sinful behaviour was encouraged. Arguably, if the practice of 'homosexuality' was an issue – and we cannot be certain that it was – this form of sexual activity was tolerated because it was not procreative, because it did not alter a woman's virginal status, or affect her entry into marriage and male/female relations, except in ways that were considered positive. Within this idealistic setting women sang of the rituals of love and the correct manner of worshipping gods, wearing clothes, garlands and headbands. In this way they were constructed into a sexual identity that presumably accorded with the models of archaic society. Dover (1978: 181) suggests that 'the relations between participants in a female chorus or between teacher and pupils in music and poetry may thus have constituted an overt "sub-culture", or rather "counter-culture" in which women and girls received from their own sex what segregation and monogamy denied them from men'. This teacher/pupil model – one of the most promulgated hypotheses about Sappho's group – is, as Parker (1993: 309–46) asserts, problematic. Evidence about the relations between Sappho and the women she sings of is inconclusive, and modes of 'sexuality', like words and terms, only have meaning – as Threadgold (1990: 18) states – 'in relation to the enormously complex discursive and semiotic systems (including the sexed bodies and subjectivities) within which and through which they are functional'.

Freud apparently thought of ancient Greece not as a separate, 'other' framework with its own complex systems and discourses, but as a primal moment in the progressive development of western culture – one that 'recorded, undisguised, the simple unrepressed desires of mankind' (duBois 1988: 22). To this end he incorporated its sexed subjects in his 'phallogocentric' theories,[4] and extracted specific examples of these unrepressed desires (i.e. the Oedipus complex) to describe both the integration of the individual into the symbolic order, and the construction of sexual identity and division. The signs/terms he employed to explicate his theories also exhibit a process of blending and innovation. By using biological terms relating to sexual desire to describe or prescribe the transition of an infant into a state of division, or nominating a sexual cause for every psychosis, he seems to pre-empt the sex-centredness that is pervasive in our culture. His account of a modern 'rite of passage'[5] might be less than satisfactory when used as a model to define female sexuality, but psychoanalytic theories have been, and continue to be, extremely influential and they provide a useful methodology for analysing and describing the processes of the mind, sexuality, and the sexing or gendering of individuals.

Rites of passage are, it seems, also celebrated within the Sapphic community. In many parts of the Greek world, female initiates pass through at least two stages, both of which are ritualised and celebrated. The first of these is the advent of sexual maturity, the second is marriage. Both stages/celebrations involve physiological changes, firstly the onset of menstruation, secondly the loss of virginity. In Sappho's songs the two stages are differently represented and shown to provoke both celebration and anguish. The movement to sexual maturity (frr. 2, 81, 94) is accompanied by the donning of garlands and wreaths, and by the love of one girl for another. Marriage and entrance into the 'heterosexual' world means the loss of such pleasant moments, the movement from an all-female environment not unlike the cloistered semi-freedom of childhood, into the assumption of adult identity in a sexually divided world. In one song Sappho represents this physiological and cultural development with a 'natural' metaphor (fr. 104a), which details a repeated sequence of loss and return, as Hesperus, the evening star, brings back the vulnerable creatures scattered by the dawn.

> Ἕσπερε πάντα φέρων ὄσα φαίνολις ἐσκέδασ' αὔως,
> †φέρεις ὄιν, φέρεις αἶγα, φέρεις ἄπυ μάτερι παῖδα·
>
> Hesperus, bringing back everything that was scattered by shining dawn
> . . . you bring back the sheep, you bring the goat, you bring the child back to its mother.

Women who marry do not return to the comfort either of mother or of the other women of the group. They have moved into a differently isolated arena where the pleasures of the Sapphic community are merely memories – an arena which could be compared with the marriages and divided public/private environments of Freud's social context – the nineteenth century.

Freud is said to have loved literature, but his discursive practices are more clinical and less poetic than Sappho's. His descriptions of the mediating force of the Oedipus complex can be used as a mirror which reflects some correspondences with a transition that occurred when female subjects of the Sapphic community entered the order of a male subject who represented law, order and authority. Grosz (1990: 69–70) summarises four 'major functional changes' that accompany the change, for Freud, from pre-Oedipal to Oedipal relations: 1. 'it introduces the sexually indifferent or polymorphous child to the (sexual/genital) differences between the sexes . . .' ; 2. 'it attempts to "match" the child's "biological" sex with its socially determined gender . . .'; 3. 'it introduces the reality principle, social law, and considerations of material existence to the pleasure-seeking, gratification-dominated child . . .'; and 4. 'it severs the constricting mutuality binding the child to its parents, especially the mother, enabling the child to establish relations, including sexual relations, with others outside the family'. There are as many disparities as equivalences in my comparison of the psychological development of an infant with the advent of sexual maturity and marriage of women of the Sapphic community. There are also similarities, however, in the transformation of the sexed subject, from a pre-Oedipal, pre-sexual state, to interaction in heterosexual relations and the assumption of a position in a sexually divided world.

Before the subject of either a Freudian or Sapphic world can take up a position in patriarchal order and discourse, she or he must move through a series of erotic relations or stages. For the infant Freudian subject, as Grosz (1990: 55–6) notes, 'the emergence of erotic and libidinal relations from self-preservative instincts is a function of lack or absence, the lack or absence of a given or pre-determined object'. The Sapphic initiate must also discover that 'lack' or 'absence' is one of the *glukupikron* aspects of erotic desire. Whether they are intended as laments, pleas or educational mechanisms, many of Sappho's extant songs (frr. 1, 16, 31, 36, 96, 131 and 168b) articulate this theme.

Lacan's psychoanalytic model also deals with lack and absence, with a movement via demand and desire towards a symbolic order and the Law of the Father. One of the most obvious differences between Freudian and Lacanian theory, is the emphasis Lacan places on language. For him, according to Grosz (1989: 20), 'sexuality and the unconscious can only be understood in terms of the peculiar "logic" of language. They are structured, organised and made meaningful only in terms of a key or threshold signifier, which represents language and embodies the Father's Law: the phallus.' It is desire which 'opens the subject to a broader world of signification or infinite semiosis: a world in which it has access to systems of meaning unregulated by any individual or group, and unrestricted in the range of its possible messages' – it is desire which 'marks the child's entry into the domain of the Other – the domain of law and language, law-as-language' (Grosz 1990: 66). But what of the non-phallic female in this order? Presumably she also demands and desires but 'her position within the symbolic must be marginal or tenuous: when she speaks as an "I" it is never clear that she speaks (of or as) herself. She speaks in a mode of masquerade, in imitation of the masculine, phallic subject' (Grosz 1990: 72). Does this form of 'lack' or 'absence' – the inability to speak or participate in systems of signification or semiosis – restrict the linguistic utterances of desiring female subjects of Sappho's songs? According to Lacanian theory, these women are also silenced, trapped within the confines of a male-dominated system.

Because of their negative sexual status, the women of our culture are said to be excluded from language, power and subjectivity, but they are positioned at the top of a phallocentric structure, a tree that Derrida (1975: 97) considers stems from 'an enormous and old root' that has been growing, reproducing itself, for thousands of years. The position/status of the women of the Sapphic community appears different. Were they considered, did they consider themselves, castrated and linguistically, sexually, repressed? Laqueur foregrounds differences in bodily perceptions and constructions throughout various stages of western culture. The bodies of the women of the Sapphic community were constructed outside the prohibitions and castration complexes of a twentieth-century symbolic order. Were they, at least within Sappho's songs, positively constructed, representative of a female body that was capable of desire or speech? Different forms of lack predominate in Sappho's symbolic register, the absence of a beloved, for example, or the immaturity of a pre-sexual subject.

Was Sappho of Lesbos small and dark, physically unexceptional, or as golden-haired and beautiful as the women and gods who decorate her songs? In antiquity, statues were erected and coins minted in her image, but the exact details of her appearance are now lost. Images of the body proliferate in her songs however, suggesting that the sexed subjects of her world were as fascinated with representations of this site of sexuality as the sexed subjects of the late twentieth century. Some of the many sculptural representations of antique bodies have lasted, reminding us of their prominence and/or the ways in which they were represented and idealised. Other cultural artefacts tell the same story. Homer's epics are full of the sight and sound of bodies straining in battle, or occasionally, and more modestly, in sexual activity; or being transformed by a god, flesh gleaming, muscles and legs as stout as oak trees standing staunchly against brutish enemies. Other preoccupations – the hours spent daily in gymnasia, the careful regimens for preserving health, athletic contests, a philosophical desire to analyse human and animal physiologies – all reflect this interest in the body. It is thought that 'women are somehow *more* biological, *more* corporeal, and *more* natural than men' (Grosz 1994: 14), and so female representations of corporeality should reveal this difference. But Sappho's representations of the body appear to be no more natural and/or less encultured than those of male poets. They concentrate on specific erotic zones, the face, eyes or heart, for example, and repeated references to these zones combine in imagistic patterns that contribute to the overall cohesion and sensuousness of her songs.

In Sappho 1.4 and 18, 'θῦμός', heart or spirit, occurs twice (and again in frr. 42 and 60), and reference is also made to Aphrodite's face and smile, while voices, mortal and immortal, can be heard throughout, alternating in sensuous oral sequences. Fragment 16.18 also highlights a shining face ('προσώπον', also used in Sappho 1) as well as the movements of a girl walking, or an army marching. In the tatters of fr. 21, as in fr. 58.13, skin is mentioned, not moist young flesh however, but 'χρόα γῆρας'. Frr. 22 and 23 introduce some new (golden hair) and some favourite images: faces feature in both fragments. Eye contact is also important between lovers or rivals who gaze or hide their eyes/emotions (frr. 137, 138 and 151). Tender ankles (frr. 44 and 57) are another conventional image, one with some Homeric parallels. Another word with some Homeric significance – 'φρένας' – recurs several times (frr. 47.2, 48.2, 96.17 and 120.2) and is usually translated as 'heart', although it can be interpreted as mind, or Homerically, as life. This presents us with an anatomical, conceptual difference between a culture that places mind and emotions together at the centre of the human body and one that assigns more importance to a later site of intelligence, the head and brain. The breast, the pulsating container of those vital parts – the *phrenes*, the breath of life and the emotions – is also mentioned several times (frr. 126, 140a, 158 and 31). In fr. 140a the breast is endowed with ritualistic significance, as the girls beat their breasts in an age-old gesture of grief. Many of the other body parts detailed in Sappho's songs seem to relate to rituals enacted by this community: it is not hard to imagine feet (frr. 103, 103b, 110a and 39) flashing, thudding in ritual movements, while curls (frr. 81 and 98) and necks (fr. 94) are garlanded by gentle hands ('χέρσιν' fr. 81.5). Likewise, soft-voices ('μελλιχόφοι' frr. 71.6 and 185), or the movements of tongues that enable speech or song (frr. 137, 158 and 31), can be heard throughout Sappho's songs, singing, talking or laughing together.

Readers searching for evidence of sexual activity might be disappointed by this modest selection of body parts: tongues that merely speak, breasts that seem more chest-like than titillating, hands that weave garlands rather than caress, etc. There are no genitals mentioned here. In our cultural context we seem obsessed by genitals, at least as visible markers of 'sexuality' or 'lack'. Smith-Rosenberg (1983: 34) remarks that we appear 'to view human love and sexuality within a dichotomised universe of deviance and normality, genitality and platonic love'. Judged by the sexual constructions of the late twentieth century, the 'sexuality' constructed in Sappho's songs is deviant and noticeably non-genital, but then perhaps Sappho did not divide the world up into those who possessed a phallus, those who lacked one. Phalloi in the representations and rituals of her social context were differently symbolised and appear in some ways less significant, and more transferable. Her selection of body parts and erotic activity might seem non-sexual, but they were obviously judged differently by her own world. In Lardinois's (191: 25) view, antique Greeks considered that she was a 'generally erotic woman', and it is not as if 'sexual' love does not feature in her work; it is the distinctiveness of these constructions that affects our reception of them. There is no doubt that Sappho 31 is a song about 'sexuality', it is intensely emotional and physical[6] in construction and impact, but no bodily contact is reported or even imagined between lover and beloved, excessive desire is demonstrated with a catalogue of one-sided symptoms while the lover/singer remains lacking, desiring.

Not all Sapphic representations are as physically excessive and overt as fr. 31. Some songs, Sappho 2 for example, sing about sexuality and body parts in a more metaphoric fashion. Within this ancient context,[7] in the terms of a more modest enunciation of genitalia and other body parts, apparently insignificant and/or natural phenomena are transformed into sexual signifiers of a different kind. The roses that overshadow the grove in fr. 2 construct a metaphoric image that has translated poetically through time into our culture – one of female genitalia – of the rosy folds of labia. Winkler (1981: 78) extends it further by associating it with *nymphê* and a variety of clitoral images, one of which is 'an opening rosebud'. The garden in fr. 2 is also the site of apple trees, a fruit that has similar metaphoric and clitoral connotations.[8] The reddening apple in fr. 105a seems to illustrate this technique of discreet genital representation. As Winkler (1981:79) remarks: 'the verb ἐρεύθω, "grow red," and its cognates are used of blood or other red liquid appearing on the surface of an object which is painted or stained or when the skin suffuses with blood'. In the few phallic representations in Sappho's wedding songs, references to the size of the groom provide another example of this form of sexual discourse. Knowledge of these metaphors adds to the interpretation/s of Sappho's representations, as well as assigning them a further sexual/genital sense.

In her quest to discover and explore 'the different terms by which the society *before* Plato conceptualised sexuality', duBois (1988: 2) also foregrounds the distinctiveness of ancient representations of the female body and 'sexuality'. Her findings and the perspective and theoretical tools through which she examines antique society present us with a more female-oriented view of this context, its sexed subjects and constructions. DuBois (1988: 26) prefaces her discussion with one of Sappho's songs (fr. 96), a song which she considers interesting because 'it is consciously subverting the hegemonic discourse about gender difference, about heterosexual intercourse, in the Greek world'. What intrigues duBois are 'the ways in which it seems deliberately to set itself against the reproductive heterosexual models of ancient culture'. Reproductive 'heterosexual' models are not the exclusive province of ancient culture, later western culture also demonstrates a vested interest in maintaining a 'heterosexual' and procreative ideal via representations of the body. In *Making Sex* Laqueur points out the prescriptive Freudian transferral of the site of female sexuality from the pleasurable but non-productive clitoris, to the site of 'mature' and reproductive sexuality, the vagina.[9] Sappho's world seems to be distanced both from the demands of reproductive sexual interaction and the agricultural metaphors which duBois believes predominate in this context.[10]

Fragment 96 is a song full of metaphors and images that could be defined as female-oriented, or as traditionally 'feminine', and are used to reconstruct the natural world. DuBois (1988: 27) considers that 'Sappho's poem celebrates the female body as unploughed earth, as ground spontaneously yielding not grain but flowers; she aestheticizes the reproductive model she inherits with a vision of the earth as parthenogenetic. Her earth is nourished only by the female dew and flowers under the female moon.' This metaphoric construction seems extraordinarily fruitful, and again sexual metaphors such as roses flourish among flower-filled fields. Mythical dimensions are added with the inclusion of female symbols such as the moon – which in combination with other elements, the *eersa* or dew for example – contrives an appropriate setting for female subjects. The song is textually coherent, circling back and forth between environments and images, integrating disparate elements into a single, eroticised body. The Lydian woman who is focused upon becomes strangely powerful, if somehow asexual, a wanderer sexually transfixed between the homoerotic and non-procreative world of Sappho's group and the potentially productive 'heterosexual' world she now inhabits. Sexually this construction seems divergent, itself caught up in the dynamics of female/male worlds, of old/new cultures, of hetero/homoerotic environments. It presents a denial of male/female reproductive processes that subverts the models of both ancient and modern worlds.

Winkler talks of a metaphoric vocabulary that is known and used by both male and female subjects of antiquity and links this to a preoccupation with sexual/bodily matters. DuBois confirms this orientation by foregrounding ancient bodily metaphors reconstructed by authors of both sexes. It is increasingly obvious that whatever form/s or concept/s of 'sexuality' existed in this ancient context, they were distinctive. Sappho's representations are relatively inimitable, but she was composing within the conventions of a genre that was used innovatively by both sexes. How similar then were the sexual and bodily constructions of the male lyric poets?

In the context of earth and reproduction, few of the lyric poets seem to share Hesiod's agricultural preoccupation – perhaps this subject is too mundane for a genre that was increasingly devoted to terse ripostes and entertainment. In fr. 36 Solon makes a typically political and didactic statement that involves 'the powerful mother of the Olympians, black Earth' ('μήτηϱ μεγίστη δαιμόνων 'Ολυμπίων' 36.4–5). Like Sappho with her image of parthenogenetic growth (fr. 96), but entirely unlike Sappho,[11] Solon represents the concept of the earth's freedom, but he concentrates on a mechanism of control and division, of mortgage stones that were fixed in her body, which he has now removed. Campbell (1983: 99) talks of the 'physical reality' of Solon's image, but despite this 'physical reality' the issue of reproduction (or human sexuality) does not surface. This poem is all about control and exchange of the mythically female body of the earth, or the bodies of slaves, and it ends with an image of the hierarchical and aggressive superiority of an animal body, a wolf ranging among a pack of dogs (36.27).

There are other less metaphoric male representations of female bodies and their sexual activity in ancient poetry, but the theme of control and/or mastery which features strongly in Solon's song, as well as in later analyses like Foucault's *History of Sexuality, Vol. 2*, remains a central focus.[12] One example of this practice – represented satirically and in a typically didactic manner – is a long composition by Semonides of Amorgos. This song is all about bodies, the female sex and their imperfections, and it tells its potent and misogynistic tale through a series of animal fables or analogies. Most of these are pejorative and appear to be designed either to instruct a woman how not to behave or to provide amusement for a male audience. This generic woman (or women) is fat and slothful like a 'bristly sow' ('ὑὸς τανύτριχος' 7.2); or too smart and changeable like a vixen; or she resembles a nosy, unmanageable bitch; or a stupid clod;[13] or this is a woman who is as fickle, unpredictable or demented as the sea (another female body). Like earth and sea or perhaps a 'much-thumped ass' ('παλιντριβέος' 7.43) she is fertile, but indiscriminate, and in need of male control unless she is as physically repulsive as a weasel or a monkey. Even female beauty is reprehensible in this context, vain and therefore expensive and time-consuming; only the bee, analogous to a modest, hard-working and productive woman, receives some praise. Women, or wives, 'the greatest evil Zeus has created' ('Ζεύς γὰρ μέγιστον τοῦτ' ἐποίησεν κακόν' 7.115) are more trouble than they are worth. The physicality of Semonides' representation can be compared with Sappho 31 which is also extremely physical. But whether the difference stems from the sex of the author or divergent poetico-social contexts, these songs and their views of women's bodies and 'sexuality' bear no resemblance to each other.

Archilochus often composed poems about women's sexual activity and male control of this ambivalent force. Like other representations of their time, the terse, satirical fragments reveal frequent, sometimes obscene, references to bodies and sexual interaction. Some of these (frr. 191, 193 and 196 for example) represent the angst and power of sexual desire in a manner that would seem similar to some of Sappho's songs if it were not for a consistently negative perspective and a tendency to equate love with battlefields and tactics of dominance and submission: 'but oh, my friend, desire, the limb-loosener, masters me . . .' ('ἀλλά μ' ὁ λυσιμελής, ὦ ταῖρε, δάμναται πόθος' fr. 196). Archilochus' longest and most recently discovered fragment, the Cologne epode, while retaining the emphasis on bodies, 'sexuality' and dominance, includes some Semonides-like animal fables, and moves from the battlefield to a more domestic context. Archilochus also taps into a vocabulary of sexual metaphors. This epode is perhaps the most graphic representation of 'heterosexual' interaction in archaic lyric poetry. The imagery within it is also structured in line with a conventional and male-oriented scheme of binary oppositions: hate/love; active/passive; whore/virgin; ugly/beautiful; strong/weak; master/mastered. After some preliminary discussion that broadcasts the idea of Neobule's[14] overripe shamefulness, the lover/singer gets down to the serious business of satisfying his 'pressing lust' ('θυμὸς ἰθύει' SLG 478.3) without deflowering his new love, a young virgin. The imagery he uses is pastoral and in this way reminiscent of some of Sappho's metaphorically sexual imagery in fr. 2. The action however, is more heterosexually oriented and explicit:

θρ]ιγκοῦ δ' ἔνερθε καὶ πυλέων ὑποφ[
μ]ή τι μέγαιρε, φίλη·
σχήσω γὰρ ἐς ποη[φόρους
24 κ]ήπους.

beneath the arch and through the portal there,
and you, my dear, be not ungenerous –
for I will stop
within your grassy garden plot.

(Burnett 21–24)

This metaphorical 'grassy garden plot' seems like the grassy fields surrounding the grove in Sappho 2 and adds a further metaphoric meaning to that flowery, body-like garden. There are flowers in Archilochus' scene too, all of them associated with the object of the lover's lust. The bloom that has been lost along with Neobule's maidenhood seems to shine from the fresh skin of this pure girl, and her fawn-like passivity can only be contrasted[15] with the frenzied sexual activity of Neobule. The actions and body of the man are portrayed less metaphorically. We are shown hands that seem surprisingly gentle (after the sharpness of his verbal attack) caressing the girl's quiescent body and a final flush of well-controlled white fluid over a grassy plot that has changed in the course of the epode to golden hair. Burnett (1983: 97) feels that the process enacted in Archilochus' epode is cathartic, that 'in modern terms the lover frees himself from fear of the feminine by the filth and rage of his anger; in allegorical terms Lust is evicted before Love is entertained', and that in this way there are positive as well as negative elements. Perhaps so, but the negative and positive factors, like the other dichotomous ingredients of this minor drama, are constructed in a way that accentuates the binary scheme that is effectively driving the epode to its physiological and poetic conclusion.

Archilochus' epode comprises various elements. One of the more obvious is a stern lesson in sexual regulations and correct behaviour. Oral poetry is much concerned with the transmission of socio-ethical messages of this kind. Sappho also transmits knowledge to the women of her community about sexual behaviour, but the songs that contain this information are not at all like Archilochus' abusive diatribe. The lover/singer in the Cologne epode is concerned with the preservation of the virginal status of his young beloved. This is a topic that the Sappho-singer also explores. Frr. 105a, 105c, 107 and 114 all highlight the importance of innocence and sexual maturity or purity and defilement. In the circle, it seems that the loss of virginity, like other physiological/social stages, is ritualised with dialogues (frr. 107 and 114) that share and/or negate the anguish that accompanies this change. The treatment of virginity in fragments 105a and 105c however, is rather different. Like the scene in Archilochus' epode, they are also set in an external, pastoral environment. The sexual metaphors used in these songs stress the ephemeral beauty of hyacinths or women, the potential lusciousness of a reddening apple. A hyacinth on the mountain-side is crushed by the careless feet of shepherds (male feet, as can be seen from wedding songs such as fr. 110a, have phallic significance), the apple is out of reach and retains its potential. Together perhaps these fragments tell a similar story to that of Archilochus' epode and despite disparities between the social contexts of these singers the value system behind the stories appears similar. The stories, however, are told very differently.

Through the medium of song, Sappho transmits other messages about 'sexuality' that have a more homoerotic, woman-centred application – examples of how to interact sexually perhaps, or the appropriate behaviour for a female subject. Some characteristics of this antique brand of poetic discourse are ideal for this purpose. Its memorableness for example, the mnemonic sequences that aurally and verbally repeat certain key points with techniques such as alliteration and assonance, leave words echoing in the minds of an audience who recognise and relate to the song's metrical structures. The rhythmic patterns and movements also add a pleasurable, physical dimension to a listening/learning experience. The questions that arise here are whether poetic discourse – even the poetry of an oral culture – acts as an ideological apparatus, a mode of social reproduction which expresses and transmits systems of beliefs, values, and practices, and whether these idealistic songs played a part in constructing the individuals of the Sapphic community and/or their 'sexuality'. Belsey (1985: 45–6) suggests that 'according to Althusser's reading (re-reading) of Marx, ideology is not simply a set of illusions . . . but a system of representations (discourses, images, myths) concerning the real relations in which people live'. Unlike Eagleton (1986: 79) who considers that because of its very eloquence poetic discourse is mask-like, defamiliarising, presenting only 'concealed truth', Althusser regards representations as neither a conspiracy nor a form of alienation. Sappho's lyrics are discursive constructs[16] which are subject to generic conventions and they therefore fit Althusser's definition of ideology. For us Sappho's songs have been reduced to an art form and as such Althusser's (1972: 83) statement that 'what art makes us *see* . . . is the ideology from which it is born, in which it bathes, from which it detaches itself as art, and to which it alludes', confirms the songs' ideological thrust. For the women of Sappho's community these songs represented a source of information about religion, ritual, myth, modes of behaviour, social relations and 'sexuality'.

It is not difficult to imagine these women gaining knowledge about homoerotic interaction from songs such as frr. 1, 16, 22, 23, 31, 47, 48, 94, 96, 102 and 130. Those poetically exalted brides who are surrounded by celebrations, rich possessions and imagery (frr. 44, 112, 113 and 141) represent an ideal of 'heterosexual' love. (An ideal which, as far as language or poetic treatment are concerned, cannot be distinguished from more homoerotic episodes.) Other songs, frr. 1, 2, 94, and Sappho or Alcaeus 16 for example, portray the irresistible power of Aphrodite as well as the pleasures of communal festivity. There is another group of fragments, mostly tiny scraps, that include details of multi-coloured leather sandals (fr. 39), or the length of skirts (fr. 57), or lovely garlands (fr. 81), or differently coloured robes and cloaks (fr. 92), or headbands (frr. 98a and b), hand-cloths (fr. 101), etc. that seem to describe or prescribe favoured or correct styles for women at certain stages of their lives. All of these fragments seem to transmit information about 'sexuality' in the sense of ideal sexual interaction, and/or 'sexuality' as in the construction of a subject into ideologically correct modes of behaviour in a segregated world.

This ancient combination of sexual and social acculturation through sexual interaction implies to some commentators that Sappho was a female pederast. One problem with this premise is its inferred reliance on the relationship between the poet and the roles of teacher/lover/pederast. Were these songs always sung by the poet called Sappho who sang of her life and loves, or indeed by any single voice? There are other complicating factors. With Sappho's poetry the biographical question is raised first by the inclusion of her name in some songs (frr. 1 and 94), and second by parallels provided by a male tradition of poets who announced their pederastic inclinations in their poetry. Pindar, for example, dedicated some of his most fervent love poetry to Theoxenus, the erotic subject of fr. 123, and Theognis addressed the bulk of his collection to a young friend and/or beloved named Kyrnus.

The tone of Theognis' poetry is admonitory and it is, like Solon's, politically oriented with an unbreachable line drawn between that indivisible Greek dichotomy, friends and enemies. As a poet of this era he speaks from a position of wisdom and authority. As the older partner/educator in a sexual relationship, he communicates to his beloved a mixture of advice, love and cynical complaints. One passage for instance, (1301–5) contains a warning, didactic and threatening, reminding this young man that youth and the 'violet-crowned' beauty associated with Aphrodite are short-lived attributes. Older bodies in ancient Greece, as Mimnermus (fr. 1) sorrowfully pronounces, are not considered sexually attractive. Another of Theognis' representations of love (87–92) displays his anger tersely with a crisp, if binary, comparison of mind/heart; love/hate; friend/enemy that again seems more politically than sexually oriented – another warning about the danger of 'a grim companion' ('ἑταῖρος δεινός' 86–7) who is more of an enemy than a friend. Whether or not male pederasts such as Theognis and Pindar have anything in common with Sappho and her relations with other women, the songs they compose to their young friends seem to lack the emotional, physiological and ritualistic emphasis that informs her songs.

In a traditional and much perpetuated binary split confirmed in representations of both male and female lyric poets of ancient Greece, women are associated with bodies, reproduction and 'sexuality'. Their capacity for physical reproduction seems to have initiated this link, while a male desire for legitimate offspring has instigated the plethora of systems and mores constructed to control a form of female 'sexuality' that is represented as being dangerously insatiable and uncontrollable. In poetry normal sexual limitations can be surpassed, female beings such as a moon-struck earth/woman can reproduce parthenogenetically (Sappho 96), and men can spring from the ground autochthonously. In socio-cultural contexts such as the ancient Greek world, via the ethical codes that order them, the bodies that are called female and considered porous, wet and unable to control their own boundaries (Carson 1990: 130) must be constrained by a variety of means. Within these constraints three aspects of female 'sexuality', sexual identity, difference and erotic activity are conjoined, at least in 'heterosexual' contexts. Sexual identity is constructed by means of accculturational processes which define and construct an ideal 'feminine' subject – one who will maintain the hierarchical structures and laws of the male public world. Sexual difference might be differently constructed in antiquity but the division is profound and appears to be constituted with the implementation of 'elaborate ideological mechanisms' by male Greek citizens, in order – to quote duBois (1988: 147) – 'to dominate the female and her body, to control its potentiality, to subdue it to his interests'. The erotic activities of female bodies are physically constrained by social constructions such as guardianship, marriage, segregation; and socially controlled by the prescriptive, public, strategies of men, or poets such as Hesiod or Archilochus. Archilochus' Cologne epode provides an illustration of the implementation of some of these humiliating, socially regulating tactics.

It also exemplifies the phallic/active/dominant characteristics that distinguish the 'sexuality' of ancient male subjects from objects such as women or boys.

I have difficulty applying this phallic/active/dominant model and its assumed binary interface – a lacking, passive, submissive object – to the sexual relations represented in Sappho's songs; but it is a model that seems, in antiquity and later, to be significant and exclusive. Halperin (1990a: 102) describes

> the extraordinary phallicism that typically . . . characterised sexual expression in classical Athens . . . Sexual pleasures other than phallic pleasures did not count in articulating sexual roles or sexual categories: caresses and other gestures that did not fit the penetration model did not figure in evaluating or classifying sexual behaviour.

This form of phallicism is different from the more linguistic and symbolically inclusive phallocentricism of the twentieth century. Halperin does not come to this conclusion, but his definition of phallic-dominated sexual behaviour appears to exclude and therefore to some extent liberate the 'sexuality' of the women represented in Sappho's songs.

In her poetic and deliberately female-oriented constructions Irigaray (1985: 28) describes the differences that could define an imaginary/specific female body: '*woman has sex organs more or less everywhere*. . . . the geography of her pleasure is far more diversified, more multiple in its differences, more complex, more subtle, than is commonly imagined – in an imaginary rather too narrowly focused on sameness'. Woman's pluralistic sexual pleasure, her *jouissance* is, in this context, a means by which a more singular phallic libidinal economy can be exceeded. In Irigaray's (1985: 28) representations, Freud's prescriptive either/or opposition between clitoral pleasure and vaginal sexuality is defused, since 'they each contribute, irreplaceably, to woman's pleasure'. The female body thus is reformulated as a site of positivity. Sappho's erotic subject in fr. 31 exemplifies this multiplicity and excessiveness by physical responses that traverse her entire body without privileging any one part; and that exceed the descriptions and represented desires of male poets. Multiple, uncentralised drives and desires and a libido that is cosmic also feature in the bodily representations of Cixous, but with some difference. She sees the female body as 'a direct source of female writing', making 'a powerful alternative discourse' possible (Jones 1985: 90). Whether or not it is possible either to write or sing the female body,[17] the suggestion that women could create art out of a peculiarly woman-centred consciousness – one linked to their physical specificity – is not unrelated to Sappho's fluid and orally pleasurable poetic compositions. Men have frequently inscribed 'female' bodies such as the earth with the phallus/plough/pen.[18] These exercises in appropriation are subverted to some extent by representations such as Sappho 96. Male representations of women's 'sexuality', whether from antiquity or the twentieth century, have focused on phallocentric models, constructing and reconstructing women's body and desire only in relation to a male norm, formulating a definition of 'lack', of powerlessness and non-entity. Sappho's metaphoric poetic representations of the body, and the erotic interaction of antique women, work to exceed male definitions and dyads, to clothe this apparently unrepresentable[19] body in a 'sexuality' that is appropriate to the desires and specificity of female subjects.

Chapter 4

'Virginity'

The bodies of the women of Sappho's songs, and that of the poet who sings of female desire and honour, are constructed differently from the bodies of men or male poets. It is in relation to men, however, through the marriage gift of an intact body, that women can attain one kind of honour, perhaps the only kind consistently valued in public arenas. These and other public/private, male/female transactions cannot be entirely different or separate; the women of Sappho's community presumably know, double-consciously, of both spheres, and are influenced by the mores and codes of the larger community. Cultural, scientific and gynaecological accounts of women's bodies in antiquity focus almost exclusively on a woman's reproductive capacity; the bodies of children and older women are considered, to some extent, culturally irrelevant. As Dean-Jones (1991: 114) suggests, it seems that for both girls and boys 'the fundamental differentiation between the sexes which occurred at conception did not become apparent until puberty'. The age/sexual status of the women of Sappho's community cannot be securely determined, evidence within the songs (frr. 21, 27, 49, 58, 98a, 121 and 122) points to a range of age groups, from childhood to older adult. Parker (1993: 316) strongly opposes the popular assumption that Sappho is older, while other members of the group are young girls. The evidence is inconclusive, but there are indications that some of these women are younger and/or sexually immature. Whatever their age, within this secluded community, where sexual maturity and the first erotic experience are mediated by ritual, song and metaphor, their 'sexuality' appears to be contained, marginalised.

In relation to the term 'virginity'[1] and its meaning/s for the women of this community of women, other problems need to be addressed. Sissa (1990b: 76) insists that 'the Greek word *parthenos* does not unambiguously signify the perfect integrity implicit in our word *virgin*', that this was the term assigned to all young women between childhood and marriage. The term, to quote Sissa (1990a: 346), is 'uncooperative and ambiguous' and bears little relation to our definition of 'virginity'. There is little doubt that the women Sappho sings of were virginal in this sense of being unmarried. Her songs on this subject also appear to conform to a conventional, heterosexual model which accords with the ideals of later commentators who consider that 'virginity' (in respect of a desirable purity in brides or unmarried girls) is all-important. This ideal was, it seems, also valued by Sappho. At times these songs have been categorised as epithalamia, in line with the assumption that 'virginity' and marriage are concomitant and that Sappho sang approvingly of both. As commodities, objects of exchange, these women were valuable only if they were physically intact. And they would have been aware of this fact. Taking a personal rather than a social view, however, what did the loss of 'virginity' or the movement into marriage and a heterosexual world mean for these women? A transitional act that is physically painful, the leaving behind of friends, possessions, home and all that is familiar, a loss of freedom – as the woman moves into the aegis/household of her husband with all the social restrictions placed upon married women – and the fear/dangers of childbirth. There is also the excitement of attaining adulthood, and the socially approved status of wife/mother. Unmarried women, like women who live with and love other women, appear to be excluded from society in various ways. In the context of Sappho's songs, the subject of 'virginity' is intriguing and raises questions about the honour and autonomy of all young females, whether mortal, mythic or divine.

Contained in the lacunose papyrus now known as fr. 44a are the remnants of another song composed by Sappho[2] to honour a female god.

4 Ἄρτεμις δὲ θέων] μέγαν ὄρκον ἀπώμοσε·
νὴ τὰν σὰν κεφά]λαν, ἄι πάρθενος ἔσσομαι
ἄδμης οἰοπό]λων ὀρέων κορύφαισ' ἔπι
θηρεύοισ'· ἄγι καὶ τά]δε νεῦσον ἔμαν χάριν.
ὤς εἶπ'· αὐτὰρ ἔνευ]σε θέων μακάρων πάτηρ.
πάρθενον δ' ἐλαφάβ]ολον ἀγροτέραν θέοι

ἄνθρωποί τε κάλε]ισιν ἐπωνύμιον μέγα.
11 κήναι λυσιμέλνς] Ἔρος οὐδάμα πίλναται

4 Artemis swore the great oath [of the gods]:
By your head, I wish to be a virgin, always
[unmarried], roaming the mountain peaks alone.
Please, accede to my desire.
So she spoke.
The father of the blessed gods nodded his consent
She is known as [virgin and shooter of deer] by gods
[and men], huntress, a great title.
11 Eros [limb-loosener] never approaches her.

This song has a mythical basis and is constructed in an epic style similar to Sappho 44 with relatively long lines and Aeolic dactyls. Featuring Artemis rather than Aphrodite, the song focuses on 'virginity', a theme which is conventionally associated with women. Not that 'virginity' was not also valued in the young men who attracted the erotic gaze of the male poets,[3] Anacreon sings of a boy's virginal glance ('παρθένιον βλέπων' 360.1) and Theognis of standards of erotic honour, of his desire for the loyalty and purity of his beloved (87–92). Whether the 'feminine', passive partner was female or male, in relation to matters of sexual honour, purity and exclusivity appear to be desirable. Two important distinctions between male and female 'virginity' centre on differences between sexed bodies: the fact that male virginity is not verified by a sign of intactness such as the hymen; and the 'natural' ability of a woman's body to bear children. The 'natural' inability of male bodies to guarantee that these children are their own results in a range of socio-ethical mechanisms or constraints such as marriage laws and/or the idealisation of 'virginity' in public statements (poetic and otherwise) shaming those who acted dishonourably. Even the flowers and fruit associated metaphorically with male/female sexuality in ancient Greece assume different significance according to the sex of the subject they define. While the advent of old age and the loss of 'the flowers of youth' ('οἶ' ἥβης ἄνθεα' Mimnermus 1.4, Simonides eleg. 8.4–5) provoke male sorrow, Carson (1990: 146) proposes that 'a woman's first sexual experience catapults her into uncontrolled sexual activity and out of the category of desirable sex-object . . . she is past her peak the moment the ἄνθος (flower) falls'. An illustration of such violent defloration seems to occur in Sappho 105c. A similar distortion occurs with the word ὀπώρα meaning 'fruit-time'. 'When used metaphorically of males, ὀπώρα signifies "the bloom of youth" or "ripe manhood," and does not exclude the pursuit of sexual fulfilment. But when used of females, ὀπώρα means virginity and is to be withheld from all erotic experimentation.'

Artemis' immortal persona appears to incorporate both sides of the *nomos/physis* divide, representing a civilising force, a tamer of nature and animals, but also an immortal who chooses to remain virginal, who inhabits wild spaces and cannot be contained within the safe ambit of marriage.[4] As the goddess of maidenhead and childbirth she was also a god to whom women could apply on ritual occasions or in times of stress related to specifically female experiences. The lacunose state of fr. 44a makes interpretation/s uncertain and pre-empts several questions. One concern is the purpose for which it was first composed. Was it created to honour this god, as part of a religious ceremony dedicated to her? Was it a tale told decoratively at a more informal gathering? Or was it didactic, an exemplar of past events or perhaps a lesson in ideal value systems? Burnett (1983: 218) suggests that 'virginity was of supreme importance' to the women of Sappho's community and that songs such as this were part of 'their education in purity'. Was it only the value accorded to an intact bride that was 'of supreme importance', or was the relative freedom associated with an unmarried state also important? Sappho's choice of legendary detail in fr. 44a presents Artemis as an actively virginal model. In lines dignified by suitably Homeric language and epithets a god petitions her father for permission to remain a virgin, to hunt alone amidst mountain peaks.[5] The scene contains few of the usual appurtenances of divinity, but it is, with the exchange between Artemis and Zeus, sufficiently familial to allow the women of Sappho's community to relate to an interaction between father and daughter. Did these women also ask permission of their fathers to remain virginal/unmarried and continue their life in this community? Finally, with the assurance that Eros never approaches her (this expansion on the theme of Artemis' 'virginity' is uniquely Sapphic), what emerges is an image of a god who chooses to remain separate from a heterosexual norm of erotic interaction or social integration and has the power to implement her decision.

There are two issues that concern the honour of Artemis, and that of the women who first listened to the Sappho-singer's tale.

One focuses on her autonomy: the desire and decision to remain virginal/unmarried, to act in a way that is godlike but presumably 'unfeminine'. By demonstrating the way Artemis makes decisions about her own sexual status the song invites a comparison with Helen's actions in Sappho 16: both women act in accordance with their own desires in a manner that seems to defy Greek norms of sexual interaction and concepts of female suppression and/or lack of control.[6] By resisting marriage, or by remaining virginal and therefore being positioned in a marginal space outside the usual processes of exchange and male dominance, Artemis – and the women of the Sapphic community – do have some freedom. Perhaps this broken song is not just pro 'virginity', but is also against marriage and the subordination of women in heterosexual relationships.

The other issue relates to the bodies of mortal women, the question of what actually constituted 'virginity' in ancient Greece. Our somewhat binary conceptions of sexed bodies, and the value accorded the inarguable evidence of bodily phenomena[7] such as a membrane that separates purity from sexual experience, appear to be distinctive, and historically and culturally specific. The split between then and now, or between term and definition/s, complicates matters. It is not, as Sissa (1990b: 87) reveals in her discussion, that this was not a sexual matter, or that the loss of 'virginity' or evidence of that loss such as pregnancy were not inexpressibly transgressive, seduction 'numbered among the gravest of threats to the kinship structure'. Two distinctions between 'virginity' then and now appear most salient. One is that antique references to a membranous veil or hymen do not link it securely to virginal female bodies (Sissa 1990a: 348–9). The other is the status this mysterious membrane acquired later in western culture. For Greeks of the ancient world the focus was upon a number of signs, some of which – the size of a girl's neck, or the depth of her voice – had a physical basis, while others, such as the test to see if a girl whose 'virginity' was in question would sink or remain above water, were more a matter of divination.

In relation to divine figures such as Artemis, or the women of Sappho's community, the issue of 'virginity' remains significant, although it is effected by a detachment that seems to be both environmental and symbolic. Physically, it seems that segregation from the larger community, and the danger of seduction inherent in a male/female environment, could provide viable reasons for the presence of these women in Sappho's establishment. Within the seclusion of this community, a woman's virginal status remains intact in both a physical and social sense. That status is also mediated, like all other essential criteria, through cultural phenomena or constructions: song, metaphor, ritual and divine figures such as Artemis. The difference is that here women, or perhaps one woman, Sappho, apparently controlled and mediated the sexuality of other women, in ways, within modes of construction, which seem relatively incomprehensible to us. Outside this community, there are fathers who administer and guard their daughters' sexual purity and arrange their marriages. Mythologically, Artemis must also apply to her father for permission to remain unmarried. The decision, however, is hers and the wildness of her chosen environment appears, symbolically, to suggest much about 'sexuality' and freedom.

According to Bowra (1961: 35), Artemis 'is to women what Apollo is to men, the spirit of purity and independence'. For the women of the Sapphic community Artemis was a paradigmatic figure, an honoured god and exemplar. In this way characteristics such as her rather masculine 'spirit of independence' assume multiple significance. But to attain honour, sexually or any other way, involves an element of choice, and active participation in a quest or confrontation. Artemis (and other virginal female gods, Hestia and Athene) appear to exemplify a standard of honour and a form of non-sexuality that is extraordinarily empowering. The sexual status of the Pythia, a virgin with oracular powers, provides an example of a mortal woman who is similarly virginal and influential. These mortal/immortal females promote a sexual state that is antithetical to the procreative ideals of Greek society. As virgins do they possess other qualities, or perform other functions, that suited the needs and representations of the public world? Their desirability, their ability to give birth, are negated, but they have been allocated other (more 'masculine'?) attributes. The application of this standard of active sexual honour to the lives of the women of Sappho's community is less clear. But 'virginity' is shown to be an ideal state, one which should be actively desired and chosen.

Representations of Artemis by male poets do not often foreground the issue of 'virginity'. Alcman was said to have composed many songs to this god, to have summoned 'Artemis from countless mountains and countless cities and from rivers too', but although these fragments are now reduced to 'the merest flotsam and jetsam, casual wreckage of poetry . . . they show that Alcman saw Artemis as a goddess of hunting and wild creatures' (Bowra 1961: 35–6). The epithets in two Homeric hymns to Artemis: 'maidenly strewer of barbs' ('παρθένον ἰοχέαιραν' IX.2), and 'terrible, austere virgin, deer-shooter and strewer of arrows' ('κελαδεινήν, παρθένον αἰδοίην, ἐλαφηβόλον, ἰοχέαιραν' XXVIII) also emphasise her warrior/hunter status and endow her with an aggressive aspect that seems more appropriate to male arenas than the quiet mountains she wanders in Sappho 44a. Although Euripides also stresses Artemis' virginal aspect in the *Hippolytos*,[8] for earlier male poets – Homeric and lyric – the most frequently represented aspects of Artemis are her affinity with the creatures she hunts and her ability to protect men and the cities they inhabit. Theognis, referring to a sacred precedent established by Agamemnon at Megara, asks Artemis as 'the killer of wild beasts' ('Ἄρτεμι θηροφόνη') to 'ward off evil fates' ('κακὰς δ' ἀπὸ κῆρας ἄλαλκε' 11–13). While Pindar produces a distinctive (compared to Sappho's solitary, virginal persona) image of a goddess caught up in a Bacchic frenzy yoking lions for Dionysus (70B), Anacreon also petitions 'the queen of wild beasts' ('δέσποιν' Ἄρτεμι θηρῶν' 348.3) in this case on behalf of the citizens of Magnesia, and asks her to rejoice since the citizens she shepherds are men who are 'not untamed' ('πολιήτας' 348.8). The remnants of Alcman's countless songs to Artemis do not depart greatly from these portrayals since they describe her as 'drawer of the bow' ('ῥύτειρα τόξων' fr. 170) and 'clad in the skins of beasts' ('ϝεσσαμένᾳ πέρι δέρματα θηρῶν' fr. 53).

The male poets are attracted to, and re-present poetically, quite distinctive aspects of Artemis. If they allude to honour at all in this context then it is the honour of being protected by this powerful god, of being able to hunt as well as her,[9] or of being civilised and not untamed. Her virginity is not as poetically entertaining a topic as the descriptions of woman/animal combinations, of savagery and Bacchic frenzy. But despite her ability to civilise and protect men, Artemis is still judged by her female status and is therefore associated with *physis* or nature. With the possible exception of Alcman's songs, these descriptions of Artemis were from songs designed for masculine occasions. Page (1955: 264) suggests a possible venue, with his remark that these were suitable topics for the skolia that became 'popular at drinking-parties in Attica in the fifth century BC'. Originally their purpose seems to have been more ritualistic – invocations to a goddess who could protect the cities of men from barbarians or wild creatures, or ensure a safe voyage – but with the conversion of prayers to skolia, former hymns can become themes for less sacred representations. Pindar's allusion to Artemis is part of an early dithyramb, an episodic narrative filled with discordant noise and wild, frenetic activity. Sappho 44a is not devoid of hunting imagery, but the features which the male poets chose to highlight – of Artemis as a hunter who subdues wild beasts and helps men – seem antithetical to Sappho's representation of a virginal divinity who elects to live forever in solitary purity. Artemis' sexual status, or the questions of female honour which her abnegation of erotic love and marriage highlight, are arguably not as relevant to male lives and desires.

Matters of male sexual honour centre on a difference between 'masculine' and 'feminine' sex roles, both of which were allocated to men. In the world of ancient Greece, there are, as Foucault (1987: 47), Dover (1978: 15), and Halperin (1990a: 33) inform us, two roles or positions, one of which – the 'masculine', active, penetrating role – is honoured or approved of unequivocally. The other – the 'feminine', passive, penetrated position – is considered dishonourable. 'Masculine' men are viewed as being capable of moderating their desires – taking pride in the regulation of excessive and therefore shameful sexual desires – or achieving sexual honour by playing an active/dominant role. The models constructed in that time/space appear to be created to guarantee their proud position as dominators[10] and/or winners in both a sexual and social sense. Carson (1990: 142–4) suggests that – at least in the eyes of men – a 'woman cannot control herself, so her *sôphrosyne* must consist in submitting herself to the control of others', but 'for the man, *sôphrosyne* is rational self-control and resistance to excess'. Archilochus' Cologne epode provides an illustration of a man who controls and/or modifies his strong sexual desires. It also contains an unflattering portrayal of two women, one who is revealed to be sexually dishonourable, catapulted by the loss of 'virginity' into immoderate sexual activity, another who is 'virginal' but passive, who lies quietly quivering, manipulated by the rational self-control of her seducer. As far as the male citizens of ancient Greece are concerned – Foucault (1987: 32) spends much time discussing this subject – it appears 'that there is a whole rich and complex field of historicity in the way the individual is summoned to recognise himself as an ethical subject of sexual conduct'. Commentary on the ethical systems or autonomous sexual conduct of women has been, however, sadly neglected, perhaps because women have been expected to comply passively with codes constructed by men, or risk being accused of shameful and dishonourable conduct by the inhabitants of the powerful public sector.

The singular patterns of homoerotic female love represented in Sappho's songs, and the distinctive versions of honour which accompany and regulate these patterns, appear to be external and/or antithetical to male modes of dominance and submission. However, whether as a symbol of autonomy or as a sign of an intact body, 'virginity' does appear to be an aspect of female experience that was of supreme importance to the women of the Sapphic community. Sappho poeticises the experience of women – commemorating a critical moment, using poetry as an anaesthetising, consolatory medium, neutralising the effect of a traumatic experience – and by doing so renders it less painful. The mock-dialogues between a girl and her virginity (frr. 107 and 114)[11] seem to represent one of these moments.

> ἦρ' ἔτι παρθενίας ἐπιβάλλομαι; – Do I still long for virginity?
> (fr. 107)

> παρθενία, παρθενία, ποῖ με λίποισ' ἀποίχῃ;
> οὐκέτι ἤξω πρὸς σέ, οὐκέτι ἤξω†.

> 'Virginity, virginity, where have you gone, deserting me?'
> 'Never again shall I come to you, never again shall I come.'
> (fr. 114)

Dialogues such as these could have been performed by two women, or perhaps by one woman on the eve of her marriage, and were formulated in rhythmic, alliterative language with a ritualistic flavour. Compared to Sappho's more imagistic songs these tiny colloquial fragments seem stark. However, in accordance with orally oriented patterns of behaviour, they exploited a set of psychosomatic mechanisms that offered some form of release from sorrow and apprehension. Although their austerity seems ironically to emphasise the importance of a change of status that greatly affected these women.

The two other Sapphic fragments representing the significance of female 'virginity' (frr. 105a and c) are different again, since the bare facts pertaining to the loss of 'virginity' are mitigated by the force of symbols and metaphors that relate aptly to the natural world.

> οἶον τὸ γλυκύμαλον ἐρεύθεται ἄκρῳ ἐπ' ὔσδῳ,
> ἄκρον ἐπ' ἀκροτάτῳ, λελάθοντο δὲ μαλοδρόπηες·
> οὐ μὰν ἐκλελάθοντ', ἀλλ' οὐκ ἐδύναντ' ἐπίκεσθαι.

> A solitary sweet-apple, reddening at the top of a branch,
> on top of the highest branch, forgotten by the apple-pickers.
> No, they have not forgotten it. They could not reach it.

Fr. 105a is, as Kirkwood (1974: 142) remarks, 'vividly conceived and subtly suggestive', skilfully playing as it does on the image of an inaccessible apple, a fruit laden with nuptial, symbolic and sexual significance. Apples also appear in fr. 2, but in this case that sweetly reddening sensuality is qualified, shown to be still unripe, and rendered unobtainable by its position at the top of the topmost branches of the tree. Its height appears to endow it with a hierarchical valuation that relates more to value systems inherent in the external world. It tells of the separateness and desirability of the women of Sappho's songs. In the inaccessibility, the detachment, of this fruit/girl resides its value, this is the condition which distinguishes it from other apples or other girls. Symbol, metaphor and human sexuality are united admirably in a poem that is primarily concerned with desire and in which both content and form cohere to re-present a state of detachment and the action of reaching. Sappho's self-corrective qualification in line 3 reminds us that the forgetfulness of the pickers is actually thwarted desire and adds further significance to an intensely meaningful few lines.[12] Physically, inadvertently, the apple is placed out of reach, but what is this positioning meant to imply for the women in Sappho's audience? Apples can hardly be anything but passive while women have some choice about where they position themselves. Was the song intended to provide another, more heterosexually-oriented, example of exemplary erotic behaviour? As an illustration of the temporary beauty and honour/value attached to what is considered (by the men who cultivate, exchange, and pick this girl/fruit?), to be the peak of female existence – the brief moment when physical intactness/perfection and sexual ripeness converge – it engages and displays ideals common to private and public worlds.

Despite the movement from orchard to mountainside, fr. 105c centres around a similar metaphoric format, except that another favourite Sapphic symbol, a flower – in this case a wild hyacinth[13] – is substituted for the apple image, perhaps to demonstrate the fearful consequences of placing oneself in a vulnerable position, and encouraging rape or seduction and the loss of 'virginity'/ honour.

> οἴαν τὰν ὐάκινθον ἐν ὤρεσι ποίμενες ἄνδρες
> πόσσι καταστείβοισι, χάμαι δέ τε πόρφυρον ἄνθος . . .
>
> Like a hyacinth in the mountains which shepherds
> tread underfoot, on the ground the purple flower . . .

In both fragments the images are of desirable, but ephemeral, natural objects, and the diverse fates which the objects attract reveals the peculiar duality of female 'virginity': it is both extraordinarily attractive and infinitely vulnerable, but only while it remains intact, or out of reach. In a typically Sapphic method of integration, perhaps the two paradoxical aspects of 'virginity' initially met in one virginal subject, one complete song. As they stand now the suggestiveness of these fragments reaps a crop of possible connotations. Is a social distinction intended? Perhaps in relation to an unwise liaison between beautiful, noble young women and country fellows (Sappho defines the sex of these shepherds: 'ἄνδρες') such as pickers and shepherds. It is also possible that this song included a warning about another form of differentiation: the difference between the graceful young women and careless, brutal young men they might marry. The trampling, destructive action in fr. 105c seems indicative (and critical) of phallocentric action. Does the song contain praise for the apple-like girl, criticism for more flower-like strayers? Or was the fragment formerly combined with fr. 105a to juxtapose two examples of untimeliness: the topmost fruit left unplucked to wrinkle and fall, and the flower that is physically grown but otherwise immature? The complex internal/external, male/female implications of these fragments also seem to co-ordinate private/public areas and their disparate inhabitants in two differently threatening contexts. An apple-like, almost ripe girl who is positioned within an environment that seems not unlike the protected garden of Sappho 2 is kept safe; a flower-like girl positioned out on a mountain is crushed, deflowered. Perhaps the hazards these songs illustrated were more complex than the loss of 'virginity' suggested metaphorically by picked apples or crushed flowers, or the form of female honour most often conceptualised by men. Perhaps they announced the beauty/superiority of these topmost, flower-like women, and of a female community which provided an alternative lifestyle similar to the mountains in fr. 44a, as well as warning of the dangers inherent in male power relations.

The male lyric poets also published poetic prescriptions on the subject of female 'virginity', but the voices that sound through the satirical and single-minded admonishments they composed, apparently for male audiences, are distinctive. Unlike Sappho's metaphoric and allusive lyrics, male songs on this subject are represented in iambics devoted to abusive, often obscene statements of blame and criticism. This is a socially regulatory genre which, as Burnett (1983: 56) informs us, 'was thought of as being as old as music itself'. Archilochus, who evidently prided himself on the skill with which he employed the sharp iambic style of this genre, frequently uses it to deride such 'unvirginal' and dishonourable subjects as female prostitutes (frr. 42W, 189W and 331W, etc.) for their 'degeneracy and greed' (Burnett 1983: 78). In the Cologne epode he not only abuses Neobule for her impurity and over-ripeness, he goes on to provide a unique male statement apparently verifying the importance of female 'virginity'. The action takes place in a poetic scenario that bears some resemblance to the scene in fr. 105c, where flowers (metaphoric and female) are crushed by the erotic interaction of a 'virginal' girl and her male seducer, and we are shown the control exerted by a man as he attempts to satisfy his desire, presumably without deflowering this girl. If Sappho was setting up a praise/blame situation in frr. 105a and 105c, the differences between her suggestive representations and the deliberately vulgar songs of Archilochus are significant. Differences between the moral perspectives behind the songs are also significant. From Sappho's woman-centred perspective we receive the impression that these men – pickers and shepherds – jeopardise the honour of graceful, fruitful young girls. The men are portrayed as brutal, careless, and presumably without honour. From Archilochus' male/masculine viewpoint men exhibit rational self-control and resistance to excess and are justifiably sexual, while women are shown to be without '*sôphrosune*' and capable of retaining honour only through the actions of men. The issue in this case is female 'virginity' or honour. It is an issue which has consistently been administered and constructed by members of the public world, such as Archilochus, who have invested much energy in ensuring the continuation of a patriarchal lineage. Arguably, however, in line with her portrayal of Artemis, and other references to 'virginity', Sappho suggests that women do have some choice, that they can exercise some autonomy and gain honour in regard to the matter of their sexual status. It seems, at least on the basis of the evidence provided in Sappho's representations, that in relation to this and other honourable issues, 'women's experiences differ from men's in profound and regular ways' (Gardiner 1983: 178).

Chapter 5

Gazing at beauty

In the world of ancient Greece, beauty, in its various aspects, appears to have been of immense value. Songs told of, or idealised, physical beauty,[1] by representing certain features of the face or body in its 'naturally' unadorned or decoratively enhanced state. Poetically, attractive sequences could also greatly increase the reputation of an aspiring lyric singer. The beauty of song formulated a cultural response or tribute to human beauty, or that of the natural world. Physical beauty (see Sappho fr. 50) could also act as a register of goodness, or excellence, or virtue. References to beautification, the donning of garlands and perfuming of bodies for example, have significance in both male and female contexts. In the public world practice/s of maintaining and beautifying the body occupied the time of male citizens, while in the Sapphic community it seems that women spent much time discussing details of beauty and appearance, dress and decoration. In both contexts the physical attributes of both gods and mortals are associated with natural phenomena, imagistically, mythically or metaphorically combining anthropomorphic beings with specific physical or topographical features. The beauty and/or power of the natural world appears often in these cultural guises, so that soft and 'feminine' or flowery images are associated with passive love objects, while stalwart, forceful images are linked to the strength of 'masculine' figures who stand tall on battlefields or in other competitive arenas.

Poets are in the business of making these sorts of connections, but the responses, the perception and expression of beauty by ancient authors do differ. Beauty is said to be in the eye of the beholder[2] and while objectification is an inherent feature of both male and female eroticism, the sexual status of the body of the gazer does affect the dynamics of his or her look.[3] The looks of the lyric poets of ancient Greece, the objects they are directed towards – as well as interactions between those who are viewed and the singer/viewer – vary, both internally (in relation to other lyric gazes) and externally (in relation to the gazes and theories of late twentieth-century culture). The distinctions, at least in the representations I consider, relate to whether the viewer is male or female and to the position which they assume in a socio-sexual economy that revolves around 'masculine' and 'feminine' definitions/demarcations, and related 'dominance–submission patterns'.[4] The erotic interchanges of Greek antiquity and the gazes that accompanied them also differ from those of later cultures which are more seriously committed to the heterosexual dyad. The men view and desire beautiful boys as much as women, although the boys are feminised and the dominance–submission patterns (and the virtues rulers admire in those they rule: virginal eyes and *sôphrosune*) remain intact. When the Sappho-singer views a female object and mediates that gaze through poetry, does she also take up a masculine/dominant position? The mechanics of the gaze must alter when it is a female viewer who does the spectating/constructing. Or when it is the sight of a beautiful woman, or an interaction between two women, that features as the object of a female poet's gaze.[5] I investigate the possibility that a woman such as Sappho could own and re-create the mechanics of the gaze, converting it to something like the form of mutual gazing that Kaplan (1983: 324) believes 'is first set in motion in the mother–child relationship'.

In Sappho 1 the Sappho-singer gazes first at Aphrodite, whose beauty she has mediated powerfully through the beauty of poetic descriptions. Here, the god of lovers meets a mortal lover on an earthly plateau, they gaze at each other with a mutuality/intimacy similar to that of mother and child, or of fellow fighters (1.28), while the object of love finally reciprocates in the same spirit. Fr. 16 reminds us of the significance of beauty in Sapphic contexts, and of the urgent desire for the sight/image of a beloved's face, the movement of her feet. The look that is constructed by the gaze/desire of the singer, telling of 'the most beautiful thing on the black earth' (16.2–3), destabilises twentieth-century patterns of dominance and submission. The viewer/speaker could be considered to take up a 'masculine' position – but through the dynamics of the song and her desirability, her poetically proven beauty – the viewed, 'feminine' object assumes a position of greater power. Other fragments, frr. 22 and 23 for example, also describe a moment when the sight of beauty inspires a desire that seems to be as mutual as a 'face-to-face' (23.3) gaze. The view of another encounter in fr. 31 differs only in its intensity, again the power resides in the viewed, not the viewer. Always the visual is foregrounded, so that it is the sight of female beauty 'like a goddess for all to see' (96.4–5), that captures the gaze of the poet/singer and of other protagonists in this scenically attractive world. Those who are viewed in Sapphic lyrics – the subjects or objects of gaze and song – are inevitably female, idealistically beautiful. Occasionally a male protagonist is included in the representation, as in fr. 31 when a godlike man sits imperviously with the object of the singer's gaze, or in fr. 112 when a bridegroom views a beautiful bride. In these three-cornered constructions the dynamics of the gaze are complex. First there is the view of the (female) singer/poet, the manipulator of the eye/mechanics of the media, then the man who is represented as gazing at a female object who often gazes back, while externally the (female?) audience or reader look on. In her discussion of cinematic gaze Mulvey (1975: 6–18) charts the interactions between a series of male gazes: director, camera, narrative, actor and audience, all of whom gaze at a female object and are described as being voyeuristic and scopophilic. The few men who gaze in Sappho's lyrics, however, are barely focused upon, their position within songs where women gaze at women takes second place to the intense emotional engagement of female singer/gazer and viewed beauty.

Outside the circle, male poet/singers also gaze intently at beautiful objects and represent the dynamics of these gazes in their songs. Can these looks be categorised as voyeuristic or scopophilic? Do they construct or replicate conventional patterns of dominance and submission? When Archilochus looks through the eyes of his singer/protagonist at a young female object (Cologne epode: 42–53) the view manifests some characteristics of voyeurism.[6] The dominance/activity of the man, the submission/passivity of the young woman, are reinforced by the dichotomous construction of the song. It is a spectacle that would be expected to excite the gazes of a male audience, to reassure them of their dominance in the arena of sexual dynamics. More generally, with the evidence of other fragments, it seems that for Archilochus, female beauty is a treacherous property. Burnett (1983: 82) considers that, in the eyes of this male poet, 'women betrayed the promise of their beauty. All were like prostitutes, corruptible where they should have been pure, and the decay of their flesh – an outward sign of their true state – was a thing Archilochus liked to mark.' This view of beauty seems antithetical to the concept of beauty visible in Sappho's lyrics. In both instances there is a process of transformation, but while Archilochus' gaze debases the women in his songs, the Sapphic gaze idealises the female objects it views. Other male gazes are less sceptical than that of Archilochus but equally voyeuristic and similarly reproductive of patterns of dominance and submission. The singer in Anacreon's songs is often seen to gaze at 'lovely-faced boys' ('καλλιπρόσωπε παίδων') with girlish or timid hearts (frr. 346, 359, 360, 407, 408); he is confounded and the patterns confused only by a girl from Lesbos who 'gapes' ('χάσκει') after another girl (fr. 358.6–9). The women of Lesbos viewed and represented by Alcaeus seem to be less exceptional: appearing either as voyeuristically inviting maidens with lovely thighs and tender hands (fr. 45); or 'Lesbian women with trailing robes [who] go to and fro being judged for beauty' ('Λ[εσβί]αδες κριννόμεναι φύαν / πώλεντ' ἐλκεσίπεπλοι' 130b.17–19); or 'pestilential' ('μιαρώταται' fr. 347a) and/or timid-hearted, deer-like creatures (fr. 10b) who are prone to 'maddened' infatuations ('μ]αινόμενον' 10b.6–7). It seems that the male gaze must always be detached from the female objects it watches, represents, desires and, paradoxically, dreads.[7]

Despite these gaze-oriented distinctions, Sappho's circle of women was not unlike the group of men who fought and drank with Alcaeus. There were, however, conspicuous differences between an environment inhabited by a group of women, and an association of men who were gathered together for different reasons, in temporary exile perhaps, or at the court of a political ally. The interests, activities (including the practices of beautification) and the cherished possessions – the extrinsic objects of beauty – of each of these groups are also divergent. The women in Sappho's songs, for example, spent many pleasant hours discussing nuances of dress and deportment. Conversely, the interests of Alcaeus' group (and other male consortiums) centre on war and political wrangles and so weapons and armour are among the objects that are represented, and/or idealised, in his songs.

Some of the smaller fragments of Sapphic songs provide us with details of robes and necklaces (frr. 22, 29 and 92), 'multi-coloured Lydian sandals' ('ποίκιλος μάσλης .... Λύδιον' fr. 39), a vanity bag (fr. 179), flowery garlands or headbands (frr. 81, 91, 94, 98a and b), or the correct way to wear a skirt (fr. 57) or perhaps soft linen shag (fr. 100). The frequent references reveal the importance such decorative objects had for the viewers and wearers of these gowns and accessories. Grace, in the divinely personified form of the 'rosy-armed holy Graces' ('Βροδοπάχεες ἄγναι Χάριτες' fr. 53), or some special quality of gracefulness or attractive appearance, is an attribute that was multifariously significant in this woman-centred environment, and signifies much about its ideals and status in the larger community. A closer examination shows that the articles themselves have multiple significance and relate closely to other aspects of, and interactions within, their original contexts. Fr. 22, for example, manages to co-ordinate the swirl of a dress with the desire of a lover, and to mingle viewer and viewed in a description ('τὰν κάλαν' 22.13). The scorn which the sight of 'a countrywoman' ('ἀγροιῶτις') and her unfashionable 'country garb' ('ἀγροιῶτιν') elicit in fr. 57 suggests a more internal/external, socially oriented split, between the women of the circle and their less graceful and therefore inferior counterparts outside the group, as well as displaying the jealousy of the viewer/singer. Similarly the decorated headbands in frr. 98a and b manage to focus on a matriarchal lineage: three generations of women – grandmother, mother and daughter – and comment on the current political situation in Mytilene, and introduce a minor culture/nature split between more sophisticated attire and the comparative naturalness of 'wreaths of flowers in bloom' ('σ]τεφάνοισιν ἐπαρτία]ιδ ἀνθέων ἐριθαλέων' 98a.9).

Alcaeus also composed a song that focused upon much loved objects and reminded his audience of the solidarity of his band of exiled nobles, the purpose which united them against external forces. Fr. 140 is a song that is almost entirely devoted to a catalogue of the accoutrements of war. It begins as a salute to the beauty of the armaments it describes, lingering on each gleaming article, fitting its essential qualities neatly into a distich, until, as Page (1955: 212) says, an 'apparently complete description of the dress and equipment of a fighting-man' is placed before us in poetic form. This song is not concerned with the beauty associated with erotic love, but as Sappho does in fr. 22, Alcaeus chooses to link the apparel with human emotion – indirectly by reminding the audience that the gleaming helmets which now adorn the roof are meant to deck the heads of men – and more directly by supplying a motive, a task for these inanimate objects. Alcaeus' descriptions seem concrete, detailed, more vivid and evocative than Sappho's. As the singer/narrator stands back, taking the role of an observer who relates an epic-like tale of warlike objects and past glories, his tone conveys a sense of detachment, unlike the Sappho-singer whose voice consistently interacts with other participants in represented emotional exchanges involving viewer, viewed and a third party. The magnificent objects that catch the singer's gaze and imagination are placed separately from the men they would normally protect and dignify so that by their physical displacement they are relegated within the song to the status of objects. This positioning can be distinguished from that of the decorative objects which proliferate in Sappho's songs – articles that seem poetically inseparable from the women who wear them.

The passage of description prefacing the Alcaeus-singer's reminder about the beauty and/or sad neglect of bright armour and weapons is longer and more detailed than Sappho's fragmentary depictions, but it is constructed in a manner which emphasises its sequentiality and perhaps in this way, its male-centredness. With a single word 'δηὖτε', Sappho amalgamates the present moment of fr. 22 with similar past occurrences. Alternatively, Alcaeus structures his list so that past and present, ordered and disordered, arms and armour, are segregated within the song. First come items which have, to quote Bowra (1961: 138), an outmoded, 'Homeric air', and the description of these shining helmets and greaves is not only close to the formulaic sequences used by epic poets, it also stresses the organised disposal of these pieces. The items that follow – corslets, hollow shields and swords – are more modern, but they are disordered, thrown around untidily on the floor, indicating or matching the unreadiness of their owners. The audience is reminded of this forgetfulness explicitly in the didactic message contained in the final lines, where past magnificence (as well as the 'masculine' form of beautification practised when men array themselves for battle) and a world of heroic battles and glory, are compared with present confusion and disuse as the singer/gazer commemorates this loss.

The question is whether or not Sappho's descriptions of the wreathing and perfuming of women differ from similar actions by men, or at least the representation of these actions by male lyric poets. Some Sapphic fragments – fr. 94 is an excellent example – are beautifully embroidered with descriptions of 'wreaths of violets and roses' (94.12–13), 'woven garlands made from flowers' (94.17) and 'perfumed oil' (94.18). Such imagistic representations contribute to the idea of Sappho composing verse, or inhabiting a social context, that is traditionally 'feminine'. Within the binary orientation of a twentieth-century gaze, flowers, perfume, and other beautiful or sensual substances are allied with female subjects and are therefore devalued. The objects and essences that decorate Sappho's poems – garlands, perfume, incense, skirts, headbands, sandals and a profusion of flowers – only corroborate this viewpoint. But it is a perspective that leads to a corresponding slur of trivialisation, the suggestion that Sappho's representations are exclusively concerned with the world of women, and that this private territory and its symbols are less important than a glorious male arena such as the great hall where Alcaeus sings of weapons and war. There could be, of course, a generic explanation: that these attractive representations are included because they incorporate some of the conventional subjects of lyric poetry (or at least a female-oriented version of them). Or it could be that wreaths, garlands and perfumed oils were applied, presumably as ritualistic beautification, by both sexes in ancient Greece, in which case the stereotypical and dichotomous distinctions of the twentieth century are amiss and the only relevant proposal is a question of difference.

In fr. 81 the speaker instructs a girl called Dika on the wearing of 'lovely' garlands ('ἐράτοις' is an adjective which combines love and beauty).

σὺ δὲ στεφάνοις, ὦ Δίκα, πέρθεσθ' ἐράτοις φόβαισιν
ὄρπακας ἀνήτω συν <α> έρραισ' ἀπάλαισι χέρσιν·
εὐάνθεα † γὰρ πέλεται † καὶ Χάριτες μάκαιραι
μᾶλλον ποτόρην, ἀστεφανώτοισι δ' ἀπυστρέφονται.

. . . and you, Dika, twine lovely garlands around your curls
weaving together young shoots of anise with your soft hands,
. . . for the blessed Graces gaze upon those whose hair is
beautifully decorated,
turning away from those who are ungarlanded.

This didactic and rather beautiful small message is gently and economically transmitted, and centres on the description of Dika binding together the stems of a scented plant. Ritualistically, as well as physically, the scene is provocative, since this form of beautification – the donning of a crown of flowers – was, according to Burnett (1983: 297), 'a sign that one was ready to please'. The act and its cultural significance do not, however, appear to be limited to female contexts. Alcaeus, for example, talks of 'youths garlanded with hyacinth' ('νεάνι [αι . . . . ἰακ[ύνθ]ω <ι> στεφανώμενοι' 296b.7–8) in a representation of the communal celebration marking the entrance into adult sexuality of a youth called Damoanactidas. Burnett (1983: 138) is unsure 'whether an actual rite inspired these lines', or whether this is an imaginary scenario, but she feels that 'in either case the song makes use of images that are ceremonious and communal'. Sappho's treatment of this theme appears more personal – in the use of the first person, the sensual images that attend this young woman and the representation of divine interaction and approval – but the imaginary/actual situation and the objects that exemplify it are not dissimilar.

Another Sapphic fragment (fr. 122) also portrays 'a tender girl picking flowers' ('ἄνθε' ἀμέργοισαν παῖδ' † ἄγαν † ἀπάλαν'), perhaps to weave into a garland and wear proudly to show that she is moving beyond childhood. Athenaeus (12.554b), the source for this fragment, states that 'it is natural that those who think themselves beautiful and ripe should gather flowers. This is why Persephone and her friends are said to gather flowers.' Stigers (1977: 93) remarks on the 'combination of eroticism and innocence' in this tiny fragment in which 'both the *anthea*, "flowers", and the *apalan*, "tender" carry a double nuance of tenderness and sensuality'. As usual Sappho imbues a few significant words with a wealth of meaning as she creates a picture of a child who is 'too defenceless to be doing something so seductive as picking flowers; too inviting to be doing something so exposed as picking flowers' (Stigers 1977: 93). Meadows where wild flowers grow are dangerous places for tender maidens such as Persephone, as Alcman demonstrates in fr. 58:

. . . . μάργος δ' Ἔρως οἷα <παῖς> παίσδει,
ἄκρ' ἐπ' ἄνθη καβαίνων, ἃ μή μοι θίγ̣ῃς, τῶ κυπαιρίσκω

lustful Eros playing like the boy he is,
coming down over the flowers – do not touch the galingale,
I beg you!

Fittingly, garlands or crowns of flowers adorn the heads of Aphrodite and Eros, and Sappho restricts descriptions of similar chaplets to contexts relating to love and/or these erotic divinities. Some of the male poets include such conventionally beautiful objects in a variety of representations connecting to other, more public, contexts.

In one of Anacreon's fragments (fr. 396) the speaker asks his boy to bring him 'garlands of flowers . . . so I may box against Eros' ('φέρε <δ'> ἀνθεμόεντας . . . . στεφάνους . . . . . ὡς δὴ πρὸς Ἔρωτα πυκταλίζω'). The song is satirical and with the image of boxing and the idea of Eros as a protagonist (or pugilist) it is male-oriented, especially since the boy is also told to fetch water and wine, presumably in preparation for a drinking party. Sympotic revels seem far away from Sappho's scenarios, but they were – if we take note of other Anacreonic songs: frr. 397 and 434, or Xenophanes' orderly banquet in fr. 1, or Theognis' representation of 'garlands set in place by the slender fingers of a young Spartan woman' ('στεφανώματα δ' εἴσω / εὐειδὴς παδιναις χερσὶ Λάξαινα κόρη' 1001–2) – male festivities at which garlands were donned not so much in preparation for love as an essential stage, one aspect of doing what is right (e.g. Xenophanes 1). In the world of literary contests and Olympic games, the crowns – of celery or bay leaves – that dignified victors and poets were symbols of honour, rather than indicators of love or beautification of the wearer, another marker of difference. As a badge of male honour these traditionally 'feminine' floral wreaths gained greater value. Other distinctions between poetic representations of the crowns and garlands that decorate the brows and/or breasts of male and female participants are subtler. It is not difficult to contrast Pindar's elaborate rhythms and language with Sappho's candid statements, to point out the sequential structure and emphasis on the maintenance of order and correct behaviour in Xenophanes' symposiastic song, or the difference between flowery garlands worn to commemorate – or indicate – the advent of sexual maturity and those put on in preparation for a night of drinking and merriment. However, it is not just the erotic perspective behind Sappho's broken songs that is distinctive, or even the objects on which her gaze focuses, but her creation of a unique and private world. The Sappho-singer's response to beauty, to the sight, sound, touch and smell of soft skin, fabrics, voices, flowers and perfume appears to be unusually sensual. These sensations are re-produced in attractive sounds and words that simply but skilfully separate the beauty that is omnipresent in that sphere from the 'τὸ καλόν' that occurs in the convivial worlds of male lyric poets.

Within each of these disparate worlds it seems that Sappho and the male poets frequently focus on, or manufacture, metaphoric links between natural objects and their cultural analogues. The beauty of the natural world is re-produced by the gaze of the poet, by the poet's response, and by the act of representation. These representations perpetuate established parallels between gods and the forces they are associated with (often reusing mythic material), or between mortals and the beautiful and/or powerful phenomena that live, flourish and die in the natural world. This analogous enculturation of nature, the poetic mingling of culture and nature or *nomos* and *physis*,[8] adds to the beauty and breadth of descriptive passages. But the conceptual category of 'nature', as wild and unpredictable, sometimes generous and fertile, otherwise violent forces, has traditionally been aligned with women whose bodies, animal-like, give birth.[9] Conceptually, the enculturation and control of these beautiful but dangerous phenomena has most frequently been the province of men. In the lyric poetry of ancient Greece both male and female poets continue the process of encoding features of physiological and 'natural' phenomena in their songs. Topographical differences between private/interiorised and public/external environments, or the physical and conceptual space between female and male bodies and/or consciousnesses result in some distinctions. But there is also, according to the dichotomous sets of twentieth-century categories and conceptual apparatuses, some suggestion that Sappho's gaze, her perspective of nature, and therefore her representations (as the creations of a woman) would be more empassioned, natural, and/or less civilised than the gazes and representations of men.

Some lines from one tattered Sapphic fragment, fr. 58, comment on and exemplify a particular version of the nature/culture dyad:

ἔγω δὲ φίλημμ' ἀβροσύναν,]τοῦτο καί μοι
τὸ λά[μπρον ἔρος τὠελίω καὶ τὸ κά]λον
27 λέ[λ]ογχε.

but I love delicacy . . .]
love has obtained for [me all] the brightness and beauty
of the sun.

Occurring at the end of a poem that seems – within its tatters – to voice the thought that poetry (a cultural production) and the success it brings can somehow defy old age and/or mortality (a natural end), these lines – and the reference to the light of the sun in fr. 56 – combine cultural constructs: wisdom, delicacy or luxuriousness, with a natural image of the sun. But is this supposedly natural image, bright and beautiful as it is, actually any more natural or any less cultured than similar male images? Sappho's representation of the sun has little to do with some distant and ever-burning planet, or even the god associated with it, but much to do with life, poetry and beauty. Likewise Mimnermus often links images of the brightness of the sun with the beauty or 'flowers' (1.4) of youth (frr. 1, 2 and 12), then contrasts them with the darkness of old age and death. But these male songs feature a dichotomous structuring that is not evident in Sappho 58, a split between young and old, light and dark, beauty and ugliness. Unconcerned as she appears to be with fear of death or the binary-type constructions that men use to voice their fears of lost beauty and life, Sappho also seems disinterested in adding to the large number of male manufactured allusions to the singular power of the sun. This fragment and the reference in fr. 56 contain her only extant acknowledgement of its existence and in both cases any natural attributes of Helios appear to be supplanted by the unnaturalness of cultural constructs such as poetic skill or the beauty that flourishes in Sappho's lyrics.

Other, more conventionally, mythically and grammatically 'feminine' celestial phenomena feature in Sappho's lyrics and the diffusiveness of their light pre-empts their 'feminine' categorisation and can be compared to the male-reported and traditionally 'masculine' brilliance of the sun. Sappho's descriptions of these celestial/mythical phenomena remain within the hegemonic language of her time but they still manage to emphasise the positive and 'female' qualities of powerful heavenly bodies. The spreading, reproductive light of the moon in Sappho 96 is an unusual image, one that blends with the land/seascape and with a glorious but melancholic human protagonist. Like the moon this woman outshines all who surround her, a theme repeated in fr. 34. Women, moonlight and female ritual are also conjoined in fr. 154 adding to the impression that this diffusive radiance is as 'feminine' as the dew that accompanies it. The moon god, Selene, is after all female, and Sappho's descriptions of her generative power and her rosy ('βρόδα-' 96.8), spreading light appear to some extent to subvert the image of borrowed, paler light usually associated with Selene, and to endow her with some sun-like qualities. The male lyric poets do not refer to the moon in their extant songs, they prefer the potent images linked with Helios to brighten their poetic contexts.

Mythically, dawn ('ἀώς' or 'ἠώς') – the harbinger of day and sunlight – is also represented as a female divinity, one who had some maternal aspects and was favoured by Sappho (the scraps of frr. 103.10, 123, 157 and 104a suggest this, and Stehle's comments [1990: 95] offer further confirmation). A dispenser of shining, spreading light (in 103.14 and 123 Sappho calls her 'golden-sandalled dawn' ('χρυσοπέδιλ<λ>[ο]ς Αὔως')), in 104a she is juxtaposed with Hesperus – the evening star – to portray a double-sided, perpetual natural process. Stars also shine in male poetic productions, but once again their representation reveals a 'masculine' perspective. Sirius the dog-star, an indication of the coming of harsh summer, is the star that shines most often in the skies of male contexts. The extant representations can be divided into two groups: the war-oriented images of Alcman (1.62) and Archilochus (fr. 61) who both equate the dog-star with their enemies; and Alcaeus' depiction of the debilitating effect that the heat associated with Sirius has upon men (not women, 'now they are at their most pestilential, but men are weak' ('νῦν δὲ γύναικες μιαρώταται, λέπτοι δ' ἄνδρες' Alcaeus 347.6–7)).[10] The solution to this inevitable 'natural' affliction, as suggested in Alcaeus 347 and 352 and Theognis (1039–40), is to bring out the wine, although as Campbell (1983: 31) remarks: 'winter offers an equally valid excuse for drinking'. The seasons, as I have stated previously, and as is apparent from Alcman's idiosyncratic review of these natural categories (fr. 20), are one of the man-made demarcations that appear more often in male songs than in Sappho's representations.

On a more terrestrial plane, the winds that swoop through male representations such as the garden in Ibycus 286 also rustle the leaves of Sappho's lyrics. Wind blows through the outer circle of the garden in Sappho 2, although these breezes are contained within its serene ambience and are unlikely to shake either hearts or apple-trees. In fr. 47 Sappho employs a conventional simile to depict an oak-like human heart that is shaken by the winds of love. Her only other reference to wind is less peaceful. In fr. 37

she integrates nature and emotion to formulate a wish that 'winds and sorrows' ('ἄνεμοι .... καὶ μελέδωναι') would carry away those who might rebuke the singer. An Alcaean fragment in which a whirlwind carries away someone's senses (fr. 336) is equally satirical and not dissimilar. Except in extreme cases such as the contrasting scenarios of Sappho 2 and Ibycus 286, the winds that blow through Sappho's female-constructed landscapes and those that shake male poetry differ in subtle ways. In more 'masculine' scenarios such as exposed campsites or ocean voyages, the wind is a force to be reckoned with, although it can be as useful as it is oppressive. Bacchylides paints pleasant pictures of the favouring winds that speed his mythical ships on their way (i.e. Epigram 1 F.G.E.) and shows 'the richest of all winds Zephyr' ('τῷ πάντων ἀνάμων πιοτάτῳ Ζεφύρῳ'), helping to winnow grain. Conversely, Simonides (fr. 27) depicts a frail ship stung by wild, Zeus-instigated winds and storms, and this scenario is re-enacted in Alcaean seascapes (i.e. frr. 6, 34, 73, 208 and 338).

Sappho's decorative land- and seascapes are sheltered both from breezes that assist farmers or sailors, and from the storms that plague such pragmatic protagonists. In place of tumultuous waves that batter real and metaphorical ships, and deluging rain (Alcaeus fr. 338, Anacreon fr. 362), Sappho offers an expanse of sea empty of waves or description (frr. 44 and 96), and dew which falls almost imperceptibly (frr. 23, 95 and 96) to nourish plants that spring parthenogenetically from untilled soil. This dew can be approximated to the enchantment that drips from the leaves of apple-trees in Aphrodite's garden (fr. 2).

The weather conditions in Sappho's poetry are surprisingly, consistently, temperate. They are controlled more by the emotions of the human protagonists, or the tranquil ambience of magical/immortal landscapes, than by atmospheric variations or the immortal anger that lashes more 'masculine' contexts. Dew does, as Boedecker (1984: 59) suggests, enhance 'the gentle, feminine atmosphere' established in fr. 96, and the subtle nature of its moisture, the generative effect it has on flourishing flowers and herbs can be contrasted with the towering waves and storms that phallocentrically overpower ships and men. Mist subdues a lover in Archilochus fr. 119W, and even the rivers in these contexts are active and forceful, pushing their way across land and flowing strongly into the sea (Alcaeus fr. 45). Sappho's references to rivers are confined to more static descriptions, for example the dewy, lotus or chick-pea covered river banks that flourish gently in frr. 23, 95 and 143. Water, to quote Hawkes (1968: 141), 'like the earth, has always been recognised in the human psyche as a feminine element', but via Sappho's descriptions the represented calmness and regenerative qualities of this fluid element render it doubly 'feminine'. The most active description of water in Sappho's poetry is the cold water that babbles through apple-branches in fr. 2. At times water babbles through male poetry also, but it is depicted differently. Anacreon (fr. 427) uses the sound of waves babbling to mimic the noisy way some unfortunate woman swills down her hearth-cup, and – in another binary construction – Alcaeus stops the energetic flow of the Hebrus long enough to view and describe a magical pool where water caresses maidens' thighs (fr. 45).

The natural world – whether topographical or poetic – also contains a variety of creatures, although few images of these creaturely and/or mythical beings stray into Sappho's songs. The most frequent of these images, as in Sappho 1, is of birds – not the portentous winged omens of epic – but the flock of tiny sparrows transporting Aphrodite's chariot down to earth. Mythically, these insignificant but notoriously fecund creatures (Page 1955: 8) are associated with the love god and are thus appropriate; contextually they provide a vivid image – one that seems to mediate between heaven and earth – to combine the trivial and great aspects of the singer's desire/torment. Despite its mythical connections, the image appears to be unique, the male poets do not refer to sparrows in their extant fragments and the snorting steeds that draw the chariots of male-represented gods are fiercer and more complementary to 'masculine' concepts of beauty and power. Horses appear in Sappho's poemscapes only in fr. 2, but there they graze quietly, unfettered by chariots, and disconnected from human glory (cf. Alcaeus fr. 259) or the contests of men.

Other species of birds that Sappho includes in her songs are more commonly found in lyric representations. In fr. 30 a nightingale is used as an example of wakefulness and 'clear-voiced' ('λιγύφω[νος') song for the singers serenading a bride and groom; and in the tiny remnant that is now fr. 136, in one of Sappho's few seasonal references, a nightingale conventionally heralds the arrival of spring. Seasonal divisions and nightingales occur quite frequently in male songs, although the men do not associate these birds with wedding-songs. Ibycus (fr. 9) and Simonides (fr. 586) both comment on the nightingale's distinctively loud, 'πολυκώτιλοι' (Simonides 586.1) cries, at dawn or the beginning of spring. Sappho, who favours the image of these feathered creatures, has two other bird images. Fr. 42 describes pigeons, plump, homely birds whose hearts, in this case, have grown cold, causing their wings to slacken. Is Sappho using pathetic fallacy to represent the death of love and hope? Or is this merely a lament for birds that are not unlike girls? For it seems that even the bird kingdom is divided according to an androcentric gender scheme, so that small timid birds such as sparrows, pigeons, partridges and swallows are associated with 'feminine' characteristics, while predatory birds (the heron and hawk in Semonides fr. 9 for example) are considered more 'masculine'. The caring female halcyons[11] who transport the singer's ageing body over flower-like waves in Alcman fr. 46 in an effective combination of myth, nature and poetry, seem – as helpmates for men – to fit into the 'feminine' side of this scheme. Conversely, the song-birds, the nightingales, swallows, or mythical swans (Terpander 1, Alcman 12b) which epitomise human song and are at times subsumed within epithets attached to male poets,[12] appear relatively gender neutral. Sappho 135, in which the singer is woken by Pandion's daughter Procne (who was turned into a swallow), again reminds the listener/reader of the mythical background operating behind these songs and gendering the birds represented there by associating them with sexed mythic figures.

The unseasonal, relatively undemarcated poetic environments re-produced by Sappho's gaze in frr. 2 and 96 provide two different, but perhaps equally imaginary landscapes. (The former seems cloistered, the latter spreads as expansively as moonlight.) Both environments are wreathed with a lavish assortment of vegetation and each is associated with a female god whose attributes match the environment, and one or more godlike female protagonists. The scented, flower-decorated and regenerative beauty of the setting melds with, and accentuates, the beauty of these women. When Sappho refers to the world in general she uses a stock epic epithet such as the 'black earth' (16.2). When she constructs one of the erotic landscapes that centre around gods, ritual and female 'sexuality', her technique and the natural features that cluster there are distinctive and inseparable from a number of cultural markers. The garden of fr. 2 appears to represent a 'virginal' setting steeped in fertile potentiality, so apart from being filled with flowers and fruits that double as sexual metaphors and emblems of Aphrodite, the central area is protected, then surrounded by a more open, median space. The expansive, moonlit environment of fr. 96 is less protected, but then the godlike woman who wanders alone is presumably no longer virginal. When Sappho's young women stray outside the confines of the circle, as Dika does when she picks wild flowers for a wreath (fr. 81), the situation seems erotically dangerous. Hearts on exposed mountain peaks are shaken (fr. 47) and a girl-like purple hyacinth is crushed beneath shepherds' feet (fr. 105c). Only Artemis, the divine perpetual virgin, can safely roam in these exposed mountainous regions (fr. 44a). Men also view and inhabit poetic environments, but again these appear to differ from Sappho's poemscapes, for example Archilochus sketches in two evocative, if binary-type scenes in frr. 21 and 21a. Two disparate places are juxtaposed, the rich river plains of Siris (21a) and the island of Thasos – which 'stands like the backbone of an ass' ('ὄνου ῥάχις ἕστηκεν ὕλης ἀγρίης ἐπιστεφής' fr. 21) – in descriptions that are succinctly effective and formulate a dichotomous *nomos/physis* split between the savage forests of Thasos and the luxuriant plains of Siris. Stark and unpeopled as they are, however, they can be distinguished from Sappho's private, dramatic and extravagant environments.

Unploughed as it appears to be, the earth[13] in Sappho's songs is usually 'embroidered with many garlands' ('ποικίλλεται μὲν γαῖα πολυστέφανος' fr. 168c). Beautiful, girl-like[14] roses, violets, crocuses, lotuses and hyacinths flower profusely throughout Sapphic contexts – in fr. 2, roses overshadow the garden adding to the impression of enclosure and an atmosphere thick with their scent. The garlands or wreaths, or headbands, which are woven from these scented blossoms (and some perfumed herbs such as anise) embellish a significant number of Sapphic contexts, most of which include erotic rituals, and contribute to the woman-centred ambience, to the 'ἀβροσύναν' (58.25) which Sappho values highly. Within the circle of Sappho's gaze, as can be seen in fr. 105a where metaphor transforms a 'γλυκύμαλον' into a young woman out of reach of eager hands; or the mountainside of fr. 105c in which hyacinths/girls are crushed; natural phenomena are combined and work intrinsically within the linguistic constructs that extrinsically formulate her songs.

Kirkwood (1974: 128) considers that 'nature's role is secondary, its portrayal slight' in Sapphic songs, but the sensuality of Sappho's responses to natural phenomena, and her collusion of natural and cultural constructs such as flowers and ritual, effect an amalgamation of dichotomous pairs. In the terms of the domain Sappho represents, dawn is sandalled; stars and moon group and gleam like a bride among her bridesmaids; the earth is embroidered, or garlanded. Trees shake like, foliage is moist or bedewed like, winds breathe like, birds sing and quiver like, water babbles like, fruit and flowers *are* like, beautiful women. Her syncretism is not only poetically effective and as diffusive as moonlight or some later descriptions of woman-made linguistic constructs,[15] it also multiplies the attractiveness of each integrated article or protagonist. When the sexuality of women is featured, the landscape she describes reflects this state. When they love or are beloved their beauty shines all the brighter. Without greatly exceeding the constraints of the lyric genre Sappho was not only selective, she also contrived to idealise, or at least embellish, every 'natural' and/or 'cultural' detail. And despite her passionate poetic avowals and the repeated use of images that befit a conventional twentieth-century scheme of 'feminine' characteristics, her creations are no more uncivilised or 'disorderly'[16] than those of the male poets of ancient Greece. However, the gaze of a woman and her responses to the scenes she beholds, as well as the reciprocal reactions of those who catch and return that gaze, are, at least in this instance, distinctive.

Chapter 6

Circles of women

Desire and sexual experience in Sappho's representations and/or circle[1] are unique, predominantly female experiences that exceed 'malestream', late twentieth-century western conceptions of erotic relationships. The woman-to-woman relationships represented in Sappho's songs still appear, however, to revolve around two participants – lover and beloved – the essential duo that replicates binary patterns of thought and language. In this chapter I investigate the possibility that the erotic emotion expressed within Sappho's songs/circle had pluralistic dimensions, that at times it involved several singer/dancers[2] who constructed a physical circle as they participated in the interactions of a 'delightful choir' ('πολυγ]άθην χόρον' fr. 70). The dramatically explicated scenes examined in the love songs reveal a consistently plural, if not extraordinary number of protagonists: Sappho 1 includes Aphrodite, the poet/singer/lover, and her beloved; fr. 16 focuses first on Helen and then on the singer's love for Anaktoria; in fr. 22 the singer urges one woman, Abanthis, to sing of her love for another, Gongyla; and we are faced with a more angst-ridden, but still triangular scenario in fr. 31. Within each of these scenes it is possible to extract and relate to a pair of lovers, and to equate these constructions with ideas about the 'natural' structures of relationships. But interactions reported by some songs (i.e. frr. 2, Sappho or Alcaeus 16, 17, 22, 27, 30, 70, 94, 96, 140a, 160) suggest that these women functioned as a collective unit, singing, dancing and worshipping together.[3] The collectivity of the members of this community, their erotic and other exchanges and their dialogue/s, as represented in Sappho's songs, seem in some ways to anticipate the future conditional state proposed by Irigaray. She 'conceives of the subject-in-process (to borrow a useful term from

Kristeva) as a subject in dialogue, engaged with the other'.[4] Whitford's (1991: 48) reading of Irigaray's work tells us that 'the conditions of emergence of female subjectivity are simultaneously, then, love between women (a female homosexual economy) which is the matrix which can generate change, and language or discourse as a process of enunciation, a dynamic exchange between interlocutors which can transfigure flesh and blood.'

Assuming that archaic contexts as disparate as Lesbos and Sparta can be paralleled – and I agree with Parker[5] that this assumption is problematic – some passages in Sappho's songs resemble the form of collective desire ascribed by Calame to Spartan female lyric contexts. One similarity is the first person pronoun that is often considered synonymous with the lyric voice and its traditional I/you formulations. Despite its usual personal, confessional, attribution, in archaic contexts such as these, this pronoun is quite possibly impersonal and not necessarily singular at all.[6] Once the autobiographical inferences that shadow lyric voices – particularly female ones – are detached, they become much less personal. Sappho's songs are often divided into two discrete categories: the epithalamia, some of which are considered to be choral; and her private, monodic songs of love and/or prayer. This binary-type division seems to have been initiated long after Sappho's songs were composed, and, in the context of archaic poetry, to be relatively arbitrary, since, as Kirkwood (1974: 10) assures us: 'nowhere in the ancient classifications is the distinction made between choral and monodic'. Questions about private/public poetic contexts or the single/multiple voices sounding behind these productions cannot be concluded easily or securely. For instance, the fragments of folk song that occasionally echo through Sappho's poetry appear to be both public and private, communal and erotic, and to present a traditional form of the I/us voice.

Fr. 102 is a song that tells, in an uncomplicated fashion, of the debilitating effect that love for a boy has had upon the singer.

γλύκηα μᾶτερ, οὔτοι δύναμαι κρέκην τὸν ἴστον
πόθῳ δάμεισα παῖδος βραδίναν δι' 'Αφροδίταν.

Sweet mother, I cannot weave my web,
desire for a boy has overcome me
because of slender Aphrodite.

Aphrodite is to blame for the singer's temporary disability, and the adjective 'βραδίναν', and the word used to describe the effect of her influence, 'δάμεισα' are words that recur in Sapphic contexts (frr. 1.3, 44b.7 and 115.2). Sweetly 'heterosexual' and 'feminine' as it appears, the song is said to have originated not from the fertile territory of Sappho's imagination, but 'ultimately from popular tradition' and Bowra (1961: 134) categorises it as 'a *chanson de toile*, such as girls sang over the loom, lamenting their loves'. Once again, within Sappho's songs, appears a fragment which apparently lingers from folk song, perhaps from a female tradition, and tells of the sorrows or loves of women via multiple voices. It presents a more impersonal and conventional statement of love than other Sapphic lyrics, one which slips uncontentiously into a framework of male poetry and/or morals. However, male poets tend not to compose songs about a young woman weaving a web who is overcome with a surprisingly gentle form of debilitation or spell-casting by a female god. Nor do they re-produce interactions between girls and mothers. The subduing of Sappho's young singer/weaver appears as a good-natured exchange between child and mother, or a young woman and a female god, that offers an excuse for a welcome escape from weaving, in addition to beginning the movement from childhood to the experience of eroticism.

Communal rituals which mark the transition from childhood to adult status feature often in Calame's discussion.[7] Some Sapphic songs could represent this form of festivity although their unworldliness and sophistication tend to distinguish them from the tribal rites Calame analyses. The original purpose of the eucharistic festival featured in Sappho 2 is obscure, but it is possible that it was a celebration marking the transition of some adolescent members of the circle from pre- to mature sexuality. In the final section of Sappho 2, Aphrodite appears and mingles nectar with festivities, and mortal with immortal protagonists: perhaps she is here to officiate, to celebrate the advent of erotic maturity with a group of initiates. The background voice, the singer who re-creates and mingles divinity, garden and festivities, seems to be singular, though as she is unnamed and relatively peripheral to the action of the song, it is impossible to be certain. The personal pronoun could be lyrically plural, this could be a choral event, with the group of initiates, or their more mature companions, begging Aphrodite to glorify this special occasion with her presence. A number of human protagonists appear to be involved, perhaps they were the singers, and Sappho – the poet whose distinctive style permeates every repeated echo of her songs – directed a choir of young women.[8] A smaller fragment, one most frequently ascribed to Sappho since the authorship is clearly Lesbian (Sappho or Alcaeus 16), draws an attractive picture of women dancing around an altar, 'treading softly on delicate flowers of grass' ('πόας τέρεν ἄνθος μάλακον μάτεισαι').

The debate about whether this community was in some way/s an institution dedicated to worship of the gods – perhaps predominantly Aphrodite – continues to flourish, fuelled by the lack of socio-historical evidence and a plurality of theses. Despite their erotic undertones, fragments such as Sappho 1, 2, 154 and S. or A. 16, encourage such hypotheses, and this religious/institutional denomination is supported by Calame's analysis.[9] There are other fragments that do appear to support this thesis and promote the idea that these women were united in some way/s, in this case as worshippers and ritual celebrants. For example, fr. 150 rather summarily announces 'that there should be no lamentation in the house of those who serve the Muses' ('οὐ γὰρ θέμις ἐν μοισοπόλων † οἰκίᾳ † θρῆνον ἔμμεν'). Gentili (1988: 84) suggests that words like 'μοισοπόλων' have 'precise religious meaning'. Other references to altars and shrines, or voices raised in holy song, occur frequently enough to imply that there was a religious focus. In a minor dialogue (fr. 140a), the women of this establishment are instructed to participate in an empathetic, ritualistic and communal episode of mourning for Aphrodite's consort, Adonis. It seems that it is not only desire that these young women experience in common with this god and each other, lamentation (at least for a divine figure) is also shared. The authoritative tone behind these and other similar pronouncements ('κ]έλομαι σ'' 'I urge/command you' fr. 22.9, or 'μέλπεσθ' ἄγι ταῦτα' 'come and sing this' fr. 27.2, or 'σὺ δὲ στεφάνοις, ὦ Δίκα, πέρεσθ' ἐράτοις φόβαισιν' 'and you, Dika, twine lovely garlands around your curls' fr. 81.4) encourages the listener to separate the implied duality of singer/audience or leader/choir into the teacher/pupil relationship which is one of the most popular modern images of Sappho's community. Since the nineteenth century, European commentators have constructed and applied this educational model to Sappho's community, in what Parker (1993: 313) believes is an attempt 'to explain away Sappho's passion for her "girls", allowing her the emotion of love but denying it any physical component, by recasting it in the form of an explicitly "Platonic" and propaedeutic love'. Since the concept of 'Sappho Schoolmistress' is implicated in the ideals/morals of later western culture, and, as Parker (1993: 322) states, reflects models 'of controlling male to controlled Other, and reveals a disturbing obsession with power and hierarchy', it appears to have very little relation to the world of Sappho and the female companions ('ἐταίραις' fr. 160) to whom she sang beautifully.

Whatever the purpose or orientation of the Sapphic community, the co-ordination of its members into some form of collective association that sang, prayed, celebrated, grieved and perhaps loved together, seems indisputable. Interactions of all kinds, from discussions of dress, music and correct behaviour to expressions of group solidarity and/or exclusion (frr. 150, 140a and 55) abound in these songs. The element that binds the circle together and distinguishes it from similar socio-poetic groups, seems to be the emphasis on love and the beauty that inspires love. Burnett (1983: 209) suggests that Sappho's community was not unlike Alcaeus' male association – that both groups were 'aristocratic, musical, and constrained only by bonds of love and loyalty'. Calame also draws parallels, linguistically and institutionally, between the lyric choirs represented by Alcman and Sappho. Despite the close bonds constraining his group of aristocrats, and the poetic re-creation of festivities such as Damoanactidas' entrance into the world of adult sexuality in fr. 296b, it has not been suggested that desire in the Alcaean community was pluralistic. Was this the case in either Sappho's community or the virginal choirs Alcman reconstructed in his lyric songs?

Desire and/or beauty in the context of Alcman's partheneia is represented as being debilitating – limb-loosening,[10] more melting than sleep or death (Alcman 3.61–2) – and competitive. This 'agonistic' atmosphere appears to arise less from the decorative compliments paid to women by other women,[11] than from the equine-centred imagery accompanying those remarks (Alcman 1.39–49). This imagery directly associates horses with women, then places these women/horses in a hierarchical scheme of faster and slower, sturdy and more glorious. The scheme identifies and highlights two women whose names proclaim them leaders – Agido and Hagesichora – and reduces the rest of the choir to a grazing herd or a team of working horses. The choice of imagery/comparison provokes awareness of the male poet behind this representation.[12] Anacreon also makes use of equine imagery, calling a girl whom the singer would like to master, with all the 'masculine' skill at his disposal, a 'Thracian filly' ('πῶλε Θρηκίη' Anacreon 417.1). In both cases the comparisons are intended to be complimentary, but the differences between this male analogy and Sappho's equitable, more woman-centred comparisons are telling. With its risqué imagery, the connotations of dominance and submission that are securely bound up in this image, and the projection of some of the symbols of a male world on to female subjects, such parallelism appears male-centred.

Behind the imagery in Alcman 1, however, the song seems to have separated its all-female protagonists into two groups, one pair of leaders who are praised extravagantly by a number of companions or cousins ('ἀνεψιάσ') who make up the chorus. The chorus are represented as singing – presumably in unison using the lyric 'I/us' – of the beauty and power of their leaders and at times this power seems to be erotic. Certainly the remarks represented in Alcman 1.74–7 give this impression. The wishes expressed: 'if only Astaphis were mine, if only Philylla were to look my way and Damareta and lovely Ianthemis' ('Ἀσταφίς [τ]έ μοι γένοιτο καὶ ποτιγλέποι Φίλυλλα, Δαμαρ[έ]τα τ' ἐρατά τε Ϝιανθεμίς') introduce a note of desire into these all-female and collective proceedings. There is some dissension about the wording of the following line (Alcman 1.77), so we are presented with two possible meanings: it could mean either 'but Hagesichora guards me' ('τηρεῖ'), or 'but Hagesichora wears me out (with love)' ('τείρει').[13] Either or both versions suggest that some erotic affiliation exists between the two leaders of the chorus, or between leaders and choreutes, and/or between members of the chorus. This atmosphere of rivalry, of 'longing to love most of all' ('ἐγὼ[ν] δὲ τᾶι μὲν .... μάλιστα Ϝαδάνην ἐρῶ' Alcman 1.87–8) other women and female divinities, ends – a little like Sappho 31 – on a note of acceptance or peace, before it resumes its complimentary interchanges, this time with references to trace-horses, ships, helmsmen and Sirens. The fragment trails off at a moment of unity, when this choir of ten are represented as singing together a 'song that is like that of a swan on the waters of the Xanthus' ('παίδων δεκ[ὰς ἄδ' ἀειδ]ει· φθέγγεται δ' [ἄρ'] ὥ[τ' ἐπὶ] Ξάνθω ῥοαῖσι κύκνος·' Alcman 1.99–100).

Alcman 3 begins with eager talk of an assembly ('ἀγών') and ritual movements before it breaks for fifty verses then moves on to 'with limb-loosening desire, and she looks (at me?) more meltingly than sleep or death' ('λυσιμελεῖ τε πόσωι, τακερώτερα δ' ὕπνω καὶ σανάτω ποτιδέρκεται' Alcman 3.61–2). It does nothing to dispel this suggestion of collective homoerotic desire. The initial invocation could have been presented by the poet or a solo singer, but the second part of the fragment once again features complimentary exchanges between women, reports of outstanding beauty and popularity as well as the representation of desire 'ἴδοιμ' αἴ πως με . . . ον φιλοῖ' (Alcman 3.79). The conditional sequence contained in the last section of reasonably comprehensible text: 'ἆσ]σον [ἰο]ῖσ' ἁπαλᾶς χηρὸς λάβοι, αἶψά κ'[ἐγὼν ἱ]κέτις κήνας γενοίμαν' (Alcman 3.80–1) continues this mood of longing and adds the touch of a soft hand. What was the original purpose or import of these exchanges? Was the representation of female-to-female desire and rivalry a conventional feature of archaic lyric? Or was there a time when women sang and loved communally in circles or choirs? The association depicted in Alcman's partheneia, some of the erotic passages included in his songs, as well as the descriptions of female beauty and superiority, seem analogous to Sappho's representations of homoerotic desire.[14]

The situation represented in Sappho 22, when the singer urges Abanthis to take her lyre and sing of Gongyla, could be construed as a representation of erotic communal interaction. This could be a singer or leader giving instructions to members of a choir of girls about correct exchanges (musical and/or erotic) and the manner in which the desire associated with the 'ἄγνα Κ]υπρογέν]ηα' (22.15–16) should be expressed and/or celebrated. The ritualistic nature of this plural form of erotic desire and interaction seems at odds with singular forms such as: 'κ]έλομαι' (22.9) and 'β]όλλομα[ι' (22.19). Was it in fact not I, but we, who 'wish', a chorus who apply together to Aphrodite – perhaps for intercession in one of the moments of desire that recur in Sappho's lyrics – moments that seem not dissimilar to the representation in Alcman 3.79–80? Sappho 23 continues in the same vein, one woman gazes at another, praises her extravagantly, likening her to semi-divinities such as Helen and her daughter Hermione who possess more than mortal beauty, then apparently (the text here is regretfully lacunose) suggests that if her love was returned it would release her from all her cares 'παίσαν κέ με τὰν μερίμναν' (23.8).[15] Some members of the Sapphic community seem to look forward to going/singing together at weddings (frr. 27 and 30), rather than assemblies, but perhaps the spirit of communal interaction and semi-public choral presentation is not all that different from the interaction represented in Alcman 3. Even fragments such as Sappho 31, with its expressions of longing for another woman and erotic debilitation, could be drawn into a list of songs representing communal interaction. Although a comparison between Alcman's conventional erotic tropes: 'limb-loosening desire' and looks more melting 'than sleep or death'[16] and the desolation of the singer/lover of fr. 31 tends to foreground the differences between these songs and/or poets.

The competitive spirit evident in Alcman's partheneia stems, not just internally from relations within the chorus, but from external exchanges such as the representation of a contest between choruses – presumably for prizes and glory. Within the Sapphic community an internal/external split is also evident, but its parameters and modes are more complex. Toward her friends, 'ταὶς κάλαισ' ὔμμιν' (fr. 41) Sappho's thoughts might be unchangeable, but to women outside the circle some representations suggest a more antipathetic attitude. Fr. 55 provides an example of this form of hostility. Associations such as Sappho's are defined as much by what lies beyond the circle as what exists within. Other fragments express a more personal view, and are directed at women who have left, or are considering leaving, Sappho's community. Mika, who is mentioned in fr. 71, is reviled as a 'κα[κό]τροπ'' for her choice of new companions.

Within the Sapphic community there is also some good-natured rivalry – apparently of an erotic nature – between its members as they engage, disengage and re-engage in romantic alliances that are in some ways reminiscent of the interplay represented in Alcman's partheneia. There is also another external component, one which appears to some extent to anneal the split between inner/outer protagonists. Some of the women now outside Sappho's circle, but still emotionally attached to some of its members, seem to have left amicably if unwillingly, perhaps to rejoin their families or to marry. These separations signify an end to life in the circle, and some of the most detailed and emotional reports of communal erotic interaction are included in dialogues that represent the sorrow of those members still within this ambience of close friendship who love others now situated outside the circle. Carson's (1986: 10) definition of eros as lack or desire for what is missing relates to a dilemma that is clearly a painful and poetically dynamic aspect of relations between these physically/socially separate lovers. Perhaps lamentation was not encouraged within a house dedicated to the Muses (fr. 150), but songs such as Sappho 96 are full of sorrow. The sense of community and choral/erotic interplay is strong in a song that represents the interaction between two women, one of whom took most delight (96.5) in the other's song.

There is another song dealing with this theme, a woman who is represented as being distraught at the thought of leaving the circle. The song centres on a list of communal activities which is richly embroidered by the Sappho-singer, apparently to console this lover. Fr. 94 has often been called 'The Confession', a label which carries a weight of possibly misleading assumptions, of singular, personal utterance, or of the iteration of some wrong-doing. The song takes the form of a dialogue, between the Sappho-singer[17] and the woman who is leaving, but the sense of community, and of an internal/external split that is, to some extent, healed by song, love and memory, reverberates through every line. Unfortunately the text is fragmentary,[18] with lacunae which can only increase its mysterious, tantalising ambivalence.

τεθνάκην δ' ἀδόλως θέλω·
ἄ με ψισδομένα κατελίμπανεν

πόλλα καὶ τόδ' ἔειπέ [μοι·
'ὤιμ' ὡς δεῖνα πεπ[όνθ]αμεν,
Ψάπφ', ἦ μάν σ' ἀέκοισ' ἀπυλιμπάνω.'

τὰν δ' ἔγω τάδ' ἀμειβόμαν·
'χαίροισ' ἔρχεο κἄμεθεν
μέμναισ', οἶσθα γὰρ ὤς σε πεδήπομεν·

αἰ δὲ μή, ἀλλά σ' ἔγω θέλω
ὄμναισαι [. . . .] . [. . .] . . αι
. . [ ]καὶ κάλ' ἐπάσχομεν.

πό[λλοις γὰρ στεφάν]οις ἴων
καὶ βρ[όδων κρο]κίων τ' ὔμοι
κα. .[ ] πὰρ ἔμοι περεθήκαο,

καὶ πό[λλαις ὐπα]θύμιδας
πλέκ[ταις ἀμφ' ἀ]πάλαι δέραι
ἀνθέων ἔ[βαλες] πεποημμέναις,

καὶ πολλωι [ ] . μύρωι
βρενθείωι . [ ]ρν[. .]ν
20 ἐξαλείψαο κα[ὶ βασ]ιληίωι,

καὶ στρώμν[αν ἐ]πὶ μολθάκαν
ἀπάλαν πα . [ ] . . . ων
23 ἐξίης πόθο[ν] . νίδων,

κωὔτε τις[οὔ]τε τι
ἶρον οὐδυ[ ]
26 ἔπλετ' ὄππ[οθεν ἄμ]μες ἀπέσκομεν

οὐκ ἄλσος .[χ]όρος
]ψόφος
29] . . . οιδιαι

Honestly, I wish I were dead!
2 Weeping, she was leaving me

with so many tears, and she said to me:
'what awful fate has befallen us
5 Sappho, I leave you against my will.'

This is the answer I gave her:
'go, and fare well, and remember
8 for you know how we cherished you.

If you have forgotten, then I want
to remind you [. . . .] [. . . .]
11 . . [. .] and the good times we had.

Many wreaths of violets,
roses and [crocuses] you put on
14 . . [. . . .] together, by my side,

and many woven garlands
made from flowers
17 you placed [round] your soft neck

and with much [. . . .] perfume
rich and flowery [ ]
20 fit for a [queen], you anointed. . . .

and on soft beds
tender [. . . .]
23 you satisfied desire.

There was neither [. . . .]
nor shrine [. . . .]
26 from which we were absent

no grove [. . . .] nor dance
28 . . . .] no sound . . . .

It begins on the second line of one of its three-line stanzas with a passionate statement which might be serious and could therefore initiate a sorrowful sequence, if there were not two voices in this song, one of which calmly enumerates the pleasures of previously shared love. Pleasures that are to be remembered, slipped through the mind like ‘rosary’ beads, or a catechism to be repeated in lonely moments. The tranquil tone assumed by the Sappho-singer clashes with the despair of the Sappho-lover who speaks first, highlighting the playful exaggeration which is a possible interpretation of ‘ἀδόλως’[19] and changing the tenor of the entire fragment. Rather than dispassionately discussing the miseries which must befall all mortals (as in Mimnermus 1), this song seems to be designed to give comfort in a way which would be almost maternal if it did not linger over erotic details. The intimacy, the choice of form (a dialogue between lovers) and imagery, and the sensuous descriptions give the impression of a distinctive and female-oriented world. The singer in Mimnermus 1 contents himself with alluding to a temporary sequence of pleasures which gently reproduce the adversary relationships depicted by other male poets: desire, a chase, then surrender and secret embraces. Placed beside Sappho’s fulsome descriptions of pleasure (which extend over seven of the remaining ten stanzas), they appear meagre, insufficient to console the singer or his audience against the despondency which he communicates at length. Filling these stanzas with luxurious descriptions representing past, present and future experience, Sappho delineates pleasures which collude to create a continuum of love, one which is seductively attractive, comparatively timeless, and is shared by the women who make up the circle.

These persuasive descriptions are multi-dimensional, with imagistic, ritualistic and symbolic significance and have a consistently ‘flowery’ aspect that appears to be conventionally erotic. The list in which they are incorporated – which is full of reminders of ‘the good times we had’ (94.11) – has links with other socio-religious festivals (Sappho frr. 2, 154, Alcaeus 296b and Sappho or Alcaeus 16) celebrated by a group of participants. As the song progresses, it moves from the intimacy of two protagonists to include all sexually mature members of the circle. The final section of another cohesive, if paratactic list, in which three stanzas begin with and are joined by 'καὶ', tells of desire that is satisfied on soft beds (94.23) and unlike Homer who uses 'ἐξίημι' in the middle voice, in Sappho 94 it is active, suggesting that it was someone else's desire which was satisfied. In spite of the switch to a single speaker the I/you mode is still apparent here ('ἐξίης' 94.23), but apart from the equivocal status of the lyric 'I', other factors suggest a more plural interpretation. Sappho's tendency to integrate past, present and future in a single moment or song is no doubt effective as a consolatory measure, but within the circle it must also integrate the various protagonists who have experienced these erotic pleasures and participated in amorous exchanges at different times. The final broken fragments hint at other socio-communal activities such as singing and dancing at shrines and groves (94.24–7) and seem again to include all members of the circle.

One important role of archaic poets – the transmission of essential information (Havelock 1986: 68–9) in oral environments – suggests some exchange of knowledge, as well as love, between the women of this community. The authoritative tone of the Sappho-singer's voice confirms this orientation. If these representations were originally created not just as love songs but as a means of initiating women, through the mediums of song and ritual, into correct modes of behaviour, then the songs appear quite different. Sappho 1, for example, represents an example of contractual obligations: if you refuse love, you wrong not only Sappho but Aphrodite, and you could be forced to comply with a code that stipulates the desirability and necessity of engaging in erotic relationships. Women like Abanthis (fr. 22) are urged to show their love for another woman. Helen in fr. 16, the Sappho-singer in 31 and other songs, appear as paradigms, as outstanding erotic figures. And the festivals described so richly, invitingly, illustrate pleasures available to the members of this circle. This represented world is idealistic, intimate and full of love and the spirit of community interaction. It was, at least within the songs that represent it, also less competitive than the world of Alcman's partheneia. Stigers (1981: 54) defines the pattern of love she traces in Sappho's poetry: 'of mutuality rather than domination and subjection, of intimacy based on comprehending the other out of the self . . . the ideal characteristic of lesbian love'.

Chapter 7

A chain of remembrance

Many of the descriptions of desire and erotic interaction in Sappho's songs are mediated – transformed and perpetuated – by the way she represents memory. In male lyric poetry, time was represented as a relentless enemy, love was temporary, exhilarating, and often violent.[1] For Sappho the manipulation of time through memory extended sweetbitter moments of love into a poetic eternity. In this chapter I investigate this mediating force and the effect it has on many of her representations. Not only those concerned with erotic exchanges, but also the time-oriented divisions in a woman's life, and the myths and rituals that Sappho reconstructs, that construct modes of poetic and communal interaction which defy temporal categories. In the context of love memory is consolatory, renewing, idealising; it also has the power to negate the pain of present anguish or separation or time-ridden distinctions such as old age. As a primary constituent of oral poetry it is represented by a divinity, Mnemosyne.[2] Association with Mnemosyne, and with the power that attends her, glorifies both song and singer.

Distinctions can be mapped between oral and literate memories, mechanisms, skills, and the value which either oral or literate cultures attach to memory. One distinctive aspect is a question of time. Vernant (1983: 89) considers that epic/oral time is cyclical and cosmological, but when, as a lyric poet

> the individual turns to consider his own emotional life, and, in the thrall of the present moment with all that accompanies it in the way of pleasure and pain, he locates the values to which he has become attached in time as it passes, he feels that he himself is being swept along in a moving, ever-changing, and irreversible flux.

Sappho combines these specifications of epic/lyric time in her songs, to retain a sense of cyclical, cosmological time, without losing the 'thrall' of present emotion. Along with poets such as Archilochus and Alcman, Sappho is situated awkwardly on an oral/literate cusp, but her representation of, and her preoccupation with, memory, appears divergent, even from her contemporaries. Sufficiently so to prompt the question of whether the recollective processes of women and men are, in general or in relation to specific cultural frameworks, differently constructed. Gardiner (1983: 188), writing in a twentieth-century context, discusses some aspects of this difference. She stresses that 'many women writers feel that women remember what men choose to forget. If memory operates in the service of identity maintenance differently in the two sexes, it will appear differently in literature by women – both in the representation of characters' mental processes and in the representation of the narrative process itself.' Sappho frequently chooses to remember aspects of love and life that male poets either forget or choose not to represent. Her dissolution of the usual barriers separating time, space and individuals via memory also suggests that women's perception and construction of temporal divisions is distinctive. As Irigaray, Cixous and Gardiner assert, women's written (and oral?) creations generally, to quote Gardiner (1983: 185): 'tend to be less linear, unified, and chronological'. Many of Sappho's songs deal with the function of memory and therefore I test these propositions by examining three repeated incidences of memory in her work: the emotional impact it has on erotic representations of present or past lovers; her treatment of divisions such as time or space or maturity; and the way ritual and myth work to eliminate what Vernant (1983: 80) defines as 'the barrier that separates the present from the past'.

Aphrodite, through her interaction with Sappho's community, complements the aura of timelessness that floats through these songs. In Sappho 1 it is Aphrodite, the wile-weaving purveyor of love, who *once again* threatens to disturb the equanimity of the singer/lover. She also appears *once again* and comforts a love-stricken petitioner. The memory of her past actions and appearances, conjoined with this particular epiphany and her words of comfort, transforms an isolated and unmemorable affair into one link in a seemingly endless chain of desire, rejection and union. The word 'δηὖτε' – a mingled word that mingles remembered and immediate erotic moments[3] – recurs three times (lines 15, 16 and 18), making the song and the occasion it ostensibly represents not only memorable but somehow timeless. Within this idealistic and timeless space anything can happen and the chanted rhythms that sing of a magical reversal hang convincingly in the air. Paradigmatically, orally, the final impression revolves around a demonstration of god-instigated, god-approved love that has occurred many times in the past and will occur again in the future. With this construction of memory, tapping into some ever-flowing stream of past/present/future encounters, erotic love – eternally the province of Aphrodite – is shown to be eternally imperative to the poet/singer and her circle. As Burnett (1983: 257) says: 'with such recollections she [the Sappho-singer] knows she cannot fail', for who could forget the cyclical, inexorable nature of eros.

This irresistible experience is most memorable when it is sharpened with longing and lack. Hegel, who is said to have inspired Lacan's views on the insatiability of desire and who was himself influenced by Plato, conceptualises desire as lack and absence. In the terms of such concepts desire appears as a fundamental lack, a hole in being that can be satisfied only by one 'thing' – the desire of another.[4] The imagistic memory of details such as a beloved's face or her walk and the represented awareness of lack of/desire for her is capable of inspiring poetic representations. Sappho 16 also tells of the power of memory: to re-awaken desire, and to idealise a beloved woman or love itself. In this and other songs, Sappho adapts mythic memory to suit the purposes of present emotion. Vernant (1983: 80) considers that one of the privileges conferred on a poet by Mnemosyne 'is the possibility of contacting the other world, of entering and returning from it freely'. In fr. 16, Sappho not only enters and returns from this other world, switching between mythic and mortal, past and present symbols of beauty and love, she reinterprets the memories it privileges in a way that best illustrates an erotic ideal – an ideal that is also a paradigm of permanence to stabilise transient relations within the circle. Helen becomes, in Gentili's (1988: 89) words, 'the incarnation of beauty and love, the two cardinal values of a unique shared experience that . . . will live on in *memory* as an eternal, inalienable possession'. The past in this song is divided into distant and recent episodes of love and loss. Helen and Anaktoria have each moved away from their lovers, leaving them grieving and remembering. But one travelled in the mythic past, one in the recent past. Behind the shining beauty of these women – a transcendent beauty that reflects from myth to mortal – mythic loss and personal loss are paralleled. The generalising tone of the song's beginning: 'whoever a person loves' (16.3–4), extends to the present, personal cycle of love and loss and transforms this affair. Sappho makes a habit of reusing elements of mythic past in a way that is idiosyncratic and elevates the status of present women. Fr. 23 includes a gaze back into the past to Helen and her daughter Hermione, who pale before the beloved at whom the singer now gazes.

The continual flux of erotic relationships within the circle provides an excellent example of Sappho's merging of past and present, remembered and immediate experience. In fr. 22, two events/times are simultaneously foregrounded and juxtaposed. Abanthis is urged to sing of Gongyla, presumably to enact an erotic, musical ritual that has occurred before but is to be newly experienced by these women. Love, as usual, is validated, paradigmatically, as past and present occasions meet. Gentili's (1988: 84) statement on Sappho's use of memory affirms its importance: 'Memory is not simply, as in Homer, a means of evoking emotions and sensations: it reactualises shared experiences in a paradigmatic fashion and offers the assurance that the life lived together exists as an absolute *reality* beyond space and time.' Paradoxically, the superiority of 'the life lived together' is most apparent when it is transposed into a memory, as it is in instances of separation.

In Sappho's songs, time is frequently telescoped so that past joins with present or present with future, and a moment – the space of a song – is rendered timeless, part of a continuous sequence. This phenomenon occurs in fr. 49 with the singer's present statement about past love, and it is a significant feature of the songs in which Sappho evokes the memory of those who were beloved but who have moved on from the circle. Carson (1986: 117) considers that 'the experience of eros is a study in the ambiguities of time', that 'the lover's real desire . . . is to elude the certainties of physics and float in the ambiguities of a space–time where absent is present and "now" can include "then" without ceasing to be "now"'. This desire – the emotional need to evade unbearable erotic and temporal limitations – reverberates in a persistent undertone throughout fr. 94. In a way that is like, but unlike Mimnermus 1, this song deals with oppositions such as now/then; life/death; sorrow/joy. It begins with a statement which is just as dramatic as Mimnermus' initial question and which also suggests that life without love (or the symbols of love presented within the song) is worthless. But in Mimnermus' song there is a time-conscious emphasis on youth and age and a sense of generalised abstraction. Not that Sappho doesn't generate an impression of generalised experience in these songs, but the general is always grounded by specifics of voice, incident and detail. Fr. 94 combines sensuality and ritual in a manner which gives the impression of immediacy yet resonates with a history of past rituals. With its rich, concrete detail, it consoles the woman who is presently leaving the circle, just as it must have seduced the imagination of the younger members who had not yet experienced these pleasures. These women were also learning that remembering past pleasures correctly will thwart future distress.

The recollections the Sappho-singer employed as a reminder of pleasure, to comfort her companion, are full of symbols that operate in a number of physical and metaphorical dimensions beyond more linear time and space schemes. The final reminders of shrines and groves impose a retrospective religious aspect on the preceding scenes. But these tattered stanzas also reveal the initial structure of a song that balances gently between past and present, love and longing, symbol and reality. McEvilley (1971: 5–6) remarks on the way Sappho unites form and content, beginning by weaving the parallel statements of the first four stanzas 'together by the repetition and development of key verbs placed prominently at the ends of lines', then shifting dramatically into a phase of recollections in which each stanza 'begins with a καὶ which has replaced the significant end-verb as the binding element'. The final integration of these elements is impressive, as is the process of dynamic evolution 'where the two aspects – form and content – start in a kernel of unity (stanza one), then gracefully diverge in a long, slow arc, which is in the end seen as a greater unity' (McEvilley 1971: 6). While I agree with McEvilley, his descriptions of Sappho's process of unification with their regenerative allusions would not be out of place in a more gynocritical account. There is a progression in the descriptive past images, but it involves the female body and moves from the hair, to the neck, to actions – perfuming and expelling desire – which suggest a total involvement of the body or bodies behind the recollections of the song, and a style that is differently unified: less linear and chronological.

The male lyric poets, who do compose songs that are structured in a linear and chronological manner, do not often combine rituals, or communal celebrations with erotic desire. Nor do they construct a list of timeless pleasures to comfort a former member of the group. Memory in the context of Greek lyric poetry can, it seems, have diverse applications and construct various social/poetic meanings. Xenophanes did, however, put together a memorable list of pleasures: an elegiac representation of a male gathering or symposium that could be compared to Sappho's list in fr. 94. Less dramatic and personal than either Sappho 94 or Mimnermus 1, Xenophanes 1 is nevertheless full of sensual detail idealising this singular occasion. Rather than choosing to remember, however, he situates his representation – presumably a composite of many similar events with a range of convivial/ritualistic symbols: garlands, food, wine, songs, perfume, frankincense and an altar – in the immediacy of the present. Campbell (1983: 40) remarks on the strong moral tone of the song: '*hubris*, outrage, is to be avoided in the drinking, goodness and excellence (*esthla, arete, khreston*) are of crucial importance in the singing and story-telling'. Sappho, like any true oral poet, also incorporates didactic messages in fr. 94, but her moral scheme and the consolatory motivation that apparently instigates the song seem quite distinctive when compared to this prescriptive and public statement. Xenophanes' song has much charm, however, and has also, like Sappho's, a pleasing balance. Both songs are constructed around two distinct, symmetrical sections and each poet takes delight in detailed, sensual depiction, but there seem to be more contrasts than similarities. For example the time scheme in Sappho 94, stark present, recent past and a pleasurable, but non-specific past episode – which mediates present anguish – seems more complex but less linear than Xenophanes' logical and progressive development. His representation moves sequentially from preparation for the festivity to the initial libations, then on to rowdier after-dinner/drinking performances. The imagery, which appears analogous to some of Sappho's images, is also treated differently in relation to these time schemes. Sappho's representation of present deprivation is bare and without images, striking a contrast with the second, recollected, section which is brim-ful of images such as Aphrodite's flowers. Other priorities order the imagery in Xenophanes' song. Campbell (1983: 40) comments on 'the poet's insistence on cleanliness and godliness', an emphasis that 'sets this exhortation in a class of its own. The word *katharos*, "clean", is used of the floor, the guests' hands and the cups (1), of the water (8), and, in the second part of the song, of the words that are to be used in the hymns (14)'. The only mention of the past in Xenophanes 1 seems to be pejorative: a ban on songs about 'the creations of our predecessors' ('πλάσματα τῶν προτέρων' 21–2), an older generation of gods that includes Titans, Giants and Centaurs. In this context it seems that gods must also be ordered into hierarchical present/past structures and pleasures, like wine, are to be mixed with prohibitions, not memories.

The vital, restorative role of memory, the sense of mutuality apparent in Sappho's community and interchanges between past and present members are also featured in fr. 96. In the remnants of the first stanzas, Sappho sings of past love and of the delights that accompanied it, and of present separation with the sweet-bitter melancholia of memories that mediate across an interstice of time and place. The singer's role is, typically, a consolatory one, as she fills the breach between Sardis and Lesbos with a song replete with images of beauty and unifying power. Aptly, exact definitions or separations of time, mortal/immortal status, season or place are dissolved by the song so that it becomes relatively timeless, a ritual enacted often and decoratively to console distant lovers or perhaps provide a formula for dealing with longing and angst. Built around a triangle which seems antithetical to more tortuous connections of lover, beloved and other lover, the interactions would seem complex if it were not for the centralising voice of the singer. One of the participants in this drama (like fr. 94 the song begins directly with a conversation) is 'like a goddess' (96.4–5), the other is surpassingly beautiful, all three are united in the imaginative visible/intangible world the song constructs. Internally the song is integrated by the love of these women, the power of memory and the spreading, shining light of its imagery. Within the song this radiant glow appears to emanate not from Lesbos, but from Lydia where this woman, perhaps newly married,[5] now outshines her female companions.

]Σαρδ . [. .]
πόλ]λακι τυίδε [ν]ῶν ἔχοισα

ὠσπ . [. . .] . ώομεν, . [. . .] . . χ[. .]-
σε θέαι σ' ικέλαν ἀρι-
γνώται, σᾶι δὲ μάλιστ' ἔχαιρε μόλπαι.

νῦν δὲ Λύδαισιν ἐμπρέπεται γυναίκεσσιν ὥς ποτ' ἀελίω
8 δύντος ἀ βροδοδάκτυλος σελάννα

πάντα περρέχοισ' ἄστρα· φάος δ' ἐπι-
σχει θάλασσαν ἐπ' ἀλμύραν
11 ἴσως καὶ πολυανθέμοις ἀρούραις·

ἀ δ' ἐέρσα κάλα κέχυται, τεθά-
λαισι δὲ βρόδα κἄπαλ' ἄν-
14 θρυσκα καὶ μελίλωτος ἀνθεμώδης·

πόλλα δὲ ζαφοίταισ' ἀγάνας ἐπι-
μνάσθεισ' Ἄτθιδος ἰμέρῳ
17 λέπταν ποι φρένα κ[ᾶ]ρ[ι σᾶι] βόρηται·

]Sardis. .[. .]
2 often turning her thoughts towards here

. . . [. . . . .] you were like . [. . .] . . . [. .]
a goddess, she thought,
5 known by all, and she took most delight in your songs

now, in Lydia, she stands out among the women
as, after sunset
8 the moon shines rosy-fingered

brighter than all the stars, and its light
spreads out over the salt sea
11 as it spreads over fields full of flowers,

the dew is shed beautifully,
roses swell into blooms and tender
14 chervil and flowery melilot.

Often as she wanders to and fro, she remembers
delicate Atthis and she must yearn,
17 her heart crying out for you.

The expanded simile which begins by describing this moon-oriented process and extends over four stanzas has attracted much controversy and a range of opinions about its function or position in the song and its relationship to the 'natural' world. Critics such as Page, Gentili and Bowra ascribe a partially biographical explanation to the simile and discuss how, to use Bowra's (1961: 195) words, 'in Mytilene the moon rises across the sea over the

Asiatic mainland' and might easily shine on two fraught and separate lovers. Certainly its effect within the song is in part to unite the protagonists, but to limit the passage to a sentimental episode or a purely physical level or even to 'a conventional figure . . . not much more irrelevant, and not at all less decorative, than the long description of Aphrodite's descent in Sappho 1' (Page 1955: 94–5) seems inappropriate and unnecessarily reductive. Each of the constituents of the simile also possesses symbolic and/or mythological qualities and Sappho's selection and treatment of these elements is suggestively complex. Other critics favour the notion that in these four stanzas Sappho creates an imaginative environment that links the song to the world outside but, on a number of levels, transmutes such objects as moon, dew and flowers into multiply dimensional symbols. Memory in Sappho's songs has also the power to transfigure and override conventional meanings. Despite its complexity, this multi-layered world of female beings and delicate flora is not only imagistically, but poetically, 'inseparably blent' (Page 1955: 94). In the first section it is united by immaterial strands of thought, memory and song, in the second by an equally tenuous substance, the woman-like brilliance of the moon's diffusive light. Stigers (1977: 93) suggests that 'the effect of the simile is to recreate the female world in its otherness'.

Suddenly, after various similes have spread light, dew and flowers over a formerly bare, apparently tranquil land and seascape, we are presented with a vision of the Lydian woman walking restlessly to and fro, disturbed by thoughts of Atthis' sorrow. The time scheme has shifted from the generality of past and recent past to a present moment full of the 'thrall' associated with lyric immediacy and eros,[6] so that the song is not 'inseparably blent' but split into three sections, with the centre, decorative section standing apart from more dramatic passages. Is the shift unprepared for, too abrupt? Or has the song actually never left this woman but somehow, imagistically and/or grammatically woven her into the simile that began by describing her? In his discussion of the song Bowra (1961: 195) states that 'unlike many Homeric similes . . . Sappho's comparison of the girl with the moon may be pressed in its main details', and that Sappho sees the girl as being moon-like in 'the brilliant and reviving power of her beauty'. Symbolically, imagistically, the links between women and the moon are significant, as are the links between these dew-nourished flowers and those that appear in other Sapphic contexts. But within the grammatical structure of the song Sappho conjoins these sections even more emphatically. As McEvilley (1973: 276) points out: 'as far as the grammar is concerned, the moon and the girl are not merely compared – they are the same being'. Despite its ostensibly disjointed structure, Sappho 96 is in fact gently but thoroughly integrated with images that match protagonists who godlike, moonlike, flowerlike, wander in the music and memories of the song, through a dew-enriched, surrealistic world.

The possible distress of the Lydian woman, a sorrow that is analogous to another lunar characteristic – the loneliness and melancholia often associated with this traditionally pale night-divinity – seems slightly disruptive in this calm context. The final six stanzas are extremely lacunose so this image lingers, subordinating the broken murmurs of godlike figures that follow. If the song was complete the sadness suggested by the comparatively restless movements of this woman might dissipate in a euphoric, ritualistic moment when beautiful gods (Adonis and Aphrodite are mentioned) and godlike humans would come together. Perhaps though, except in memory,[7] the Lydian woman, separate from the group as she is, would be excluded from the ceremony and her sorrow is therefore paradigmatically indicative of the state of women who are considered superlatively beautiful during their time with the circle but then relegated to the status of outsiders. Memory, and the thoughts, songs and music of those remaining within the group can close the gap briefly, subtly, for the space of a song. Within the closeness of these circular constructions of community and song an enticing world can exist – at least on a poetic level – a recollected, re-created world that transmutes the time schemes, inhabitants, rites, objects and topography of everyday existence.

The processes Sappho uses to organise these recollections, this world, are in various ways – poetically, imagistically, ritually, temporally – distinctive. The events she chooses to remember and the manner of her remembrance are, arguably, unlike the recollective processes of male lyric poets. They not only choose to forget, or are perhaps unaware of, the nuances of more reciprocal relationships or the construction of female identity and desire via memory; their perception of time seems to construct temporal schemes that order their songs in a more logocentric manner.

These schemes Sappho chooses to forget. As a woman who manifests an understanding of and an ability to transverse both private and public sectors, Sappho presumably knows of the definitions and divisions of such time schemes, but in her songs she often chooses to represent an alternative, atemporal, state. This state, as is suggested by songs such as frr. 96, 34, 154, or Sappho or Alcaeus 16, or perhaps even fr. 2, involves a cyclical sequence that resembles the regular, circular patterns and time schemes of the moon.[8] It is divided not by hours, days or seasons[9] or the rising/setting of the sun, but by a series of rituals, songs, erotic couplings and dissolutions, and the rhythms and stages, the waxing and waning of a continuum of female bodies.[10]

According to Moi (1986: 187), who refers in this instance to Kristeva's ideas, 'female subjectivity would seem to be linked both to *cyclical* time (repetition) and to *monumental* time (eternity), at least in so far as both are ways of conceptualising time from the perspective of motherhood and reproduction. The time of history, however, can be characterised as *linear* time: time as project, teleology, departure, progression and arrival.' Physiologically, Sappho's represented conception of time seems to precede the rhythms of motherhood and reproduction, but to link closely to Kristeva's definition of a time scheme constructed in line with female subjectivity. To describe the representation and function of memory in Sapphic lyrics as '*cyclical*' and '*monumental*' does not seem inappropriate. Several of Sappho's fragments foreground physiological changes and social stages that seem infinitely more *cyclical* than *historical*, since they compare a past and present that relates to the female body. They also juxtapose the memory of youth/immaturity with the festivities and rites accompanying the next age-classes, sexual maturity, and then marriage. Carson (1986: 7) suggests that 'boundaries of body, categories of thought are confounded' by desire, but these physiological boundaries and categories appear to remain as intact as an apple reddening on the top branch of a tree (fr. 105a). Only the sexually mature are associated with desire in Sappho's lyrics. The others wait, listening to songs composed in memory and anticipation of a series of rites and symbols celebrating love and beauty, learning of these gradations of female time, identity and sexuality.

Sappho 24 and 27 both sing of the memory of a younger stage that is now past. Fr. 24 requests remembrance of the lovely things they did in their youth (24.3–4), fr. 27 instructs all the members of one age-class, women who are reminded that they were once tender children, to 'come and sing this' (27.5), for they are going to a wedding. The garlands Dika is told to place around her hair (fr. 81) seem to be a further representation of the barriers and symbols separating age-classes or stages of maturity. Fr. 125 again confirms the connection with, and movement away from childhood, through a reference to the garlands that signify sexual readiness or love. The tiny dialogues about virginity (frr. 107 and 114) also represent a process of looking back to a former stage, via memory, with the nostalgia that is often associated with recollection. The past moment when Atthis, a young woman who in a confusion of age-classes still seems like 'a small and graceless child' ('σμίκρα .... πάις .... κἄχαρις') was loved by the singer, 'πάλαι ποτά', (fr. 49) once long ago, is another representation that destabilises exact definitions of time. Perhaps *once again* however, it is desire or *erôs* that conflates and confuses the emotions of the singer and affects her representation of time.

The question of whether, as Gardiner (1983: 188) believes, memory operates differently in the service of identity maintenance in the two sexes, or whether representations of male memory operate 'differently from female memory, at least in terms of the memory of emotional states', is complex. Whether it is posed in relation to the context of Greek lyric poetry, or the twentieth-century representations on the basis of which Gardiner formulated her comments. Sappho has a habit of telescoping or infinitely expanding time. Theognis (425–8) also telescopes time, poetically eliding the interval between birth and death. But Theognis' emphasis seems typical in its scepticism and the portrayal of an ephemeral human time span, and it is effectively foreshortened. Other more sequential male representations, such as Mimnermus' elegiacs, dwell upon particular stages, glorious youth or depressing old age, for example. The physical symptoms of advanced age – white hair, withered skin, feeble limbs – also occur in Sappho's songs (fr. 58), but the effect is represented differently, apparently nullified by delicacy, love, and the 'brightness and beauty of the sun' (58.25–6). Old age, as (1988: 87) Gentili remarks, is 'an unavoidable episode', but its representation in Sapphic songs is 'one that has failed to destroy the essence of the reality Sappho has constructed within the circle of her friends'. In Sapphic lyrics the physiological facts and stages of life appear to be as intangible as an oral song, as permanent yet impermanent as a plant that blooms every spring and dies every autumn. Solon (fr. 27), like Sappho, also charts and reviews the stages of life according to physiological, not historical or chronological phenomena, but his representation again reports a 'reality' that is more concrete than intangible, more linear than cyclical. Its sequence is hierarchically ordered, reminding the audience that at one particular stage: 'everyone is easily at his finest in strength, which men have as a sign of excellence' ('πᾶς τις ἐν ἑβδομάδι μέγ' ἄριστος ἰσχύν, ἥν τ' ἄνδρες σήματ' ἔχουσ' ἀρετῆς' 27.7–8) while the weakness of old age and the inescapable and final moment when a man receives 'death's portion' ('ἔχοι θανάτου' 27.18) are much lower down on a scale of human happiness and worth.

In memory-oriented songs such as fr. 94, and other fragments, 31, 55 and 95 for example, Sappho also sings of death, but not as incontrovertible fact or a sequential reference to the end of life. Her statements about death are instead dramatically motivated and delivered[11] and relate more to artistry and erotic desire than to the end of an existence which has been measured out in consecutive, seven-year segments (Solon 27). Time shaped by memory tends to zigzag back and forth rather than move forward relentlessly towards a pre-determined finish. In the Sapphic circle, as Burnett (1983: 300) says, 'memory preserves, and the conceit of the ritual confers a permanence, for a rite holds within itself all of its past and all of its future performances'. The symposium Xenophanes describes (fr. 1) should also manifest this ritualistic form of permanence, but his representation chooses to ignore what Sappho remembers and re-creates: a preservational mnemonic force. This dynamic force seems to relate more to epic than to lyric poetry, and to retain the energy and monumentality of an oral age. Sappho, as an expert integrator of contradictory elements, combines the time schemes of epic and lyric genres, just as she mingles past and present moments by manipulating memory and ritual in the production of her memorable songs.

Chapter 8

Epithalamia

Weddings are one of the few socio-poetic occasions in which 'heterosexual'[1] love is represented in Sappho's poetry. Her epithalamia present later commentators with an opportunity to view archaic marriage ceremonies through the gaze of a woman, to investigate a genre which is distinctively woman-oriented. These songs have been welcomed by commentators who believe that all ancient poetry was created for particular occasions, and by social historians attempting to glean details of ancient customs from poetic artefacts. In epithalamia the inhabitants of female/male, private/public spheres are merged, and the Sappho-singer assumed a relatively public, conventional role, possibly as a monodist who recited at such festivals or as one of a group of singers. Perhaps for these occasions she employed a ritual voice, like that used in folk songs or partheneia, so that, to quote Stigers (1979: 477), 'the "I" of the poem is communal or generalised', and can represent either female or male personae. In these wedding songs, the Sappho-singer addressed both male and female participants, at times with a form of epithalamic humour which was conventionally, if discreetly, bawdy. Sappho was well aware of the mixed character of such celebrations, and her wedding songs diverge to some extent from her usual style, effected as they are by the conventions of a public genre, or by the rhythms of a heterosexual occasion.

Page (1955: 120) proposes that Sappho's epithalamia differ 'from the whole of the extant remainder of her poetry in style, metre, and apparently also dialect'. I investigate whether or not they differ noticeably from wedding songs composed by male poets. When constructed from the perspective of a female participant, the experience and representation of a wedding could, it seems, be expected to be distinctive. For the women involved it is a momentous occasion, one in which imminent sexual experience is foregrounded and thinly veiled by ritual, in which a veiled bride features as both an honoured participant and a young woman who is about to be displayed to, and integrated within, the adult community. Mythically, a man has been credited with instigating this institution. Legend tells us that Cecrops 'devised the institution of marriage, to put an end to sexual license and clarify the lines of patrilineal descent; for this service he was regarded as a culture hero, who led the Athenians "out of savagery into civilisation"' (*schol.* Aristophanes *Plut.* 773).[2] If Sappho's epithalamia are any indication however, it was women who played a larger part in the rites attending this socialising process.

Two of these songs, frr. 27 and 30, are contained in Book 1. Both songs, with their references to brides and weddings, appear to be epithalamic, to represent songs sung by age-mates of the bride. Burnett (1983: 218) ascribes a didactic purpose for them, asserting that they taught the young women of this community 'just what to do'. More relevant to my discussion is the sense of excitement and ritual activity they convey. Sappho 27 begins with an invitation 'to come and sing' (27.2) and a reminder that the addressee was once a child herself. Age was clearly a determinant in the allocation of parts played by the various participants. The anticipatory exhilaration indicated by 'for we are going to a wedding' ('σ]τείχομεν γὰϱ ἐς γάμον' 27.8) suggests that this was an occasion which excited and involved most members of the circle. With a request for favours (as in frr. 1, 2, 5, 15 and 17), the song represents another prayer or invocation; while the final mysterious allusion to the gods and Olympus suggests that this event is to be blessed by the gods, or perhaps, as in frr. 1 and 2, actually attended by Aphrodite. Fr. 30 is addressed to the groom and depicts a later stage in the proceedings, possibly some time after the wedding the group of serenaders in fr. 27 were preparing to attend. Now it seems that a singing contest is to take place throughout the night[3] and the singer's words imply that male/female interaction at these affairs involved not only the bride, and the groom who is playfully exhorted to 'wake up' ('ἐγέϱθεις' 30.6), but also these girls and some young bachelor friends of the groom. For the girls who appear eager to sing alongside or in competition with these young men, it seems a wedding presents an opportunity for enjoyment and social activity that is out of the ordinary. The urgency evident in fr. 27 is repeated, converted into this attempt to wake the bridegroom, and an atmosphere of communal festivity enlivens this all-night occasion.

Considering the dearth of extant epithalamia from male poets, perhaps this was a more female-oriented genre. When men do compose songs about mortal weddings, the scenes they describe are quite distinctive. The first lines of Pindar's *Olympian Ode VII* depict a wedding feast complete with an ornate 'solid gold' ('πάγχρυσον') bowl, plentiful draughts of fine wine to celebrate this honourable alliance, and much male conviviality. Finally, before the mythical episode and the real theme of this song – the congratulation of a sporting hero – harmonious love (or at least the marriage-bed 'εὐνή' VII.6) is mentioned. As usual in Pindar's poetry, emotion takes second place to more serious male concerns: glorious objects, the expedient exchange of women in an aura of male solidarity, the envy of friends and a plenitude of good wine. There is no sign of any female participant, not even the bride who would be likely to incite envy, to shine brightly in Sappho's epithalamia. Pindar's luxurious language, his opulent descriptions and the role his singer plays at the wedding feast – commentator rather than participant – are all factors which further differentiate these songs. There is a clash, not just of disparate eras, genres and social circumstances, but of value systems – the male poet concerned with grand events and public adulation and a woman composing and singing for a private wedding party or proffering a poetic illustration of correct behaviour.

As part of another song commemorating the success of a sportsman (fr. 179) Stesichorus takes time to describe a wedding feast which features maid-gifts of 'not only sesame cakes and groats and oil-and-honey cakes, but also other cakes and golden honey' ('σασαμίδας χόνδρον τε καὶ ἐγκρίδας ἄλλα τε πέμματα καὶ μέλι χλωρόν'). Alcman, who had a reputation for gluttony,[4] also portrays what appears to be a wedding feast in fr. 19. This time there are loaves with sesame seed and bowls of linseed and honey set out on many tables, around which, for extra comfort, there are seven couches. These scenes are appealing, reminiscent as they are of the sumptuous epic banquets or symposia enjoyed by both mortals and immortals, but Sappho's view of marriage ceremonies seems different. Her wedding songs are full of the sounds of music, of people interacting, of beautiful brides, and ritual. The tables groaning with rich food and drink dwelt upon by the male poets do not seem to appeal to her. Her wedding scenes are occasionally expanded by legend (frr. 44 and 141), but the way the male poets interpolate their wedding scenes with eulogistic descriptions of feasts appears alien to the world she constructs. It seems that, even in these semi-public affairs, she is preoccupied with the representation of primary and personal relationships. Her focus is upon interactions between the people who take part, singing and rejoicing at an all-important, female/male occasion.

For the bride, the young woman moving from the safety of her parent's house or the sensual, female environment of the Sapphic community, the experience is perhaps more ambivalent than this atmosphere of unqualified festivity would suggest. On this day she is honoured, she receives gifts, she meets, perhaps for the first time, the man who now takes possession of her body, and she moves from girlhood to wifehood, from the position of cherished child to the role of mother, from the house of her parents to that of her husband.[5] In her new role she may be as outstanding as the Lydian woman in Sappho 96. But much must be left behind, and like the virginal state that represents one of these leavings, the bride will presumably never return to this space or state. Details of what could literally represent a darker side to married life – social and/or physical seclusion and the dangers of childbirth – are omitted from Sappho's epithalamia. Later poets often represented the correlation between marriage and death, perhaps in recognition of the fact that the ceremonies that most frequently accompany marriage also go with funerals.

In some of her epithalamia Sappho represents the lighter side of weddings with a relatively bawdy, sexually suggestive and traditional form of humour. Frr. 110a and 111 are two examples of such songs, fragments that were couched uncharacteristically in language that seems, as Demetrius (*Eloc.* 167) noted, more prosaic than poetic. Both fragments are presumably intended for choral, public performance and the humour in these songs focuses on size: the enormous feet of a doorkeeper who prevented the bride's friends from rescuing her (fr. 110a), or the roof-raising, godlike height of a bridegroom. Is Sappho making 'very cheap fun of the rustic bridegroom and the door-keeper' (Demetrius *Eloc.* 167)? Is she simply using hyperbole in an effective and amusing manner? Phallocentrically, some critics assume that these references to oversized male protagonists are sexually suggestive, and in that way in keeping with the spirit of much ancient wedding poetry. Was this Sappho's intention? Or does the roof in fr. 111 have more in common with Archilochus' arch and portal in the Cologne epode, so that it relates metaphorically to female bodies? Perhaps other explanations, such as Kirk's (1963: 52) interpretation, whereby the groom is endowed with an impetuosity not unlike that of Ares rushing into battle, are equally viable and indicative of disparate female/male perspectives. This godlike groom who must approach marriage armed with the bravery needed for battle diverges substantially from Sappho's amusing descriptions. Her other image of a groom, in which she likens this young man to 'a slender sapling' ('ὄρπακι' fr. 115), is also potentially productive of numerous interpretations. This groom could be just slim, strong and flexible like a young tree, the image is effective and not unpleasant. Although it could be considered to contain some phallic symbolism.

Sexual symbolism is not, as Winkler and Bagg remind us,[6] a modern invention. Sappho's lyrics often refer, suggestively and/or symbolically, to female and male body parts and this form of symbolism seems particularly appropriate in an epithalamic context. The references to male genitalia are treated by Sappho with humour and playful exaggeration. References to female genitalia occur less frequently, although the chorus of 'Hymenaeus', 'Hymenaeus' ('ὐμήναον, ὐμήναον' 111.2 and 4) in one of Sappho's epithalamia implies that the nineteenth–twentieth-century symbol of maidenhead, the hymen, was not entirely neglected. Sissa (1990b: 106) suggests that 'the seemingly incontrovertible association of the hymen with *hymenaios* was not made by the ancient Greeks'. In corroboration of her statement, she recounts several alternative stories of the origin of this word, showing us the 'signs' of virginity constructed by an 'other' culture. These signs are now reduced to minor narratives which offer – to us – decidedly inferior proof of something as socially approbated as a perfectly intact female body. On the subject of hymens, the most frequently told and accepted tale is of a youth called Hymenaeus who fell in love with a young virgin and secreted himself among a group of virgins so he could gaze upon her. The young women, and unwittingly Hymenaeus, were abducted by pirates, but when they fell asleep he killed them and returned 'the pride and joy of his city's most notable citizens'. As a reward 'he obtained in marriage the virgin he desired. And since this union was a happy one, it pleased the Athenians that the name Hymenaeus be present in all marriages' (*Mythographi Vaticani* III.1; Servius, *Ad Virgilii Aeneidem* IV.99). Here, in an unusually romantic tale of male/female love, is an unusual and apparently girl-like hero. Who can tell now if Sappho, who was composing epithalamia on Lesbos, not in Athens, associated the word Hymenaeus with a mythic episode or a thin membrane ('ὑμήν') that would be torn away as the bride and groom consummated the marriage. The question, one which has stymied generations of scholars and commentators,[7] is not directly addressed in Sappho's representations.

The remaining epithalamia suggest that Sappho was more interested in the ceremony itself and the events which preceded it. Frr. 108, 112 and 113 all focus on the beauty of the female participant, the bride. Bathed, prepared and veiled, this young woman is brought to the home where the ceremony and festivities are to take place. The climax of the nuptial ceremony is the moment when she is unveiled, either by her attendants or her new husband. In antiquity bridal veils appear to signify much more than modesty or correct attire[8] and Sappho, with her knowledge of symbolic images relating to female 'sexuality', would be aware of this multiplicity of meaning. Carson (1990: 163) suggests that 'this action, called the *anakalypteria* ("unveiling"), gives its name to the whole first stage of the wedding ceremony. It signifies the official consecration of the marriage: henceforth, the bride is considered to *be married*.' The gaze of the bridegroom and the wedding guests upon the unveiled, newly exposed face of the bride represents an act of touching, a crossing of boundaries, a violation[9] that is preliminary but significant. At this stage the detachment that is a vital aspect of virginity is disturbed and her physical attributes are revealed. In frr. 108, 112 and 113 Sappho appears to be singing of this gaze, of this significant moment. She sings eulogistically of the grace and beauty of the bride (fr. 108), and of the good fortune of a bridegroom who is blessed with an exceptional wife (fr. 112). Woman-centred as always, Sappho's epithalamic poetry becomes truly lyrical only when it focuses on the female protagonist:

> ὄλβιε γάμβρε, σοὶ μὲν δὴ γάμος ὠς ἄραο
> ἐκτετέλεστ' ἔχῃς δὲ πάρθενον ἂν ἄραο . . .
> σοὶ χάριεν μὲν εἶδος, ὄππατα δ' . . . .
> μέλλιχ' ἔρος δ' ἐπ' ἰμέρτῳ κέχυται προσώπῳ
> . . . τετίμακ' ἔξοχά σ' 'Αφροδίτα

Happy bridegroom, for the marriage you prayed for
is taking place, and you have the girl you prayed for . . . .
'Your shape is graceful, your eyes . . . .
sweet as honey, love streams over your beautiful face
. . . . Aphrodite has honoured you greatly.'

The compliment to the bride in the second part of Sappho 112, which lingers on her eyes and love-illuminated face, cannot help but dominate. Transformed by love and the gaze of the singer, her face and eyes – the most expressive human elements – reflect the dual attributes of lover/beloved (frr. 16, 22 and 31), and good/beautiful (fr. 50), that shine through Sappho's songs. Aphrodite, as usual, has a part in this process and the bride of fr. 112 has been honoured outstandingly by the god of love, with the result that once again Sappho's songs infuse a mortal subject with immortal characteristics, for the occasion, and for the space of the song.

The melodious, decorous language of fr. 112 is similar to the language in Sappho's description of an immortal wedding in fr. 141.

(a) κῆ δ' ἀμβροσίας μὲν
κράτηρ ἐκέκρατ',
Ἔρμαις δ' ἔλων ὄλπιν θέοισ' ἐοινοχόησε.
(b) κῆνοι δ' ἄρα πάντες
καρχάσι' ἦχον
κἄλειβον, ἀράσαντο δὲ πάμπαν ἔσλα
γάμβρῳ.

(a) There was ambrosia
mixed in the crater,
Hermes took the jug and poured wine for the gods.
(b) Everyone there held drinking cups
and they offered libations
praying for blessings of all kinds
for the bridegroom.

As in Sappho 112, praise, blessings and prayers are a feature of this representation, but in some ways it also resembles the few weddings, and many other celebrations, described by male poets. There are parallels with Pindar's *Olympian Ode VII*. For example the singer of fr. 141 is detached from the proceedings, as she is in fr. 44 where she assumes the role of narrator, rather than participating and/or addressing the bride and groom. It is Hermes[10] who officiates here, and in a stately manner reminiscent of Pindar's wedding feast or Aphrodite in Sappho 2, pours wine so the gods can offer libations to the groom. The sumptuous descriptions of food that decorate the weddings of male poets are not dwelt upon, and although there are some Sapphic scenarios where wine or nectar are poured, the portrayal of wine drinking and male solidarity in an epithalamic context is unusual for Sappho. The scene in fr. 141 does seem, however, to present a further conjunction of female/male worlds, another crossing of sexual boundaries. It becomes particularly obvious in her representations in this genre, that, to quote Winkler (1981: 77), 'there are two sides to double-consciousness: Sappho both re-enacts scenes from public culture infused with her private perspective as the enclosed woman and she speaks publicly of the most private, woman-centred experiences'.

Elements of Sappho's songs which do not appear to conform to a characteristic style, language or form have been labelled 'abnormal' (Page 1955: 120). A narrative song which abounds in such abnormalities and has a distinctly Homeric ambience is fr. 44, a song in dactylic metre which describes, and evokes, the excitement aroused in Troy by the marriage and return of Hector and Andromache. This song, like other unaccountable Sapphic creations, has been linked to her epithalamia, but it seems in fact to be an expansion of myth, one of many antique poetic and/or dramatic re-creations based on epic. As Kirkwood (1974: 145) remarks, Sappho's choice of theme is, in a conventionally 'feminine' sense, not inconsistent: 'Sappho, poet of love and the world of women, would, in choosing a Homeric theme for treatment, be attracted to a story of marriage.' Her language in this song is not as predictable, since it is full of epic forms rarely encountered in Sappho's extant songs. Access to epic tales was a privilege enjoyed by most Greeks, including it seems, the female inhabitants of Lesbos, but Sappho's inclusion of forms usually considered Attic in origin is still significantly irregular. Textually, with its long lines, instances of epic correption and Homeric phraseology, this song is distinctive. It is possible of course, that such apparently uncharacteristic elements were deliberately inserted to fit the tone, metre and subject matter of a mythical episode, and that ancient rules of prosody were more flexible than later critics imagine.[11] Alternatively, Gentili (1988: 58–9) suggests that such instances 'should be taken not as borrowings but as phenomena inherent in the nature of the verse technique itself'. Both epic and lyric songs could be derived from a common, more ancient, source. Whatever the origin of these apparently anomalous forms, it seems that fr. 44 presents another combination of male and female elements, as it focuses on a scene extracted from 'public culture' and infused with a 'private' perspective.

Κυπρο. [ ]ας·
κάρυξ ἦλθε θε[ ]ελε[. . .] . θεις
Ἴδαος ταδεκα . . . φ[. .] . ις τάχυς ἄγγελος
deest unus versus
τάς τ' ἄλλας Ἀσίας . [.]δε . αν κλέος ἄφθιτον·
Ἔκτωρ καὶ συνέταιρ[ο]ι ἄγοισ' ἐλικώπιδα
Θήβας ἐξ ἴερας Πλακίας τ' ἀ[π' ἀι]ν <ν>άω
ἄβραν Ἀνδρομάχαν ἐνὶ ναῦσιν ἐπ' ἄλμυρον
πόντον· πόλλα δ' [ἐλί]γματα χρύσια κἄμματα
πορφύρ[α] καταύτ[με]να, ποίκιλ' ἀθύρματα
ἀργύρα τ' ἀνάριθμα ποτήρια κἀλέφαις.
ὣς εἶπ'· ὀτραλέως δ' ἀνόρουσε πάτ[η]ρ φίλος·
φάμα δ' ἦλθε κατὰ πτόλιν εὐρύχορον φίλοις·
αὔτικ' Ἰλίαδαι σατίναι[ς] ὐπ' ἐυτρόχοις
ἆγον αἰμιόνοις, ἐπ[έ]βαινε δὲ παῖς ὄχλος
γυναίκων τ' ἄμα παρθενίκα[ν] τ . . [οσφύρων,
χῶρις δ' αὖ Περάμοιο θύγ[α]τρες[
ἴππ[οις] δ' ἄνδρες ὔπαγον ὐπ' ἀρ[ματ-
π[ ]ες ἠίθεοι μεγάλω[σ]τι δ[
δ[ ] . ἀνίοχοι φ[. . . .] . [
π[ ]ξα.ο[
desunt aliquot versus
ἴ]κελοι θέοι[ς
]ἄγνον ἀολ[λε-
ὄμμαται[ ]νον ἐς Ἴλιο[ν,
αὖλος δ' ἀδυ[μ]έλης [κίθαρις] τ' ὀνεμίγνυ[το
καὶ ψ[ό]φο[ς κ]ροτάλ[ων, λιγέ]ως δ' ἄρα πάρ[θενοι
ἄειδον μέλος ἄγν[ον, ἴκα]νε δ' ἐς αἴθ[ερα
ἄχω θεσπεσία γελ[
πάνται δ' ἧς κὰτ ὄδο[ις
κράτηρες φίαλαί τ' ὀ[. . .]υεδε[. .] . . εακ[.] .[
μύρρα καὶ κασία λίβανός τ' ὀνεμείχνυτο·
γύναικες δ' ἐλέλυσδον ὄσαι προγενέστερα[ι,
πάντες δ' ἄνδρες ἐπήρατον ἴαχον ὄρθιον

Πάον’ ὀνκαλέοντες ἐκάβολον εὐλύραν,
ὔμνην δ’ Ἔκτορα κ’Ἀνδρομάχαν θεοεικέλο[ις.

Cyprus [. . . .
the herald came [. . . .] running
[He said] ‘Idaeus, the swift messenger [. . . .]
and of all of Asia [. . .] undying fame.
Hector and his companions are bringing a lively-eyed girl,
in their ships, over the salty sea from holy Thebes
and the ever-flowing stream of Placia –
delicate Andromache. With them are many golden bracelets,
purple robes, and elaborate trinkets,
and countless silver drinking cups and ivory.’
So he spoke; and quickly Hector’s dear father leapt up
and the news spread to his friends throughout the spacious city.
Straightaway the sons of Ilus harnessed their mules
to smooth-running carriages, and a great crowd
of women and [tender-] ankled girls climbed in.
The daughters of Priam came separately
and unmarried men yoked horses to chariots
[. . . . .] and greatly
[. . . . .] charioteers [. . . .]
[. . . . .]
(several lines missing)
[. . . . like to gods
[. . . . holy, all
together [ ] went to Ilium.
The sweet-sounding flute and [kithara] were mingled
with the sound of castanets, and girls
sang a holy song, and a wondrous echo
reached to the heavens [. . . .]
everywhere along the roads
bowls and cups were raised [. . . .]
and myrrh and cassia and frankincense were mingled
while older women let out a joyous cry
all the men gave a glorious shout
calling on Paean, the archer skilled in the lyre,
they sang hymns of praise for godlike Hector and Andromache.

Taken singly the sumptuous, jubilant descriptions which proliferate in Sappho 44 are not unusual. In conjunction, and considering their purpose – the celebration of a mortal marriage – they appear less common. There are no extant male songs that contain and combine similar descriptions of mythical, mortal weddings. The song is set during the time just prior to the celebration, as Burnett (1983: 223) reminds us, 'Hector and his bride are ever approaching but never here'. The scene-setting begins with the arrival of a herald and the news of Hector's imminent arrival from Thebes with 'delicate' (ἄβραν) Andromache. A verbal announcement introduces the chorus of sounds that resonates through the song, and is followed by a comprehensive list of the abundance ('πόλλα' and 'ἀνάριθμα') of valuable objects that they are bringing with them, 'over the salty sea' ('ἄλμυρον πόντον' 44.10 and 8). Simple, paratactic,[12] this list has some features which identify it as Sapphic. The all-inclusiveness of the catalogue – the almost overwhelming richness of these wedding gifts is one feature – but the manner in which they are described seems equally inimitable. Aurally the sounds merge, caught up in alliterative patterns with repeated 'κ', 'α' and 'π' sounds, and the bracelets, cups, robes, trinkets and ivory[13] are also conjoined in as little metrical space as possible, so that they are amalgamated into a single magnificent entity.

Remaining within the single moment of a present description of a legendary past event – Sappho's paratactic construction seems to exclude sequentialness – the song moves on to capture the eagerness with which the report of Hector and Andromache's arrival is received. After an instant of stasis while the news is relayed, the contrasting burst of action – the immediate dissemination of these glad tidings and the eager movements of Priam, and of the inhabitants of this 'spacious city' (44.12) – can only add to the vigorous excitement. The response is, like the list of objects, all-inclusive, incorporating all the inhabitants of Troy. And the action of the song, as Bowra (1961: 230–1) states, does not conform to a progressive or continuous sequence, but dwells 'affectionately on certain chosen episodes'. The next of these episodes supplements the first eager reaction, adding a spate of forward movement which looks toward a merger of townspeople and those newly arriving from Thebes. The transience of all personae adds to the fluidity of the song, and as with previous images the presentation is pictorial, although this time the image/s convey an impression that is more visually than aurally oriented.

In the epithalamic representations of frr. 27 and 30, the most significant feature is the sound of people singing, participating vocally in a wedding. Despite a proliferation of other voices, sights, even smells, the sound of singing and musical instruments appears to be equally prominent in Sappho 44. Amongst the sweet, mingled tones of flute and lyre and the noise of castanets, maidens can be heard singing a holy song, so that a religious dimension is added to a festive scene, and earth is joined to the heavens in the echo that follows. Within each of these episodes a mingling process, 'ὀνεμίγνυ[το' (44.24) is enacted, combining several elements in a single, sumptuous phrase. The next set, comprising three fragrances, is also united with this verb (44.30), continuing the process of amalgamation, adding a sensual component to the religious atmosphere invoked by the resonance of holy song. Bowra (1961: 231) notes that Sappho also uses a mixture of new and old objects to decorate her song, 'the silver, cups, the carriages in which the women ride, the noise of the cymbals, the myrrh and cassia and frankincense, all belong to her own world and help to make the scene from the past lively and contemporary'.

The images placed together in the last lines draw further, perfectly conducive, elements into Sappho's pictorial song. Older women add to the voices of maidens with their own joyous cries and men raise a loud paean to Apollo. So old and young, nobles and townsfolk, men and women, are also intermingled, along with the strains of various songs, a range of musical instruments and a mixture of fragrant smoke. The song they sing, within another song, likens Hector and Andromache to gods and dissolves a further polarity, one that is often rendered insecure by Sappho's representations, that of mortals and immortals. 'Godlike' (44.34) is an epithet also used to endow worthy humans with divine status in Homeric songs, an element which gives this song the feel and sound of epic. The similarity to Homeric poetry is increased by Sappho's unusually objective viewpoint, the dactylic metre and the stateliness of her delivery. There is also the inclusion of non-Lesbian forms such as: 'ὅσαι', 'ἴερας', 'φίλοις' (44.31, 6, 12). Bowra insists (1961: 230), that in spite of these inclusions, 'the art of this poem is not Homeric', and I agree. The disparities in technique, choice of episode, and the presentation of these episodes are obvious, and they appear to separate this Sapphic production not only from the Homeric tradition, but from other, namely male, poetic narratives of her time.

Celebration of marriages was apparently not a popular theme among the male lyric poets, and in their representations these public, *polis*-oriented authors never equal the mood of undiluted joy pervasive in fr. 44. Engagement with the female in the interior space allotted to women, whether within marriage or in the course of other interaction/s, appears to represent an ambivalent experience for the male citizens and poets of ancient Greece. Such perilous encounters or alliances are not often represented or celebrated, although the male poets do at times choose mythical wedding episodes and expand these themes in line with personal inclinations and contemporary trends. Alcaeus 42 is a mythical expansion comparing two legendary unions, that of Helen who is in many ways the traditional antithesis of Andromache, with the ideal coupling of delicate Thetis and Peleus.

Like Sappho 44 the song takes the form of a lyric narrative, but this appears to be one of the few similarities. Burnett (1983: 197) feels that 'it is as a complementary pair . . . and not as a pair of foils, that Alcaeus has set his two weddings side by side'. Her view is not shared by Kirkwood (1974: 89) who considers that 'the poem is built on a contrast between the ruin brought on Troy by Helen and the glory that came from the marriage of Thetis'. On this point I side with Kirkwood, since the act of juxtaposition, the placing of two marriages, one which is explicitly extolled, one which is damned, side by side, must necessarily invite comparisons. Unmoralistically, unlike Alcaeus' song in which moral judgement is passed and announced, there is no good or evil in Sappho 44, merely a superlative state that could be defined as excellence, and the multiple features and descriptions contributing to the portrayal are in no way divisible into a binary-type scheme. Whatever the motivation behind the story Sappho tells, her depiction of this mythic event is not negatively didactic – it does not provide an illustration of right and wrong, or productive/destructive alliances. Alcaeus' language is also decorative, with some Homeric echoes, and his descriptions are evocative and dignified, particularly when he dwells on the ideal love of Peleus and Thetis, the pure, immortal maiden. But beside the extravagance of Sappho's all-inclusive, multi-faceted lists, they appear economical and single-minded. Even the mixture of mortal/immortal personae is divided by the emphasis placed on the difference between a disastrous mortal union and a glorious mortal/immortal match. Like Sappho 44, Alcaeus' song appears to be relatively complete, framed within a tight and effective scheme, but its binary construction and the overt condemnation of a woman who has chosen to defy laws made by men, suggest that behind the song the mechanics of a male-centred value scheme are operating. The single extraneous item in Alcaeus' song, Achilles' 'chestnut fillies' ('ξάνθαν .... πώλων' 42.14) also links this poetic scenario to the world of men and 'masculine' interests. A feature that is missing from his song is the cacophony of sounds reverberating through fr. 44. Alcaeus 42 fits some of the criteria of an orally oriented song, concentrating as it does on a lesson imparted within a mythical tale, but apart from an indirect invitation to the gods, the only sound we hear is the distanced voice of the story-teller.

It is possible however, that in public, male culture, hymns, music and paeans are restricted to specific occasions. Alcman tells us that 'at the meals and banquets of the messes it is right to strike up the paean in the presence of the feasters' ('θοίναις δὲ καὶ θιάσοισιν ἀνδείων παρὰ δαιτυμόνεσσι πρέπει παιᾶνα κατάρχην' fr. 98). Theognis also includes a sequence that seems similar to Sappho's celebration: 'rejoicing with the kithara and pleasant feast, with dance and cry of Paeans around your altar' ('τερπόμενοι κιθάρηι καὶ ἐρατῆι θαλίηι / παιάνων τε χοροῖσ' ἰαχῃισί τε σὸν περὶ βωμόν' 773–82), but he seems to offer these festivities to Apollo as a bribe, expecting in return that 'Lord Phoebus (will) be gracious and guard this our city' ('Φοιβε ἄναξ, αὐτὸς μὲν ἐπύργωσας πόλιν ἄκρην' 773). In some of his epinicians Simonides also sings of beautiful paeans with hymns (frr. 61 and 78) of cheerful revels and mingled shouts (fr. 519). In a song composed for a similar occasion, a victory ode (3) praising Hieron, the victor of a chariot race at the Olympic games, Bacchylides presents first the sound of a great crowd shouting in unison, and then provides – in his usual ornate style – a rich vision of festivity and religious ritual. Although the male poets do not often represent marriage celebrations, it seems that they do include similar passages in choral songs created for more male-oriented experiences and festivities.

When Burnett (1983: 222) discusses fr. 44, she describes the cumulative effect as dreamlike, 'quite unlike that of any epic event . . . for it is rendered by details that are rich, insubstantial and not quite germane'. But the song begins with a list of precious gifts – golden bracelets, trinkets and robes – which appear not unlike the very substantial objects often referred to in Homer, or the flashing gold tripods in Bacchylides' choral ode. Are they different? Sappho's gifts are, of course, varied, multiple and secular, they also are not actually present, they are merely reports of objects travelling across the sea. (Perhaps the lack of stasis, the mobility of the gifts, ships, men, women, carriages, etc. contributes to the fluidity, the overall aura of insubstantiality.) When compared to the solidity of items which are firmly located in public ritual they are less substantial, and by their diffusiveness, their surprising richness and heterogeneity they appear relatively dreamlike. Variously, this song announces that it is a product of the imagination, perhaps a specifically woman-centred imagination. The exaggeration and multiplicity that contribute to its abundance and vividness could be considered traditionally 'feminine' qualities. Sappho seems to be proclaiming her 'femininity' in the excessiveness of descriptions that take over this song. Apart from the tripods, altars and oxen which endow the male paeans/hymns with a definably ritualistic aura, the smell of feasting seems more tangible than mingled scents of frankincense, cassia and myrrh (44.30). In Sappho's song the religious component is also noticeably insubstantial, reduced to songs, scents, echoes and likenesses. Gods and mortals of both sexes are, like all other elements, merged together. Paeans, hymns and the sounds of voices and musical instruments feature in the male songs, but in less profusion, for example, only the kithara (Theognis) or flute (Simonides) is joined with the sound of male voices, and these men honour a god, or a victory, never a marriage.

By her diffusiveness, her consolidation of multifarious components in a song that is filled to overflowing with movement, scents and sounds, with the delight she transmits in her descriptions of nuptial celebrations,[14] Sappho is once again declaring her female-centredness. She converts some elements of male culture, adds a perspective and technique which appear idiosyncratic, and finally presents us with a creation that is unlike any of the extant songs of male poets. Behind this poetic representation, with its proliferous music, gifts and sights, smells and sounds, a woman, even a woman as noble and graceful as Andromache, is exchanged between men,[15] taken across the sea from the *oikos* of her father to that of her husband. Within this genre, from the perspective of a female poet constructed into this culture and its modes of exchange however, it seems that weddings and the epithalamia that celebrate them can still be represented as moments of unqualified joy.

Chapter 9

Immortality

μνάσεσθαί τινά φαιμι † καὶ ἕτερον † ἀμμέων

(Sappho, fr. 147)

'Someone, I say, will remember us . . . and in other times . . .' In this small fragment Sappho again sings of the significance of memory in ancient socio-poetic contexts. The remembering in this case is to be done by future generations and the act of remembrance will transmit the fame of a singer whose songs have overcome mortal ephemerality. She was not forgotten.[1] But this desire for poetic immortality, the creation of songs powerful enough to gain admiration and reward in contemporary contexts, as well as to influence future audiences is not exclusive to Sappho. Many of the Greek lyric poets, and their epic counterparts, seem preoccupied with the creation and dissemination of poetry that excelled, that spread the news, not only of the song's content, but of the greatness of its author. One feature of archaic and ancient Greece that is rarely disputed is its 'agonistic' nature, a salient characteristic that is also evident in the more private arenas represented in Sappho's lyrics. In later antiquity when her songs were written down and her fame established, Sappho attracted the epithet 'mascula',[2] perhaps, as Davison believes, as a result of the sexual behaviour associated with her and other Lesbian women, perhaps because of her reputation as an exceptionally skilful poet. Often it appears to be a male, 'masculine' voice and viewpoint that affects or assaults audiences sited in public forums. In the competitive poetic context of antiquity, Sappho's success and position seem exceptional, equal or perhaps superior to many other poets. Was it because her songs – her entries in an ongoing competition – were superior and/or in some way/s distinctive? Or was it due to the conditions within which they were composed; or her socio-poetic functions; or her responses to her environment? Why did public responses to this woman poet differ from those of male poets? I suggest that such distinctions could arise from or relate to the fact of her femaleness, the fact that a woman's voice initially sang these well-crafted, authoritative and long-lasting songs, that they emanated from a woman's body, to some extent out of her relations with other female bodies, voices and symbols.

If we accept Friedrich's (1978: 110) statement that 'Lesbos may have been the most distinguished in . . . an early pan-Hellenic "women's culture" of colloquial poetry', then Lesbian women may have had greater access to an established female-oriented tradition of poetry, and to some chance of fame. Sappho herself sings: 'superior, as the Lesbian singer to those of other lands' ('πέρροχος ὡς ὄτ' ἄοιδος ὁ Λέσβιος ἀλλοδάποισιν' fr. 106). If we believe in the oral orientation and correlative authority of Sappho's songs, then she was endowed with justifiable prestige. As the maker of songs designed – at least in part, as ideological apparatuses to construct people as subjects – she had some power within the wider community, a position in a competitive market that she guarded somewhat jealously. As a poet she must also have competed with other poets. Lyric poetry – the genre chosen as a vehicle for these constructions – has been retrospectively devalued, at least in comparison to the grand structures and themes of epic poetry. Sappho, squeezing epics, hymns and philosophical tropes into her lyrics, apparently attempts to redress any imbalance, but forms associated with women, emotion and personal expression seem certain to be depreciated. Unaware of this distinction perhaps, the creators of both epic and lyric songs apply to certain – predominantly female – divinities for inspiration, renown and information outside their own knowledge, enhancing songs and personal status by this interaction.

Another aspect of the ancient world that differentiates it from later and more Christian contexts, is the prevalence of female divinities, immortals who might be less powerful than Zeus – patriarch of the Olympians – but who retain some traces of the ascendancy of older gods. Several of these divinities, the Muses – the daughters of Mnemosyne and Zeus – and the Graces or Charites, were, like Aphrodite, frequently invoked or referred to by Sappho (frr. 32, 53, 58, 81, 103, 127, 128, 150, 187). Invocations such as fr. 128: 'Come once again now, delicate Graces and lovely-haired Muses' ('δεῦτέ νυν ἄβραι Χάριτες καλλίκομοί τε Μοῖσαι') seem conventional, but there are indications that the relationship between these deities and the Sapphic community was unusually close. Fr. 150 suggests that these women served the Muses, a proposal that seems to confirm the poetic/religious orientation of the circle and imply that the association between these mortal/immortal women differed from the usual interaction of poet and divine helpmate.

Sappho's represented alliances between herself, her community and female gods do, quite conventionally, endow the human elements with some reflected glory, but the relationships seem more intimate and equitable than similar male mortal/immortal associations. Like Aphrodite, Sappho is concerned with erotic love, like the Muses she sings beautifully and creates songs, like the Graces she attends Aphrodite. She and her community focus on the attributes that Friedrich (1978: 106) considers are epitomised by these kindly and harmonious spirits: 'personal beauty, loveliness', graceful 'deeds and words' and 'gratification through pleasure and beauty'. So close is the affiliation that in the second century BC Antipater of Sidon (*Anthologia Palatina* 7.14 and 9.60) classed Sappho as 'other', 'not among the leading male poets of her time, as the ninth great Greek lyric poet, but as the tenth of the female Muses'.

The male poets, despite their frequent invocations to the Muses, engage in different interaction/s. In the eyes of the male poets and philosophers, the Muses and Graces, as females, even immortal females, are sometimes represented as 'other': deceptive,[3] merely capable of assisting men with their productions, and 'forever outside the activity of philosophizing'.[4] While poets such as Hesiod (*Theogony* 99) and Archilochus (fr. 1) do, like Sappho, announce themselves as servants of the Muses, their representations suggest that interacting with these divinities or 'having knowledge of the Muses' lovely gifts' ('Μουσέων ἐρατὸν δῶρον ἐπιστάμενος' Archilochus 1) is simply a formal point of departure, an invocation that leads to the poet's personal glory. Pindar, who constantly and diversely addresses the Muses, deliberately seeks new ways of linking himself with them and then surpassing them:

μαντεύεο, Μοῖσα, προφατεύσω δ' ἐγώ.
Give your oracle, Muse and I will be your spokesman.

(fr. 150)

ἐμὲ δ' ἐξαίρετο[ν κάρυκα σοφῶν ἐπέων Μοῖσ'.
Me the Muse has appointed as chosen herald of wise words.
(fr. 70b.23–4)

The male poets can usurp some of their attributes but they cannot, in the way that Sappho can, be *like* these female divinities. Theognis continues the theme of self-glorification via the Muses:

Χρὴ Μουσῶν θεράποντα καὶ ἄγγελον, εἴ τι περισσὸν
εἰδείη, σοφίης μὴ φθονερὸν τελέθειν,
ἀλλὰ τὰ μὲν μῶσθαι, τὰ δὲ δεικνύεν, ἄλλα δὲ ποιεῖν.

The servant and messenger of the Muses, if he has an abundance of knowledge, must not begrudge others his wisdom:
he must seek out some things, reveal other things, create others.
(769–71)

Campbell (1983: 256) considers that by the time of Solon (fr. 13.51–2) 'we see that the image of the Muses' "gifts" is already fading, since they "teach" the poet their gifts'. This transferral of knowledge depletes their power, and Solon, like Theognis and Pindar, then converts the gifts into '*sophia*', wisdom or skill that emanates from the poet rather than from the Muses. Often it is not the poets that are servants, but the deities: 'Muse, carry the fame of this song throughout Greece, as is right and just' ('Μοῦσα, τοῦδε τοῦ μέλεος κλέος ἀν' Ἕλλανας τίθει, ὡς ἐοικὸς καὶ δίκαιον' Timocreon 728). The tone of these representations suggests that the power originally possessed by such female divinities is being eroded or appropriated, that they have been relegated to the position of a base for men to leap from, a vehicle for self-glorification. Whitford interprets Irigaray's comments on this subject to suggest that 'the body that subtends language is the phantasied body of the mother'.[5] As the lyric poetry of antique Greece becomes more sophisticated, the bodies of female divinities such as the Muses – who were once represented as controllers, possessors of the powers of inspiration, wisdom and composition – are gradually superseded, thus suffering a similar fate to that of the phantasied body of the mother, the buried and neglected maternal-feminine described by Irigaray. Sappho also seeks renown via her association with divinities such as the Muses, but requests for their presence in an earthly environment (frr. 127, 128, 103.8 and 53), or the desire for honour (frr. 32 and 58), or approval (fr. 81), suggest a different relationship.

The 'agonistic' socio-poetic context that is evidenced by pleas to the Muses, or self-publication of greatness and wisdom, or rivalry between poetic establishments, is also represented in Sappho's songs. Her pronouncement about the superiority of Lesbian singers (fr. 106) implies that this traditionally 'masculine' competitiveness included both public and private spheres throughout Greece, but her 'agonistic' representations more commonly deal with personal relationships within her community on the island of Lesbos. In one fragment the Sappho-singer suggests that 'those whom I treat well harm me the most of all' ('γὰϱ εὖ θέω, κῆνοί με μά]λιστα πά[ντων σίνοντα]ι' fr. 26). Sappho herself is certainly not above harming others with her poetry however, and a lack of poetic skill or non-association with the Muses is destined to provoke an excess of scornful abuse, and to remind the audience of the opposite, positive side, the Sapphic community's link with the Muses and the expectation of a fame that will not be forgotten, even after death:

Κατθάνοισα δὲ κείσῃ οὐδέ ποτα μναμοσύνα σέθεν
ἔσσετ' οὐδὲ πόθα εἰς ὕστεϱον· οὐ γὰϱ πεδέχῃς βϱόδων
τὼν ἐκ Πιεϱίας, ἀλλ' ἀφάνης κἀν 'Αιδα δόμῳ
φοιτάσῃς πεδ' ἀμαύϱων νεκύων ἐκπεποταμένα.

When you die you will lie there, forgotten.
Afterwards no-one will remember you or long for you.
For you have never shared in the roses of Pieria.
Unseen in the house of Hades,
you will flutter to and fro amongst shadowy corpses.

(fr. 55)

The language Sappho uses to formulate her insult is striking, and visually, imagistically balanced, emphasising the insubstantiality of a woman who was unpoetic. Effective as it is, it does not stray far from Sappho's usual mode and the store of attractive images and/or metaphors that ornament more pleasant environments. The Pierian roses she refers to have no counterpart in ancient poetry, but they once again effect a transposition, conflating poetry (the Muses) and female beauty (roses), in a way that diminishes the negativity of her uncommonly decorative abuse. Men, to be properly 'masculine', would be expected to be more competitive and abusive, and the male poets certainly fulfil that expectation. Many of them use the position of poet as a mechanism for abuse, employing the power and public nature of their verse to demolish rivals and enemies.

In a context where poetry was the preferred medium for philosophical statements and warlike exhortation, some poets were renowned for the power of their invective, the poetic rendition of superb abuse. Men like Archilochus – who stated poetically that he understood one thing: 'to come back with deadly evil at the man who wrongs me' ('τὸν κακῶς μ' ἔρδοντα δεινοῖς ἀνταμείβεσθαι κακοῖς' fr. 126) – used abusive songs as weapons against enemies or friends who had betrayed the speaker and/or his associates. According to Burnett (1983: 57) 'successful blame was bitter and degrading; it searched out what was shameful, obscene, deformed or grotesque'. A prescription that makes Sappho 55 seem quite moderate, although for Sappho a lack of poetic skill was shameful and/or obscene. The male poets directed their barbs at a wider range of targets: Archilochus seems fonder of vilifying unfaithful women than denigrating other singers, Alcaeus, Theognis and Solon all used poetry as a platform from which to discredit their political enemies (Alcaeus frr. 129 and 348 for example) with a spirit of blame that fits Burnett's description. As can be seen by Pindar's metaphoric swoop against lesser opponents, poetic rivals receive much the same treatment:

> ἔστι δ' αἰετὸς ὠκὺς ἐν ποτανοῖς,
> ὃς ἔλαβεν αἶψα, τηλόθε μεταμαιόμενος
> δαφοινὸν ἄγραν ποσίν
> κραγέται δὲ κολοιοὶ ταπεινὰ νέμονται.
>
> The eagle is swift among winged creatures:
> searching from afar, it suddenly seizes
> the bloody prey with its talons.
> Cawing jackdaws inhabit lower levels.
>
> (*Nem.* 3.80–2)

The metaphoric association of birds with poetry is not uncommon, but the choice of images[6] and the way they are portrayed and hierarchically compared seems, along with the aggressive tone, to possess characteristics that could be defined as traditionally 'masculine'. Campbell's (1983: 280) description of these lines confirms this orientation: 'Pindar's manner, in other words, is elevated, and his aim is unerring, whereas rival poets are pedestrian, noisy and ineffectual.' Other Pindaric metaphors – chariots (fr. 124a and *Nem.* 5.19–20); athletic competitions (*Nem.* 5.19–20); arrows, bows and targets (*Isthm.* 5.46–7, *Olympian*

2.83–5 and 89–92 and *Olympian* 9.11.12) – befit the contexts in which they were originally performed and are equally male-oriented, but they also remind later audiences of the 'agonistic' desires of a poet who must compete for reputation and reward.

Contained within the abusive and/or lyrical utterances of both female and male lyric poets, particularly those of Pindar, are announcements that focus on the brilliance of the poet and the capacity of poetry to advertise and immortalise the author and his or her themes/characters. Sappho, as is implied by fr. 147, is aware of this function of poetry, but she rarely sings directly of her own greatness. Was this because she did not have to offer her songs for patronage or other financial reward? Later poets were forced to consider the desires of those who commissioned their songs and paid for the privilege, a mercenary aspect of authorship that was not always welcomed. As Pindar shows when he sings nostalgically of earlier times when poets did not have to sell their labour for a living. Once again he converts the traditional characteristics of the Muses, in this case into more mercenary qualities:

ἁ Μοῖσα γὰρ οὐ φιλοκερδὴς
πω τότ' ἦν οὐδ' ἐργάτις·
οὐδ' ἐπέρναντο γλυκεῖ-
αι μελιφθόγγου ποτὶ Τερψιχόρας
ἀργυρωθεῖσαι πρόσωπα μαλθακόφωνοι ἀοιδαί.

For then the Muse was not yet greedy for gain,
nor a hired worker.
Sweet songs were not sold abroad
by honey-faced Terpsichore, their faces silvered over.
(*Isth*. 2.6–9)

Whether to secure a living, or to entertain a court, or remind a group of women about the power of poetry, the majority of these songs were created with the idea that immortality could be guaranteed by the production of exemplary lyrics. One example is the gift of poetry which Theognis proudly claims has the capacity to endow his beloved Cyrnus with wings, fame and 'an imperishable name forever' ('μελήσεις ἄφθιτον ἀνθρώποισ' αἰὲν ἔχων ὄνομα' 245).

In his article on ancient monody Russo (1974: 708–9) asks some questions such as '*when* does the poet recite, and for *whom*?', questions which can attract a number of answers depending on the situation of the poet or even that poet's sexual status. Pindar's *Olympian* hymns, for example, were intended to enhance public occasions and to be sung to large audiences. Other male songs, like Anacreon's entertaining lyrics, were intended for a more convivial setting, a court scene where amusement – sometimes at the poet's expense – takes priority over more serious pronouncements. Soldier/poets such as Archilochus, Mimnermus, Tyrtaeus and Callinus apparently recited their songs on the battlefield or in the soldier's barracks in quiet moments between battles, but usually to an audience composed of men similar to themselves. The warlike themes they favoured can also be found in the poetry of Alcaeus, although the songs of this aristocratic Lesbian feature a more symposium-like atmosphere where wine and song mingled to inspire lyrics reflecting the activities and discontents of a group of men involved in political struggles.

Sappho knew of the songs of the external world, but her own songs, and even the language used within them, appear internalised, restricted by the closeness of the circle and its physical/social boundaries. The 'when' for Sappho is occasioned most often by events within the circle, familiar rituals or moments of love or sorrow or special beauty; the 'whom', except for semi-public occasions such as weddings, seems to have been the women of her community. Sometime, perhaps within her lifetime, her poetry was circulated and ensured the immortal fame she desired and finally attained, but socially and poetically Sappho seems to have been more constrained than her male counterparts.

Singing to this audience, composing a song about the conditions of performance, she tells us:

> τάδε νῦν ἐταίραις ταὶς ἔμαις † τέρπνα † κάλως ἀείσω.
>
> Now, for my companions . . . to delight them . . . I shall sing these songs beautifully.
>
> (fr. 160)

Two features of this broken statement stand out: the beauty of her singing and the consequent delight of her companions. It is Segal's (1974: 155) opinion that the Greeks of the ancient world 'take natural pleasure in fine shape and sound which we too sometimes recognise as beautiful but only after we have first pulled ourselves up by our own boot straps to an educated level of perception'. The sounds of Sappho's songs, the aural dynamics of the finely crafted patterning of assonant and musical syllables was an experience that, along with the physical rapport of singer and audience, is denied later readers. But this, along with the sweet sounds of her 'divine' (δῖα fr. 118) lyre and 'more golden than gold' ('χρύσω χρυσοτέρα' fr. 156) harp, was intended to, and presumably succeeded in, delighting her listeners. Within the enclosed space of the circle she was constrained, but the pleasure of singer and audience – a delight incited by the rhythms of words and music, and the rituals they accompanied – seems physically engaging and/or liberating. Segal (1974: 152), working within Havelock's definition of oral characteristics, considers that 'oral recitation of this type relies upon 'the manipulation of verbal, musical and bodily rhythms' and exploits 'a set of psychosomatic mechanisms . . . for a very definite purpose'. The purpose and practice of this form of recitation add a further therapeutic and magical[7] dimension to the function of ancient poets. The language used and manipulated by Greek poets of both sexes appears, as Havelock suggests,[8] to be ideally suited for these purposes. Surely however, despite their common linguistic basis, these sensual utterances cannot be treated as sexually neutral. Consistent with the rhythms and needs of human bodies they sing out of the throats, the consciousnesses, of male and female poets who, in the segregated world of Greek society, are not only contextually separated, but sing to audiences composed predominantly of members of their own sex. So female to female or male to male bodies are linked and participate together in these psychosomatic sounds and movements.

Segal (1974: 144) suggests that Sappho 'draws upon this reciprocal relation between poetry and the physical reactions of the body: poetry as *thelxis*'. One aspect of the gendering of human subjects, both now and in antiquity, is that women have been associated (and likewise devalued) with the body. Not because of unmediated anatomical differences, but through the mediating symbolic and linguistic systems that frame these environments. Within her representations and the ritualistic practices they describe Sappho frequently amalgamates bodies and songs. Extrinsically this combination is manifested in songs such as Sappho 1 or frr. 94 and 96, where erotic anguish is soothed by poetic music and its inherent, transforming, magic; or fr. 31 where an unusual lack of synchronisation between ordered poetic and disordered bodily rhythms re-enacts the disintegration of an erotic subject. Intrinsically it is visible in Sappho's idiosyncratic and 'sensual'[9] choice of words/sounds, themes and metres, and her structural, aural, co-ordination of these poetic building blocks. She constructs her songs in an auditory and paratactic fashion, sketching in one verbal/visual picture before proceeding to the next and finally integrating all of these pictures in a coherent nexus that unites sound and sense.

If skilfulness is considered a 'masculine' attribute, then later commentators have every reason to call Sappho 'mascula'. Do her sensual rhythms, her ability to produce modulations and tempos that relate to a form of female specificity, or an apparent desire to heal through the transforming, magical capacity of song, act as markers of difference – at least in the context of ancient lyric? Within the multi-meanings and fluid structures of her poetry, Sappho contains or conflates private and public worlds. As Segal (1974: 155) notes, 'Sappho's artistry lies in her power not only to create and utilise such rhythmico-ritualising effects, but also to move between this public, social form of utterance and quieter, more relaxed, more private moments.'

While Sappho was reaching for her lyre to entertain her circle within the private world,

ἄγι δὴ χέλυ δῖα † μοι λέγε † φωνάεσσα † δὲ γίνεο †

Come, divine lyre, speak through me and find yourself a voice (fr. 118),

other, male, voices were earning prestige in the public world by continuing an age-honoured and apparently male-dominated tradition of formulating philosophical statements in poetic metres. This form of 'truth' seemed, to Sappho and her contemporaries, to be:

πόλυ πάκτιδος ἀδυμελεστέρα . . . χρύσω χρυσοτέρα . . .

More sweet-sounding than a harp . . . / more golden than gold . . .

(fr. 156)

combining as it did the mnenomic, didactic qualities that epitomised excellence. Poetry, over the course of western civilisation, has been allied with a number of predominantly unfactual 'truths'. In the seventh to sixth centuries, various strains of rhetorical, metaphoric, oracular or mythic 'truth' were consolidated under the title '*philosophia*'. At this early point in the formalisation of a discipline of rational thought or 'truth'[10] that has continued throughout western culture, the prophetic, wise and 'true' sayings of philosophers were still structured within, and transmitted by, the memorable metres of poetry.

Lyric poetry seems an inappropriate medium for such weighty thoughts, but *philosophia* of various kinds continued to find a place in these innovative songs, augmenting the reputation/status of lyric poets. Gentili (1988: 55) considers that 'poetic performance, whether epic or lyric, was conceived as more than a means for allowing audiences to see themselves in the mirror of mythical or contemporary events; it could also serve to arouse in them a new perception of reality and political activity which new needs and goals demanded.' The male lyric poets actively participated in this give and take of wisdom and/or ideology through poetry, delighting in the poet's right to disseminate new and often prescriptive ideas. Xenophanes (fr. 2) even maintained 'that the civic honours awarded to successful Olympic athletes ought rather to be given to him because of the contribution which his *sophia*, "skill", "wisdom", makes to the well-being of the city'. Sappho, as a creator of songs, should also be considered a sage, a disseminator of wisdom and of a new and different perception of 'reality'. Women have frequently been excluded from the privileged world of *philosophia*, emerging from its dichotomous systems as, to quote Gatens (1991: 92), 'less than human, as bound to their bodies and the exigencies of reproduction, as incapable of a certain kind of transcendence or reason that marks the *truly* human individual'. Statements of an abstractive, conceptual kind are relatively rare in Sappho's poetry, but the less than rational construction and perception of 'woman' in western culture invites the question of whether representations of wisdom formulated by a female poet would differ from those of male poets who stepped undisputed into the prestigious role of sage, in part because of their sexual status.

A reader investigating the history of ideas in antiquity would perhaps be disappointed if he or she perused Sappho's poetry. For although the reference to 'σοφία' in fr. 56.2 suggests that she valued poetic skill or wisdom, very few of her extant songs deal with this form of abstract conceptualisation. Bowra (1961: 223) supplies a reason for this deficiency, he considers that: 'in the presence of strong passions it is absurd to argue or to preach'. This statement again associates Sappho only with poetry of a subjective nature – cries or songs springing direct from her heart – and brings to mind the reason/emotion split, the logocentric notion that men are capable of conceiving and then correctly organising abstract ideas, while women, as McMillan (1982: 28) states, 'do not reason but live on an animal-like level of subjective intuitions'. Although the Sappho-singer often proffers advice or instructions, few of Sappho's extant fragments are concerned with the type of philosophical or aphoristic maxims that flourish munificently in the songs of the male lyric poets. Is this shortfall due to the random manner in which her fragments have been preserved, or to Sappho's female status, a status which allegedly reduces her cognitive perception to the extent that 'only what is intuitive, present and immediately real truly exists',[11] so abstract ideas were incomprehensible to her or of little consequence? Perhaps the private nature of her socio-poetic context determined and/or limited the kind of knowledge or advice relevant to the present and future situations of female subjects. Philosophic discourse seems traditionally to be enmeshed with the interests of the public world. Whatever the reason, apart from the pseudo-philosophical proposition that enlivens Sappho 16, there are only two fragments that resemble the many 'γνῶμαι' attributed to Theognis and other male poets: tiny (two or four lines) poetic statements which articulate some general thought.

One of Sappho's aphoristic fragments (fr. 148) deals with a subject dear to the hearts of men and often mentioned in male poetry, that of wealth.

> ὀ πλοῦτος ἄνευ † ἀρέτας οὐκ ἀσίνης πάροικος,
> ἀ δ' ἀμφοτέρων κρᾶσις† εὐδαιμονίας ἔχει τὸ ἄκρον†
>
> Wealth without . . . virtue is no harmless neighbour.
> The blending of both . . . brings the peak of good fortune . . .

Stylistically similar to male songs, the choice and blending of the two elements she combines – wealth and virtue – appear to be relatively conventional. Like her proposition in fr. 16 the maxim she presents appears quite easy to comprehend. If possessed separately these positive qualities could be less than fortunate, in fact potentially harmful. Bowra (1961: 223) feels that 'she did not accept the possession of wealth as an unqualified good in itself, but saw its dangers and realised its obligations'. The two negatives in the first line are compounded tightly enough to cast doubt, obliquely, on this proposition. Is Sappho's usual terse technique of combining oppositional motifs less effective when applied to gnomic statements than it is for descriptions of sweetbitter love? The second line, incorporating a more typical and unbinary merger (κρᾶσις), and a reference to superlative good fortune indicates a return to Sappho's usual style and idealistic ethos. Theognis, a poet who is inordinately fond of disseminating maxims, composes gnomic verses which Podlecki (1984: 148) considers 'are tinged with a shrewd pragmatism', with 'a note of tough-minded realism, even cynicism', and has much to say on the subject of wealth and virtue. His contributions to this genre are constructed in a more precise and dichotomous fashion and point out a standard contrast between good and evil. Lines 145–8, for instance, warn his listeners that it is better to be pious than to have wealth that has been gained unjustly: righteousness and virtue are ideally concomitant (ἀδίκως and δικαιοσύνη are juxtaposed internally to make his point perfectly clear).

Sappho's other small maxim, fr. 50, also consists of only two lines, although within these lines the idea seems complete:

> ὀ μὲν γὰρ κάλος ὄσσον ἴδην πέλεται <κάλος>,
> ὀ δὲ κἄγαθος αὔτικα καὶ κάλος ἔσσεται.

> For he that is beautiful is beautiful as far as appearances go,
> but he that is good will immediately also be beautiful.

This fragment reproduces many of the characteristics of male γνῶμαι. It is succinctly 'pithy', it presents a 'general thought' and its structure is balanced, circular, and revolves neatly around a scheme of internal repetitions. It focuses on what Burnett (1983: 229) defines as a general, but more personal 'Sapphic law according to which beauty demands love and love, in turn, creates the beautiful'. In this instance beauty creates goodness and goodness creates beauty. Sappho's train of thought appears simple – beauty can be only skin deep, but is always present in 'he that is good'. These sentiments are not represented in any of the extant maxims of male poets. Nor are they as hierarchically organised, as exclusive, as Bowra (1961: 223) considers – with the result that beauty in this case is placed 'second to true nobility'. I believe that beauty, 'καλός', the word that recurs in this fragment, is represented as being of at least equal importance to goodness, 'ἀγαθός'. Rather than being subordinated to goodness, beauty is the quality that acts as a certain indicator of its presence. The idea of beauty is the factor that provides a vital link between these conjoined, but not contrasted, statements. In his discussion of Hesiod's aphoristic poetry, Beye (1975: 58) states that 'what is critically important in such poetry is not the thought in each line, but what the combination means; the joining is the poetic act'. Sappho's two statements are welded together (by the idea of beauty) in a circular fashion that makes dissection difficult. So tightly are they joined that the full meaning of each of these lines is dependent on the content of the other line. It is a technique that is apparent in fr. 148 and one that is recognisably Sapphic.

Sappho 50 introduces a type of poetic/philosophic discourse that is distinctive, because of the way it combines both outer and inner aspects of the human body; because it is spoken by, or sings out of, a female body; and because it provides a further example of the beauty of Sappho's language. Beauty is a theme that is relevant to the philosophies and priorities of Sappho's community. By virtue of her discussion of this topic, Sappho could assume a female version of the authoritative role of poet/sage/adviser and instruct the women of her circle in a form of wisdom that bears little resemblance to the 'shrewd pragmatism', 'tough-minded realism, even cynicism' (Podlecki 1984: 148) practised in the public world. But Sappho believed that her songs were superior because female divinities such as the Muses 'made me honoured with the gift of their works' ('αἴ με τιμίαν ἐπόησαν ἔργα τὰ σφὰ δοῖσαι' fr. 32). Honour, in her representations (keeping fr. 55 in mind) is defined not as prowess on a battlefield, but as the ability to compose superlative songs, to claim association with the Muses. Some male lyric poets – i.e. Anacreon, Simonides and Pindar – would agree with her. Often the difference between the wise sayings of the female and male poets of antiquity seems to have less to do with a split between emotion/reason; bodies/minds; and concrete/abstract ideas and more to do with the space and conceptual apparatuses that separated female bodies from male, private from public environments, and idealism from scepticism. The idealistic attitude expressed in much of her poetry, the emphasis on beauty and goodness and love, and her inimitable mode of construction, ensured Sappho's fame in contemporary and later milieux. The beauty of this woman's voice is not easy to forget.

Chapter 10

Honour

Adkins considers that a man's honour or 'τιμή'[1] was of the utmost importance in archaic Greece. He (1972: 14) proposes that the concept was conventionally rendered as: 'honour, compensation, penalty' and links it to punishment and *arete*, to a split between *agathoi* and *kakoi*, or aristocratic/good and inferior/bad men. These definitions, and the general tenor of Adkins's book, suggest that 'moral values and political behaviour in ancient Greece' were activities engaged in and constructed exclusively for/by men. Presumably honour or *time* was also of considerable value in the private world, in a community such as Sappho's, and in that group's internal interactions and its dealings with the public sphere. At times Sappho sang of honour, directly in fr. 32 in relation to the Muses who honoured her with 'the gift of their works'; less directly in hymns announcing her close relationships with female gods and in songs telling of the superiority of singers from Lesbos (fr. 106), or the honourableness of her relations with others (frr. 3, 120 and 137). The dishonour associated with her brother (frr. 5 and 15) or with a woman who was not poetic (fr. 55) are further indications of the importance Sappho placed on honour. But female and male bodies, particularly in the segregated world of archaic Greece, are constructed differently. Klintz's (1989: 127) suggestion that 'a subject is born into and lives her or his body according to certain ways of representing male or female difference, and these representations are related to a broad variety of institutions', seems relevant here. Both the male and female variety of institutions in archaic Greece were constructed on the basis of certain ethical mores/ideals – one of which was honour. In more public contexts, honour was vigorously competed for by differently represented male bodies. It was necessary to earn it with displays of bravery and/or excellence and seemed at times synonymous with death. It was also a matter of material value – part of a hierarchical system constructed to ensure that 'fair and just' (*dikaiosune*) reward (Adkins 1972: 85), gifts or compensation would pass from vanquished to victor – or to those who excelled, or ruled, or from men to gods. Later discussions reconstruct the dichotomous pairs inherent in this concept: winner/loser, honour/shame, good/bad, debt/payment, active/passive, and so on. A reminder that honour is inherently social – an accepted, controlling and constructed feature of interactions between the individual and the group,[2] or between those whom society favours and those it condemns.

Sappho's community was also a centre of social interaction and within her songs she represents relationships which have an ethical, honourable basis. One honourable anomaly that is relevant to the context of representations such as Sappho 31, suggests that to exceed the status quo is sometimes more honourable than to remain within its constraints. This private and female version of honour, like other Sapphic ideals, appears to differ from the honour gained in battles, oratorical, political and athletic competitions, as well as from ideals structuring more personal engagements in the public world. Perhaps it is in the area of personal and/or erotic interactions, one of few themes common to both sexes, that differences can be identified and compared. Sappho's preoccupation with personal relations provides a wealth of material for the investigation of female honour. An attempted definition of a woman-centred, or at least Sapphic, conception of honour or *time*, as well as some analysis of the exact nature of differences between male and female versions, are my objectives in this chapter.

In the previous chapter I discussed Sappho's reputation, her poetic prowess and consequent honour in the ancient world. According to the reports of ancient commentators and poets who were greatly impressed by her songs,[3] as well as the evidence of vase paintings, statues and coins perpetuating her image, Sappho was honoured by contemporary and later Greeks. Aristotle (*Rhetorica* 1398b.12), notes the qualified respect paid to Sappho and other poets: 'the Parians honoured Archilochus even though he was sharp spoken; the Chians Homer, though he was not a citizen of their country; and the Mytilenaeans Sappho, although she was a woman'. Later, it was her sexual status – the dual dishonour or reprehensibility of being not only a woman but one who apparently loved other women – which obscured her poetic honour. This occurred, to quote Snyder (1989: 7), sometime 'after the beginning of the Christian era', although it seems 'not to predominate until the Victorian period and its aftermath'. This retrospective dishonour, a product of the sexual bias and hetero-sexual obsessions of later ages, has affected not only Sappho's reputation but the reception and analysis of her songs. Despite these later and poetically irrelevant recriminations, Sappho was aware of her own honourable position within and without the group. Frr. 106, 160 and 147 tell of the superiority, beauty and memorableness of her songs. Adkins (1972: 13) foregrounds the significant contribution made by aristocratic leaders at this time: 'those who are able effectively to defend the group . . . must unite in themselves courage, strength, wealth and high birth . . . further-more . . . it is by success, not by good intentions, that the group continues to exist'. Likewise the honour of Sappho's community depended upon her skill and success, and it seems that Sappho's high status fulfilled its expectations. While we cannot know the extent of the honour or even the 'fair and just' rewards bestowed upon her in antiquity, it seems that in her lifetime and the centuries immediately following, Sappho's female status did not prohibit her fame.

As private, female-oriented institutions, families were con-sidered unworthy of mention in the wise, glorious and/or abusive songs of male lyric poets. From her place in an enclosed, female space however, the Sappho-singer addresses two songs to her brother, frr. 5 and 15, both of which sing of family honour and highlight an internal/external split that seems integ-ral to both public and private sectors: between group/outsider, citizen/barbarian, friend/enemy. These fragmentary songs are hymnal and invocatory in form and both are addressed to Aphrodite, a god who watches over those who cross the sea and who is honoured by Sappho's circle. The subject of these broken songs – statements concerning Sappho's brother Charaxus – and the relative lack of metaphor and symbolism, makes them more circumstantial than her other invocations to Aphrodite.

Fragment 5 begins with a plea addressed to Aphrodite and the Nereids, female deities who have charge of both love and the sea and are therefore suitable addressees for a petition of this nature.

Κύπρι καὶ] Νηρήιδες ἀβλάη[ν μοι
τὸν κασί]γνητον δ[ό]τε τυίδ' ἴκεσθα [ι
κὤσσα ϝ]οι θύμωι κε θέλη γένεσθαι
4 πάντα τε]λέσθην,

ὄσσα δὲ πρ]όσθ' ἄμβροτε πάντα λῦσα[ι
καὶ φίλοισ]ι ϝοῖσι χαραν γένεσθαι
κὠνίαν ἔ]χθροισι, γένοιτι δ' ἄμμι
8 πῆμ' ἔτι μ]ηδ' εἶς·

τὰν κασιγ]νήταν δὲ θέλοι πόησθαι
ἔμμορον] τίμας, [ὀν]ίαν δὲ λύγραν
11]οτοισι π[ά]ροιθ' ἀχεύων

[Kypris and] Nereids, grant me this,
that my brother arrive here free from harm,
that all he desires in his heart
4 be fulfilled.

Grant also that he atones for all his past errors
and becomes a joy to his friends,
a bane to his enemies, and may no-one
8 ever be a grief to us again.

And grant that he may be willing
to bring honour to his sister, grievous sorrows
11] past suffering . . . .

These female divinities are asked to bring Charaxus home unharmed and effect a reversal of the suffering which his love for Doricha has supposedly imposed upon both Charaxus and his sister. The paratactic list with which Sappho conveys her wishes for Charaxus and herself consolidates the impression of a sincere plea, a prayer proffered by a woman to female gods in order to gain some consolation or assistance in a familial predicament. Sappho's nomination of the characters involved in this poetic drama, and the hints it supplies of adherence to a common moral code, can only add to this impression. Without the historical background reconstructed by Page (1955: 48–50), the song becomes an infinitely more general statement about the dangers of sea voyages and love affairs, or the dynamics of filial relationships and family honour. Most of the action takes a future and therefore conditional tense, and this contributes to the uncertainty of the song. A voyage is mentioned, but the point of departure is not specified, the all-inclusiveness of the way in which the singer's wishes for every one ('πάντα') of Charaxus' desires to be fulfilled (5.4), and all ('πάντα') his past mistakes to be atoned for (5.5), adds to the generality of this statement. Enemies are also reviled, but not named, honour and anguish are referred to but not dwelt upon. The plea is non-specific. It requests simply that no-one ('μ]ηδ' εἶς' 5.8) should ever be a grief to us again, that from now on Charaxus should bring only honour ('τίμας' 5.10) to his sister. But however generalised their representation, the moral lessons which add a disturbing note to this prayer linger on, and a conventional split seems to be drawn between such opposite entities as honour/dishonour, friends/kin and their enemies, or joy/suffering, or good/evil, which is unusual in a Sapphic context. Is this song didactic, a way of disseminating ethical knowledge about the honour and dishonour attached to love and life?

There is an elegiac prayer by Solon (fr. 13) which begins with an invocation to Zeus and the Muses similar to that which initiates fr. 5, although in this case the singer requests fame and prosperity 'so I can be sweet to my friends and bitter to my enemies' ('εἶναι δὲ γλυκὺν ὧδε φίλοις, ἐχθροῖσι δὲ πικρόν' 13.5). In the context of Solon's direct politico-moral pronouncements, binary oppositions such as friends/enemies; right/wrong; sweet/bitter; appear appropriate. Frr. 5 and 15 also deal with a love affair, one which seems to be definably sweetbitter and in which other conventional oppositions are also confused or decentred: Doricha, the enemy, is also Charaxus' friend, and the wrong that he has committed is also right, at least if erotic love is considered all-important. Sappho is delineating a male environment in these fragments, and an event that relates to 'heterosexual' interaction external to the circle, with all the prohibitions normatively attached to male/female love. It is to be expected therefore that her treatment of this version of honour would differ from representations dealing with more internalised erotic interactions. In the world outside this community, there exists a stringent, logocentric ethos, a set of moral rules and obligations. A poetic depiction which focuses upon an external/public arena must inevitably take on some of its standards, producing a mingling of public and private worlds as well as incorporating standards of honour.

One rare example of a male poet singing about family honour is a song by Alcaeus (fr. 350) which was apparently composed to welcome Alcaeus' brother Antimenidas on his return from a

Babylonian campaign. Even if he does, as Burnett (1983: 142) suggests, let 'his joy take the form of friendly raillery', the tone of Alcaeus' song suggests that he is genuinely pleased to welcome his brother back into his circle of exiled noblemen. Friendly raillery, extravagant, rather ironical exaggeration of Antimenidas' distant exploits and the sense of affectionate brotherhood which is uppermost in this fragment are all suitable accompaniments to a male-to-male speech of welcome. Serious topics such as the questions of morality, honour and self-justification that weigh down Sappho frr. 5 and 15 and Solon's elegiac song are forgotten for the moment, as Alcaeus and his companions enjoy a familiar and light-hearted form of intra-fraternal sport. But behind the enjoyment this fragment highlights two important aspects of male honour: one is the suggestion that Antimenidas has contributed to a victorious campaign and is therefore to be honoured; the other is the description of the 'fair and just' spoils he brings with him, a sword which has a hilt that is 'ivory bound with gold' ('ἐλεφαντίναν λάβαν τὼ ξίφεος χρυσοδέταν' 350.2). With these trappings of success, he can be welcomed unreservedly and some honour must reflect on his family and friends. Whether or not they provide evidence of honour in a male circle, such symbols seem less important to the Sappho-singer who (16.17–20) would rather see Anaktoria's 'graceful walk and the brightness of her face than the gleam of Lydian chariots and heavily armed infantry'. A man might also take a different view of Charaxus' distant erotic exploits. Despite reports of the fortune apparently wasted on Doricha by Charaxus (Bowra 1961: 209–11) Sappho is less worried about material loss (which she does not mention) and more concerned about erotic honour, the possibility that Doricha might boast 'telling how he came the second time to a longed-for love' ('τὸ δεύ[τ]ερον ὠς πόθε]ννον εἰς] ἔρον ἦλθε' 15.11–12). Only Aphrodite can prevent this form of dishonour.

Other extant fragments about her family and the forms of honour that pertain to families include only female members – tracing a matriarchal lineage from mother, to Sappho, to daughter.[4] This signals a return to the usual woman-oriented ambience of Sappho's songs. All three of these fragments involve Kleis, the golden-haired girl who was said to be Sappho's daughter. Frr. 98a and 98b tell of a decorated headband – not the usual subject to provoke a discussion of honour, except that Sappho's comments on this headband appear to relate in various ways to personal, family and political pride. In past, and perhaps politically freer and more luxurious times in Mytilene, it seems that to bind hair with 'a purple headband was indeed great adornment' ('πορφύρωι κατελιξαμέ[να πλόκωι / ἔμμεναι μάλα τοῦτο δ[ή' 98a.4–5), a source of pride and 'feminine' honour. After political upheavals and the exile of the aristocratic Cleanactid clan, such decorations are either unavailable or terribly wasted away ('αἶνα διέρρυει[ν' 98b.9). Within the tatters of this song the fate of decorated headbands becomes metaphorically entangled with the fate of displaced, dishonoured leaders. The Sappho-singer's pride and love show, as she sings of a girl who has hair that is 'yellower than a torch' ('ξανθοτέραις . . . . ταὶς κόμαις' 98a.6–7) or the beauty of a child who looks 'like golden flowers' ('χρυσίοισιν ἀνθέμοισιν' 132.1), who is more valuable than 'all of Lydia' ('Λυδίαν παῖσαν' 132.3).

According to Sappho's poetic reports, her dealings with other people were perfectly 'fair and just'. Alcman presents us with a more competitive but perhaps equally honour-oriented set of relations relating to another group of young women. In both environments love between members of the group is represented and women who love and are loved are praised for their beauty. To refuse love in the Sapphic community, as is evident in frr. 1 and 22, is to act dishonourably,[5] and these non-participants are shamed by Sappho's lyrics. Apart from erotic interactions between women, there is also the honour of being loved by the singer/poet whose songs provide a focus for the circle, an honour which, if we take note of the avowal of love for the Sappho-singer in fr. 94.3–5, appears to be much desired. Adkins (1972: 16) discusses relations between the men of archaic Greece, foregrounding *philotes*-type relations of mutual dependence and co-operation which bind men together against the adversities of an agonistic society. The concept changes but continues to dominate in later and more political contexts and alliances, as Pindar suggests when he sings that: 'honour departs from a man when he is deprived of his friends' ('οἴχεται τιμὰ φίλων τατωμένῳ φωτί' *Nem.* 10.78–9). Within Sappho's community *philotes*-type relationships also flourished, but they were of a more erotic and female-oriented nature.

The context in which Adkins places these male *philotes*-type relationships is internally and externally agonistic. It is within the stress of heroic battles or athletic competitions that honour or *time* is displayed, won or perhaps lost.[6] Songs by male poets glorify the acquisition of honour in these arenas, singing the praises of heroes and victors, contributing to their honour, and at the same time prescribing approved modes of behaviour. A Spartan poet of the seventh century BC, Tyrtaeus,[7] provides an illustration of this dual mode of praise/prescription in his poetry. Apparently composed to spur soldiers into battle, Tyrtaeus fr. 11 exhorts Spartan troops to count 'life as hateful and the black spirits of death dear <like> the sun's rays' ('ἐχθρὴν μὲν ψυχὴν θέμενος, θανάτου δὲ μελαίνας/ κῆρας <ὁμῶς> αὐγαῖς ἠελίοιο φίλας' 11.5–6), and in fr. 10 he asserts that 'it is a fine thing to lie dead, having fallen in the front rank' ('τεθνάμεναι γὰρ καλὸν ἐνὶ προμάχοισι πεσόντα' 10.1). If they were unable to prove their valour and gather honour and prizes in battle these men often chose an alternative means – contending with others in athletic competitions. Tyrtaeus (fr. 12) clearly considers this form of excellence to be second rate.

Later lyric poets, such as Pindar and Bacchylides – the authors of almost sixty victory odes or epinicians celebrating and immortalising the honour awarded to the victors of the athletic festivals that prospered in the sixth and fifth centuries BC – would clearly disagree with Tyrtaeus' Homeric viewpoint. The glory and honour that Homer associated with war and athletic contests, as well as his representation of heroes and gods in mythic settings, is reproduced, albeit distinctively, in the epinicians of Bacchylides and Pindar. The resultant rise in status of these victor/heroes, as well as the envy they roused in the hearts of their fellow men, are indications of the honour they were awarded. Packed with allusions to myth and suggestions that gods, heroes and victors (and perhaps poets) had much in common, these songs appear intended not only to promote the excellence of athletes, but also to exhibit the excellence of a poet who can represent these contemporary events distinctively, and in as dignified a manner as a past tradition of epic poets:

εἰ δ' ἀρετᾷ κατάκειται πᾶσαν ὀργάν
ἀμφότερον δαπάναις τε καὶ πόνοις,
χρή νιν εὑρόντεσσιν ἀγάνορα κόμπον
μὴ φθονεραῖσι φέρειν
γνώμαις. ἐπεὶ κούφα δόσις ἀνδρὶ σοφῷ
ἀντὶ μόχθων παντοδαπῶν ἔπος εἰ-
πόντ' ἀγαθὸν ξυνὸν ὀρθῶσαι καλόν.

If a man devotes his every impulse to excellence,
sparing neither expense nor hard work,
it is right to bring noble praise with heart
that feels no envy with those who find
excellence; for it is an easy gift for a wise man
to speak good words in return for the man's various hardships,
and so to extol his splendour for the community to share.
(Campbell – Pindar's *Isthm.*1.41–6)

The honourable achievements of the public world are, to reuse Winkler's (1981: 69) statement about male discourse, 'displayed as the governing norm of social interaction "in the streets"' for the admiration and edification of all citizens. Representations of quests for honour or even poetic contributions towards a definition of a 'norm of social interaction' in female sectors of the ancient world are neither as numerous nor as easily accessible.

The representations which describe exchanges between Sappho and female divinities are both beautiful offerings which must have endowed honour on their creator, and constructs of mortal/immortal relations of an extraordinarily intimate nature. Sappho was favoured, honoured by the female gods to whom she gave honour with 'fair and just' dedications through her songs and ritual offerings. This divine favour appears to have added to her own status as well as to that of the women of her community. In Sappho 1, Aphrodite appears and speaks to the Sappho-singer, and is asked to assume a more 'masculine' position of honour: to be the Sappho-singer's 'fellow-fighter' (1.28). Winkler (1981: 68–70) considers that 'poem 1 contains a statement of how important it is to have a double consciousness', he also states that the Homeric heroes of the *Iliad* 'give and receive gifts as Sappho does; they wrong each other and re-establish friendships with as much feeling as Sappho and her beloved'. Sappho 2 involves another transaction between female and female god. Frr. 5 and 15 remind us again of Aphrodite's willingness to intercede in Sappho's affairs, fr. 140a details a ritual where women grieve with Aphrodite, and fr. 112 tells of a bride who has been honoured by the god of love.

Aphrodite is not the only female god honoured and/or appealed to by Sappho. In fr. 17 Sappho again takes a revisionist perspective, one which appears to involve a local myth and a female ritual.

πλάσιον δή μ' [εὐχομέναι φανείη,
πότνι' Ἦρα, σὰ χ[αρίεσσα μόρφα,
τὰν ἀράταν 'Ατ[ρείδαι κλῆ-
τοι βασίληες·

ἐκτελέσσαντες μ[άλα πόλλ' ἄεθλα,
πρῶτα μὲν πὲρ Ἴ[λιον, ἔν τε πόντωι,
τυίδ' ἀπορμάθεν[τες ὄδον περαίνην
οὐκ ἐδύναντο,

πρὶν σὲ καὶ Δι' ἀντ[ίαον κάλεσσαι
καὶ Θυώνας ἰμε[ρόεντα παῖδα·
νῦν δὲ κ[ἄμοι πραυμέντες ἄρηξον
κὰτ τὸ πάλ[αιον

ἄγνα καὶ κά[λα
π]αρθ[εν

Please appear near me [while I pray
Lady Hera, it was to your [graceful form
the [illustrious] At[ridae kings
prayed,

after they had accomplished [many labours]
first around I[lium, then on the sea]
they began to make their way to this island,
but could not complete their journey

until they [called upon] you and Zeus, the god of suppliants
and Thyone's lovely [son].
Now please be [gracious and assist me]
in accordance with that ancient precedent.

holy and beautiful
maidens. . . .

This could be a cult hymn, one of the forms produced in 'great antiquity', an example of which is the song sung by the women of Elis to invoke the presence of Dionysus at their festival. The hymnal tone of fr. 17 suggests that it is either an invitation to an appropriate female god to honour a religious occasion with her presence, or a plea for her to assist the suppliant/s' journey to a shrine. A 'masculine' note is introduced by the myth referred to in this song, the story that Agamemnon and Menelaos visited Lesbos together after they had left Troy. This is a non-Homeric, apparently local, epic tale, a version that differs significantly from other reports of quarrels and separation. While on Lesbos the Atridae apparently prayed to Zeus, Hera and Dionysus for assistance to complete their journey. Adkins (1972: 19) proposes that Homeric heroes and their gods differed only in the way that the gods '"have more *aretê*, *timê* and strength than men" (*Iliad* IX, 498)' and do not die. Both parties have similar values. If 'a *philotês*-relationship is set up between man and god' the man can make a claim for divine help. And so when the singer in fr. 17 – who appears to have a *philotês*-type relationship with a female god – is beset by problems, she recalls the prior situation as a precedent for her prayer.

Sappho's mention of this trinity of immortals and the inclusion of the legend about the Atridae, implies that parallels are deliberately being drawn between the two situations. The suppliants in Sappho's song are not 'Atridae kings' (17.3–4), but 'unmarried girl]s' (π]αϱθ[εν 17.13–14) and whatever their request it seems likely that it relates to some present need, one which is woman-centred and unheroic. Sappho also chooses to address her invocation only to the female member of this divine trio, Hera, cutting out the male power figures, a further indication that this petition involves a female occasion. These male figures: Zeus, Dionysus, Agamemnon and Menelaos, feature significantly in what remains of the song however, as the instigators of an honourable 'ancient precedent' (17.12), one which the singer would now like to reinstate. Winkler's (1981: 68) comments about Sappho's intrinsic 'many-mindedness', her double view of female and male, private and public cultures, are particularly appropriate to this discussion. The dynamics of this male/female, past/present representation are interesting. In fr. 17 these oppositional pairs are not openly contrasted but placed together so that they invite comparisons by their proximity. The potent connotations inherent in each of these sets are also increased by the choice and representation of character and event. These are not just any males, they include the two most influential male gods and mortal characters who are greatly honoured within the heroic arena of the Greek world. As the precedent they set is ancient and therefore venerable, it seems an inappropriate model for the private, present nature of requests sought by Sapphic suppliants.

Alcaeus also has a song (fr. 129) in which he seeks aid from Hera, Zeus and Dionysus. Discussing the differences between this song and Sappho's supplication, Kirkwood comments (1974: 126) that 'Alcaeus's poem is strictly contemporaneous, immediate, and bound up with political strife; and it is rather sprawling and loosely organised. Sappho's is a neatly formed unit, beginning and ending with a personal prayer, but containing a mythical reference that expands the theme.' While I don't disagree with these remarks, I consider that there are other distinctions which are relevant. In fr. 17 Sappho incorporates an allusive mythical segment 'neatly' between two dignified pleas to Hera. To some extent the male or 'masculine' impact of the mythical segment disrupts the conventionally religious, woman to female god, interaction that marks the beginning and end, although the connection between the singer and the heroic status of these kings effectively adds to her honour and/or status. Whether or not the inclusion of an episode reporting a heroic event is somewhat incongruous in this female religious context, the tone and treatment of the song are consistent and to some extent integrate past and present, male and female, public and private elements.

Also referring to a local religious context, Alcaeus begins by describing the establishment of the worship of these divinities on Lesbos, mentioning the naming of these gods, stressing the grandeur and consequence of this event and invoking (in another male-to-male *philotês*-relationship?) their aid. He reminds his listeners that a relationship exists between these gods, the male forebears who initially established their worship, and his band of noble[8] followers. A relationship that can be compared to the proud patrimonial claims of heroes who increase personal *timê* by tracing their ancestry back to an immortal father. Burnett (1983: 157) describes Alcaeus' circle as 'men sure of divine indulgence for their own group, and of divine justice for outsiders who opposed them'. This certainty, of aristocratic right and the honour of the group – comes across strongly. Often in Greek poetry the gods are represented as fearsome and malevolent, immortal enforcers of laws made by men, and this attitude is evident in Alcaeus' song. The description of Dionysus as an 'eater of raw flesh' ('κεμήλιον' 129.8) sets up the vengeful ethos that informs Alcaeus' enterprise. Sappho's motivation in frr. 5 and 15 might seem similar, but her method and purpose, as well as the qualities she projects on to the gods she invokes, appear very different from the aggressive, hierarchically oriented tactics and projections of male suppliants.

The Alcaeus-singer's tone, in the first two and a half stanzas of fr. 129 is reasonably solemn. It includes a range of suitable epithets, and accords with the events he describes. His request for assistance is also appropriately, graciously worded, but once he begins his request for the vengeance he would like to have wreaked on Pittacus, it changes dramatically, and sounds more like the rhetoric of abuse than a petition to the gods. The violence – vividly expressed in yet another scheme of oppositional pairs – takes the form of scenes of death and destruction. And although some links are forged by the theme of Pittacus' betrayal of the moral code which was presumably instigated by Alcaeus' forebears and perpetuated by his followers, this section, in contrast with the initial stanzas, seems to indicate a complete departure from a religious theme or tone. The song sprawls out, as misshapen as Pittacus with his 'pot-belly' ('φύσγων' 129.21) or his splay-foot. It never (as far as we know, the last section is missing) returns to the original theme or the stately articulation of divine characteristics and mortal altars and precincts.

The final stanzas of Sappho's song are also missing, although the few words that remain retain the religious emphasis. We will never know whether she also departed from her original theme and moved on to some personal request, such as a safe voyage as in the case of the Atridae, or for the appearance of a god at a mortal occasion. Whether or not Sappho was employing a revisionist perspective in her use of myth in this song, whether her combination of female/male, private/public, present/past elements or her use of a particular, possibly male generic form, are at all distinctive, is perhaps less relevant than those questions invited by the clash of internal/external value systems. Alcaeus' reference to an ancient precedent explicitly defines a male code of honour – rules which are time-honoured and noble. These rules are now being defiled by a man who has 'recklessly trampled the oaths underfoot' ('βραϊδίως πόσιν / ἔ]μβαις ἐπ' ὀρκίοισι' 129.22–3), dishonourably placing himself beyond a code which men have constructed and established, and which other men should respect. This might be merely a war of words, a poetic slanging match in a shame-oriented culture, but the sense of political competition, of a clash between rival clans and disparate codes is strong. It is improbable that Sappho would be ignorant of such codes of honour, as unlikely as her ignorance of epic songs or generic forms. Although, as Winkler (1981: 69) suggests, 'her participation in the public literary tradition always contains an inevitable alienation'. Within the circle Sappho seems alienated from participation in political wrangles or civil warfare, from male struggles for *time*, *arete* and power. Her knowledge of the ethical codes which structure these engagements and transactions between mortals and immortals however, seems clear. Sappho's frequent conversion of these elements of male culture, into a female-dominated context structured according to different ideals, brings into play a multi-faceted perspective. In fr. 17 the interplay between illustrious male heroes and a female god results in the glorification of a god whom great men must bow before to plead for a safe voyage. To this much-honoured god the Sappho-singer composed her appeal, placing herself in an identical position to the Atridae. Female and male honour are juxtaposed. In Sapphic representations prayers from a woman to a woman god are answered with sufficient frequency to suggest that this present plea will succeed, as surely as we know that the mythic plea succeeded. Within the action of these songs the honour of a female suppliant is validated, and is seen to be as valid and valued as the form of honour or 'τιμή' that was manifested and revered within other, more public and male-oriented, spheres of ancient Greece.

Chapter 11

Symbolic realms

The lack of divine female symbols in a twentieth-century western context,[1] and the dilemma, foregrounded by Irigaray, that female-oriented images and/or symbols cannot be inserted in place of male images/symbols in a cultural framework which accords no specificity to the female, contributes to the powerlessness of modern women. For Sappho and the women of her community, however, Aphrodite, and other female gods, functioned as symbols of divinity and female power. The status of these women was augmented by their close connection with divinity. Vernant (1989: 18–47) separates the dim bodies of men from the dazzling bodies of gods, but the represented bodies of the women in Sappho's songs often take on a godlike luminosity. Many significant similarities can be traced between the characteristics of the female god of love and the symbols, the decorative objects, creatures and flora that proliferate and are associated with female personae who wander through a 'forest of symbols' (McEvilley 1971: 11) in Sappho's representations. With his statement that 'the relation to the divine or supernatural, whose presence within oneself, in and through one's own body, like the outer manifestations in the case of a god's apparitions or epiphanies, expresses itself in the same symbolic register', Vernant (1989: 22) re-connects mortal bodies with the bodies of gods. The power of Aphrodite, as a symbol of female sexuality, enchantment, grace and beauty, spins a golden web which appears to overlay all aspects of the Sapphic circle. In Sappho's lyrics it seems to infiltrate the bodies, to run with 'subtle fire' (31.9–10) through the veins of these women. Symbolically, Aphrodite's associations with birds, fruit and Sappho's favourite flower, the rose, with goldenness, ornamentation and luxury, as well as eroticism and wile-weaving, all contribute to this representation of divine/mortal syncretism.

One Aphrodisian symbol, the 'beautiful swift-winged sparrows' (1.11) that pull her chariot in Sappho 1 seems similar to other birds that flutter through Sappho's lyrics, those girl-like birds who slacken their wings in fr. 42, for example. A mythical woman who manages to fly the coop, and thus emulate the erotic power and independence of female divinities, is Helen of Troy. In Sappho 16 she is represented as a dazzling figure who symbolises, both within and without Sappho's lyrics, an extraordinary quality of beauty and love. For men she is a symbol of war and death and the war-oriented male symbols that Sappho compares with 'whoever a person loves' (16.4) highlight a sexually specific contrast. For Sappho she appears as a symbol in her own right, but also a mediating figure in recurring incidents of divine/human symbiosis, a semi-divine woman influenced by a god – Aphrodite – who reminds the singer of a human symbol: Anaktoria. Within the golden web of erotic interaction, the shining qualities of gods and women are merged.

Sappho 2, with its description of a grove that abounds with Aphrodisian symbols, is a song that offers another illustration of the symbolic integration of godly characteristics, scenery, ritual and young women. Every decorative element in this rose-shadowed garden replicates Aphrodite's best-known attributes and provides a focus for her worship. The atmosphere, caught up as it is in the cyclic time scheme of repeated rituals, the aura of Aphrodite, eroticism and enchantment, is unworldly, dreamlike. Even the nectar, drink of the gods, that is poured into golden cups by Aphrodite, symbolises a shared and imbibed immortality. In his discussion of fr. 2 McEvilley (1972: 333) focuses on 'the immense suggestiveness of the song . . . the grove is a symbol and as such has not one identity only, but many'. The varied constituents of the grove recur in other Sapphic contexts conjoining divine, scenic, and mortal symbols, until they unite overall in a multiply relevant patterning.

Caldwell (1989: 26) considers that the 'most widespread symbiotic state' involves 'mythic and religious fantasies . . . of an original paradise'. The setting in fr. 2, with the eucharistic interaction of god and mortals and the central and perfect garden is suggestively paradisiacal. Was Sappho's song to some extent derivative, re-presenting some conventional symbols, traces of past descriptions of golden ages?[2] One marker of paradise – interaction between gods and mortals – occurs often in Sappho's songs. As do the flowers, fruits, incense and golden objects that are common religious symbols, and a pervasive atmosphere of ritual celebration. It is the sleep which drips from shimmering leaves that completes the trance-like effect, but this seems to be an all-consuming sleep that entrances any or all inhabitants of the garden, like death, or perhaps the lethargy that follows sexual satisfaction. Sleep, death[3] and eros are also linked together in Sappho's lyrics, suggesting supernatural influences or a state that is beyond the bounds of conscious, mortal existence. The influence of Aphrodite's magical aspect is pervasive here, but Jung's (1968: intro. viii) suggestion that the symbolic language of the unconscious is communicated through dreams is also relevant. Dreams, like myths, facilitate the expression of repressed images from individual and collective psyches. The unconscious does not distinguish between fantasy and the world of perception, and neither does Sappho in her construction of this other-worldly terrain. This and other songs were consciously constructed, but the symbolic world created by Sappho often seems dreamlike: full of images and 'ideas beyond the grasp of reason' (Jung 1968: 4). Other Sapphic references to death, in frr. 55, 94 and 95, are also accompanied by floral symbols and, in frr. 94 and 95, by a longing for death that is associated with erotic desire. The sensual aspects – the scent, beauty and soft petals of roses, violets, lotuses, hyacinths, chervil blossoms, the anise and celery plants that flourish there – as well as their symbolic, erotic and ritual connections, greatly effects the representation and significance of death. Like the flowers that symbolise it, it appears regenerative, numinous and attractive.

The symbols employed by the male poets to represent death and the divine male symbols controlling the lives/deaths of mortals are distinctive and distinctively unfloral. The hierarchical, agonistic relations which provide a focus, a recognisable if disruptive order, for the lives of these men are reproduced both in representations of their gods and interactions with these divine symbols. 'Loud-thundering' Zeus ('βαρύκτυπος' Semonides 1.1) dominates poetic descriptions and it is the inexorable motif of his undying power (as compared to the ephemerality of mortals) that recurs most frequently. On the subject of death, the sceptical statements of the male poets foster an atmosphere of hierarchical imbalance, of lives overshadowed, not by roses, but by the spectre of death. For them it is

> always Death, in person or by delegation, who sits within the intimacy of the human body, like a witness to its fragility. Tied to all the nocturnal powers of confusion, to a return to the indistinct and unformed, Death . . . denounces the failure, the incompleteness of a body of which neither its visible aspect – contours, radiance, external beauty – nor its inner forces of desire, feeling, thoughts and plans are ever perfectly pure.
>
> (Vernant 1989: 25)

Just as their erotic interactions are fraught with unequal exchanges between men and divinities such as Eros that torment, pierce, bombard and weaken them; death and the symbols associated with it also represent a battle that must, ignominiously, be lost. In some ways death, like Eros, is expropriation, since, to reuse Carson's (1986: 32) description of Eros, it 'robs the body of limbs, substance and integrity'.

Men are 'destroyed by fierce Ares' ('θοῦρος Ἄρης ὀλέσῃ' Tyrtaeus 12.34), washed away by 'the waves of the roaring sea' ('πολυφλοίσβοιο θαλάσσης' Archilochus 13.3), 'devastated by wretched diseases' ('βροτῶν φθείρουσι νοῦσοι' Semonides 1.12–13) or, in the throes of a despair that seems for some[4] to be a habitual condition, they choose to 'fasten on a noose of wretched death' ('οἱ δ' ἀγχόνην ἅψαντο δυστήνῳ μόρῳ' Semonides 1.17). The realisation that:

> ἀνθρώπων ὀλίγον μὲν
> κάρτος ἄπρακτοι δὲ μεληδόνες,
> αἰῶνι δ' ἐν παύρῳ πόνος ἀμφὶ πόνῳ·
> ὁ δ' ἄφυκτος ὁμῶς ἐπικρέμαται θάνατος·
>
> men's strength is slight,
> their plans impossible
> within their brief lifespan toil upon toil
> while death hangs inescapably over all alike
>
> (Simonides fr. 520)

seems to impend upon their lives and poetry. In these songs Hades is symbolised as a dark and tortuous place (even Anacreon's singer 'often weeps in fear of Tartarus: for the recess of Hades is grim' ('ἀναστραλύξω/ θαμὰ Τάρταρον δεδοικώς, / 'Αίδεω γάρ ἐστι δεινὸς μυχός' fr. 395.7–10), although one of Pindar's dirges does feature some pleasant and not unSapphic-like components. In Pindar fr. 129 there are meadows with red roses, 'shady frankincense-trees' ('λιβάνων σκιαρᾶν' 129.4) as well as 'trees that bear golden fruit' ('χρυσοκάρποισιν βέβριθε' 129.5) and here men take pleasure in 'horses and bodily exercises' ('τοὶ μὲν ἵπποις γυμνασίοισι' 129.6). This is the place of the pious, a reward for virtuous citizens, as we see in Pindar fr. 130, criminals inhabit the usual binary interface: a dark and noisome pit. The garden he represents is full of 'delightful perfume' ('ὀδμὰ δ' ἐρατὸν' 129.8) and blossoming prosperity and it would bear close resemblance to the grove in Sappho 2 if it wasn't for obtrusive male symbols: horses, bodily exercises, cities, sacrifices and prosperity. Despite the superficial similarity of some of Sappho's and Pindar's more conventional symbols, it appears that these poets dream of death and of life, and represent the symbols that emanate from those dreams, somewhat differently. The bodies of gods and men are separated by the symbols of death and immutability with which each is associated, and by an irreversible perishable/imperishable split. The evidence of Sappho's lyrics suggests that her attitude to death, and to man's or woman's relationship with the imperishable bodies of gods such as Aphrodite is distinctive.

One of the symbols which features in heavenly and median environments such as the grove in Sappho 2 – the flowers which bloom profusely in Sappho's songs – more frequently symbolise life than death. Although the relation to erotic interaction is a constant factor in this symbolic register. In fr. 2 the garden is the site of a festival, an occasion which Aphrodite is asked to honour with her presence. Despite the ritualistic atmosphere, the roses and wild flowers in fr. 2 adorn trees and meadows, not the necks and/or curls of young women, although they are significant as symbols of Aphrodite, and of burgeoning growth and 'natural' beauty. McEvilley (1973: 265) states that in Sappho's songs 'there are thirteen occurrences of specific kinds of flowers, six mentions of garlands of flowers and seven compound epithets involving flower names'. But when does this, or any other sign, cease to be termed an image and take on the qualities assigned to a symbol? Does this occur when the sign accumulates multiple significance, when, as Jung (1968: 87) suggests, it is 'charged with emotion', or when it recurs persistently, when it relates simultaneously to a god, to poetry, to women, to ritual, as well as to the sensual plants that spread over fields or river banks, that are considered beautiful, that wither and die too soon? The significance/s of these floral symbols in Sappho's songs overlap and overflow. It is

McEvilley's (1973: 265) opinion that 'overall, so frequent and so patterned are their uses that we are especially justified in suspecting them of a clear and conscious symbolism.' Sappho's descriptions of these flower-decorated landscapes do provoke further questions.

Western frameworks have positioned women (like nature) outside definition or categorisation, conceptualised them as formless and non-differentiated. 'The problem as defined by Irigaray is that the female has a particular function in symbolic processes: to subtend them, to represent that which is outside discourse.' 'Within this sexual symbolism, the determinate, that which has form or identity, belongs to the other half of the pair, and is therefore male' (Whitford 1991: 66). Nature has featured, within these symbolic frameworks, as some form of pre-cultural residue which must be suborned, which is classified, in Whitford's (1991: 94) words, as 'the raw material for symbolisation', or 'the support of representation', or 'the maternal-feminine' or 'that which is referred to by the sign "nature" in male discourse'. In her songs Sappho repeatedly represents elements which have, at specific times in western culture, been schematically constructed into a category referred to by the sign 'nature'. Such 'natural' elements are counted as inferior, at least in relation to those incorporated under the category/sign referred to as 'culture'. This tendency has provided confirmation of the ultra-feminine, emotional, naive and 'natural' ethos of this woman and her songs. Conversely, her discursive strategies and her treatment of a chosen few of these linguistic constructs effectively defy this classification. Sappho's construction or re-symbolisation of a representational poetic territory, her reuse of some key elements or signs which have generic or mythic, or ritualistic bases – but can be defined as products of culture – appears to affirm her own 'cultural' allocation. If, as it has been suggested by Winkler (1981: 68–72), Sappho was appropriating and/or reworking discursive elements which already possessed some pre-determined cultural attributes, her project should be interpreted as a secondary process which was therefore doubly encultured. I believe also that her representations, which are not sited within an underlying structure in which no specificity is accorded to the female, but in a poetic terrain where female gods, mythic and even mortal women were accorded some specificity, could be capable of transcending – or at least destabilising – the nature/culture split and other conventional classifications.

Pertinent to this discussion are the many ritualistic Sapphic contexts which foreground the cultural aspects of the flower, the 'key symbol of her work' (McEvilley 1973: 269). Conjoining the bright beauty of flowers with the beauty of women adds further significance to the scented wreaths and garlands that encircle another 'key symbol of her work' – the divine, mythical and mortal female personae upon whom these songs focus. Sappho 94 is a song that is full of symbols and reproduces, albeit differently, the timeless atmosphere of fr. 2. For the two women who sit sorrowfully at the centre of this song, caught in the angst of imminent separation, these symbols are living, ritualistic mechanisms. But Sappho represents a view of their past that is symbolic, that overrides the contingencies of erotic temporality and sets in place a time-defying sequence of consolatory motifs. The 'good times we had' (94.11) and the objects featured in them have been repeated so many times (the repetition of πολύς – πό[λλοις, πό[λλαις, πολλωι – in lines 12, 15 and 18 reinforces this sense of multiple objects, multiple occasions) that single instances are now merged. Arguably, the objects themselves, the usual accompaniments of Sapphic ritual – wreaths of violets and roses for the hair, woven necklaces of flowers to adorn a soft neck, perfumed oil, and the places where they are worn: sacred hills, temples, streams, groves – are repeated frequently enough in Sapphic contexts to attain the significance of symbols. The two women involved also symbolise equally recurrent erotic roles or states: the Sappho-singer is the lover who must stay, the other must go; one takes a mature and consolatory role, the other declares her love and sorrow with the passion of youth. As an analogue of the mother and daughter relationship, 'the unsymbolized maternal-feminine',[5] they contribute yet another systemic element to the female-centred world created by Sappho. Through their interaction they also reconstruct the sign of eros in its most familiar and sweetbitter form, as a sign that resonates with desire for whoever is missing.

A similar form of erotic symbolism occurs in fr. 96. In this Sapphic poemscape however, one female protagonist wanders through a moonlit world crowded with flowers and symbols, apparently irrevocably distanced from the consolatory rituals of the circle, while within the circle her lover suffers an agony of desire. McEvilley (1973: 275) considers that 'both flowers and the moonlit night are symbols of an emotional rite'. Certainly the emotional impetus adds further dimensions to the already proliferous meanings. The diffusive radiance of the moon – itself a symbol with divine relevance – is conjoined with the radiance of this goddess-like (96.4) woman; with the precipitation of tear-like dew; and with the flowers and scented plants that grow and spread over unploughed earth, while an inestimable breadth of salt sea symbolises the distance between estranged lovers. The female-oriented nature of these many-meaninged and interwoven symbols is difficult to ignore; duBois (1988: 27) announces that 'Sappho's poem celebrates the female body as unploughed earth, as ground spontaneously yielding not grain but flowers . . . Her earth is nourished only by the female dew and flowers under the female moon . . . As in other songs, Sappho seems deliberately to take up the hegemonic language of Greek culture . . . and to offer a parallel universe, one that refuses the aims of the male culture'. With the exclusion of phallic symbolism, the productive input of the male parent is elided from this and other Sapphic representations.

In terms of this representational system it is not only the curls or the bodies of young women that are decorated with wreaths and garlands, but also 'the earth [which] is embroidered with many garlands' (fr. 168c). A deliberate coupling that suggests a link between the Greek female symbol of Earth, Gaia, as well as later conceptions of 'Mother Nature', and the women who weave and don these floral wreaths. Such representations support an ideology that duBois (1988: 28) refers to, of the woman's body as fruitful, spontaneously generating earth, an ideology which apparently pre-exists 'a cultural appropriation of the body that responds to and rewrites that primary image'. The woman who wanders through the fertile scenery of Sappho 96 seems to symbolise a productive sexuality and fittingly the earth blooms with her. Generally, those who remain in the circle appear to be divided between sexually immature and more mature women. Fr. 27 talks of children, of sending the maidens away from a wedding rite; fr. 81 instructs Dika on the correct wearing of garlands; frr. 98a and 125 connect youth with wreaths of flowers; fr. 105a highlights an unreachable and presumably immature fruit/girl; while fr. 105c appears to conflate hyacinths and youthful 'virginity'. Floral garlands are not always present in these scenes, but the wearing of garlands appears, for both sexes, to indicate that the wearer is sexually mature or ready for love. They are erotic symbols.

As part of his discussion of Sappho's 'double-consciousness' Winkler (1981: 77) introduces the notion that Sappho's use of sexual images is based upon 'a large family of natural metaphors for human sexuality and, conversely, sexual metaphors for plants and body parts'. 'They would constitute then scattered fragments of a locally variegated, tenacious symbolic system which was operative in Sappho's time and which is still recognisable in modern Greece.' Some of Sappho's favourite images assume in this way yet another level of significance. A further connection is also suggested between such 'sexual metaphors' and the sexualised bodies of the human symbols who enliven her lyrics. For example, an association between *nymphê* (bride) and the clitoris is made by some medical writers (Rufinus ap. Oribasius III.391.1, Galen II. 370E), while *nymphê* is also associated with '*to pteryges*', wings/labia, as is shown by the name of a kind of bracken, the *nymphaia pteris*, 'nymph's-wing' (Soranos *Gynaecology* 1.18). *Mêlon* also has a broader range of meanings and is associated with various clitoral objects. In all cases these objects and their symbolisation provide examples of discursive processes which effectively enculturate 'natural' phenomena. Winkler stresses the private, almost secret, quality of this symbolic language about female 'sexuality'. This is a discourse that represents women's bodies and their 'sexuality'. It is also a form of discourse, using a group of linguistic constructs that have some female specificity, that women appear to have engaged in within more private territories.

The phallocentric orientation of the public, male sphere indicates the presence of a form of symbolic discourse that is not entirely dissimilar. This discourse focuses on an alternative set of objects and body parts which in some cases also have ritual significance. Halperin's (1990a: 102) discussion foregrounds 'the extraordinary phallicism that typically . . . characterised sexual expression in classical Athens. Sex was phallic action . . . it revolved around who had the phallus, was defined by what was done with the phallus, and was polarised by the distribution of phallic pleasure'. Halperin (1990a: 35–6) also separates an 'acquisitive and object-directed' form of male desire from the 'undifferentiated appetite for sexual pleasure' normatively associated with women's desire. The singular aspect of male desire, compared to the apparent plurality of women's eroticism, brings to mind another symbolic female construct: the pluralistic, constantly touching lips that Irigaray employs to represent female 'sexuality'. When compared to the phallic signifier that transcends all other symbols in the psychoanalytic symbolic world constructed by Lacan, the phallocentricism of ancient Greece appears similarly entrenched, but distinctive. Men of the twentieth century do not carry enormous phalloi in religious festivals, and our street corners or house fronts are not enhanced by herms displaying erect penises. Lacan's transcendental signifier might be equally transferable but it is detached by various linguistic and psychoanalytic strategies from the phallic-oriented sexual activity of male subjects. Ancient phalloi were directly associated with fertility in a way that is less apparent in later western culture. In both sites and times however, the power of those sexualised subjects whose bodies are actually phallic over those whose bodies lack a phallus is undisputed.[6] Derrida (1975: 97) suggests that Lacan, like Freud, 'does nothing else but *describe* the necessity of phallogocentricism, explain its effects, which are just as obvious as they are massive'. The symbolic value of the phallus appears, undeniably – if distinctively – to be dominant in the social and representational constructs of each of these cultures.

Manifestations of the phallocentric orientation of the male poets of ancient Greece are usually more oblique than other representations, such as the ritualised phalloi and erect herms that were displayed conspicuously, like male culture, in the streets. Alcaeus sings of 'ploughing free furrows' ('[τῶγας ἀροτρώμμε[. ἐ]λευθέραις' fr. 120) and the reiteration of this phallic agricultural symbol in later contexts says much about a symbolically 'male/female' division between 'culture' and 'nature'.[7] Only Archilochus refers explicitly to phallic activity (frr. 42W, 43W, 46W, 66W, 82W and 189W) and his animal-oriented symbolism affords an illustration of a satirical one-to-one correspondence that seems simplistic and obscene. More indirectly Archilochus tells us often of spears and other pointed weapons which gain further phallic or erotic connotations when juxtaposed with his description of a lover 'pierced through the bone' ('πεπαρμένος δι' ὀστέων' fr. 193W) with desire. Perhaps desire, as Eros the divine symbol, can pierce or overpower men, but more frequently the phallocentric active/passive, dominant/submissive split that is a prevalent feature of erotic relations seems to be constructed into the imagery and symbolism of these songs. This is obvious in the sexual interlude depicted in Archilochus' Cologne epode where the male lover controls his lust and the release of white sperm (SLG 478.52) while the girl lies trembling 'like a fawn' ('τὼς ὥστε νέβϱ[' SLG 478.47). Other poets, Anacreon in frr. 346, 408 and 17, Alcaeus fr. 42, Ibycus fr. 287, confirm this trend and again young animals: fawns and fillies, are symbolised as fearful, passive objects which must be caught and mastered by a skilful male subject. Although Sappho does not use animal symbols, with her representations of an apple that could be picked, a hyacinth that is trampled, she remains within the hegemonic language of her own culture and does not transcend the dynamics of this masculine/feminine, active/passive split.

It would be expected that these timid 'feminine' objects would fear invasion, but in fact it is men who seem most fearful that walls, ships' hulls or armour will be breached and overcome, that they will be reduced to a feeble, passive state. Considering their association with interiorised environments, it is significant that the women in Sappho's poemscapes often dance or wander through externalised and relatively open spaces – mountainsides, gardens, fields – despite erotic/symbolic dangers (i.e. frr. 2, 96, Sappho or Alcaeus 16). In other parts of the ancient world the phallic male body, erect and powerful as a marble herm, or stone walls, or bronze armour, or oxhide shields, seems to be symbolised by the strength of upstanding barriers, by the ignominy of their fall or loss. An analogy can be drawn, in twentieth-century discourse and perhaps also in archaic Greece, between phallic identity and stable form. Symbolic barriers, such as armour, musculature, or other culturally constructed outer skins,[8] are inserted between the frailty of mortal bodies and a threatening 'natural', or barbarous, force. Like the overthrow of life by death, the breaching of these constructed barriers results in loss of stable form and identity, and an enforced changeover from active to passive positioning. Alcaeus assures his audience that: 'warlike men are a city's tower' ('ἄνδϱες γὰϱ πόλι]ος πύϱγος ἀϱεύι[οι' fr. 112.10), but he also tells them of ships (frr. 6, 208, 249) swamped by storms, and city walls (frr. 70 and 298) that are trampled. Archilochus is another poet who represents invasions (frr. 94W and 98W), and storms at sea (frr. 105W and 13W). The control he recommends in the phallically oriented symbolism of fr. 128W: to firm a grieving heart, to 'rise, fight, thrust a hostile breast against the enemy' ('ἀναδευ † δυσμενῶν δ' ἀλέξεο πϱοσβαλὼν ἐναντίον / στέϱνον .... ἐχθϱῶν' 128.2–3), to win and lose without excess; appears structurally and symbolically analogous to the representation of the violence/control displayed by the lover at the beginning and end of the Cologne epode. For Archilochus, and Anacreon, who also used and confused the accoutrements of war and love, it seems that Eros and Ares were divine male symbols which possessed some similar aspects.

The weapons used in these endeavours, accoutrements of war that are juxtaposed with the sight of a desired face in Sappho 16, are symbolised in various ways in male lyrics. These objects represent not only a protective barrier against invasion, they also signify pride in regard to a specifically male form of beautification and glorification, and they are linked to the status, ancestry, identity and prowess of their wearer/bearers. In fr. 140 Alcaeus lingers over the gleaming details of armour that symbolises old and new, action and inactivity, order and disorder, glory and dishonour. The list of armaments in Alcaeus fr. 140 is comprehensive, but such symbols of war also appear frequently in other male contexts. Tyrtaeus sings enthusiastically of 'hollow shields' ('κοίλης ἀσπίσι' 19.7) and 'man-killing spears' ('ἀνδροφόνους μελίας' 19.9), Archilochus of spears, bows, slings, swords and javelins (frr. 2W, 3W, and 98W), Anacreon of shields (frr. 349, 388, 401 and 111D), and of weapons such as javelins and a scimitar (frr. 445, 501 and 465). This equipment seems to be highly valued as a source of pride and protection. Without weapons/armour the fighting-man stands naked, bestial and vulnerable. Comparing these martial symbols with more luxurious symbols: the robes and accessories that feature just as frequently and as pridefully in Sappho's representations, must, it seems, foreground the question of value. It is a comparison which results in a resonant clash of symbols. For not only does it focus upon disparate, 'masculine/feminine' attitudes related to the objects that represent variant lifestyles and ideals; it also juxtaposes the private space of the circle with a public sphere where battles are fought and valour proved. With recourse to 'double-consciousness' Sappho knows of and represents the symbols of both private and public territories, but it seems that she views and values them differently. The paratactic lists she includes in her songs, that linger on bright objects of ritual, and the robes, headdresses and jewellery worn and delighted in by her circle, are sensual and pluralistic, gathering together a collection of valuable items that are not hierarchically categorised but listed together in a way which foregrounds their 'mobile, fluid, protean, and unstable' aspects (Whitford 1991: 37). With the frequency of these lists and the richness and comprehensiveness of their description/s Sappho also glorifies these ornaments, validates their worth poetically. Male/female symbolism has been used consistently to express subordinate relations between elements of a divided human nature. Symbols which possess a female or 'feminine' aspect are subsequently devalued, except perhaps in an imaginative world constructed by a woman.

In Sappho's world the face and walk of a beloved are valued above armies and chariots (fr. 16). The bodies of women move in unison with musical rhythms of songs sung for and about women. The rituals integrated with these songs contribute to the construction of a time scheme that defies temporality, as repeated instances of prayer, ritual movement and emotion, as well as sequences of musical and metrical accompaniment, connect in familiar patterns. An atmosphere of celebration, in which voices and/or instruments sound and merge, incense burns, floral garlands and perfume cover bodies, pervades these songs. And there are moments of seduction, rejoicing or sorrow, in which everyone participates. Time here seems to be measured in accordance with the cycles and stages of a woman's body or her 'sexuality'. Even the symbolic death of Aphrodite's young lover Adonis (fr. 140a) presents an instance of ritualised lamentation that marks a particular, cyclical moment. The dim bodies of women, the dazzling body of an immortal, are joined in sorrow for the death of a lover who dies as vegetation dies – but returns, cyclically – to life. In ritual movements, the women of the Sapphic circle beat their breasts in lamentation for Adonis (140a), their feet tread delicate flowers of grass (Sappho or Alcaeus 16), their bodies move to the rhythms of music and love and, throughout these songs, female voices sound and merge so that 'a wondrous echo reached the heavens' (44.26–7).

Erotic love, the intense, sweetbitter emotion that affects divine, mythic and mortal protagonists, is sung of with sufficient frequency to ensure that it features as one of Sappho's most pervasive symbols. Always, as is demonstrated in Sappho 31, it affects the bodies of the women who inhabit an erotic, emotionally dynamic, space. Mythically, through her relationships with Adonis and other divine and mortal males, Aphrodite is also affected by the emotion she herself represents. Within the Sapphic circle, love and Aphrodite seem to combine as the god instigates new affairs, blesses or reprimands lovers. In this idealistic territory, it is a crime or a breach of contract to refuse love and every woman is expected to experience the 'grief and bitterness' (1.3), the ecstasy, of erotic love. The Sappho-singer sings of her involvement in these affairs (frr. 1 and 31) and at other times (fr. 22 for example) she encourages the desire of one young woman for another. Aphrodite also has a darker side however, an aspect of extreme erotic desire that can cause madness in besotted lovers: the Sappho-singer sings of her 'maddened heart' (1.18) and at times the male poets sing of similar afflictions (i.e. Anacreon 428, Ibycus 286). These antique poets acknowledge and accept the transgressive power of sexuality. The response of the erotic subject in Sappho 31 is as pluralistic as it is excessive, traversing her entire body,[9] shaking her heart, stilling her tongue in a way that exceeds the descriptions of male poets. Trapped in the linguistic, psychoanalytic and sexual constraints of a symbolic world that appears to have been constructed by men for men, women of later centuries are not only denied the favours or reflected status of a female god or symbol of desire, they are also denied the right to want.[10] In the symbolic world constructed by Sappho the love of one woman for another – a love that is based idealistically on reciprocal and mutual relations and approval of excess – provides a reason to rejoice, to a greater extent perhaps than 'the holy Cyprian' (22.15–16).

Irigaray believes that 'it is necessary for symbolism to be created among women in order for there to be love between them. This love is in any case only possible at the moment between women who can speak to each other.'[11] Within the symbolic register formulated by Sappho and the ambit of the Sappho-singer's gaze, women love and speak/sing to other women. Outside the circle and this woman-made symbolic world, in a phallocentric symbolic order, the sexual and discursive freedom of these women is severely limited. But here, in a secluded and marginally sexual environment, they are represented as subjects who speak and want. As it is represented by Sappho and theorised much later by Irigaray (1985: 25–6), women's eroticism is distinctive. In Sappho's lyrics, erotic love, like the beauty that accompanies it, is a force that constantly affects these women. Here, female gods can flourish and affect the sexual interactions, status, thoughts and songs of mortals. Within the terms of this representational system, gods, mythic figures and godlike women are converted to symbols which take up the position of active desiring subjects, and women's eroticism is viewed with approbation. As cultural constructions and/or constructional mechanisms, the representations – the imaginary and symbolic worlds and hegemonic structures of the public sphere – appear to have phallically reinscribed women's bodies; reconstructed them as passive, irrational, uncontrolled objects or bodies who 'lack', who are subject to 'nature', who must be excluded and/or transcended.[12] From Aristotle to the twentieth century the structures that appeal to male subjects are hierarchical – formulated in binary-type configurations – in which 'one of each pair is a positive term, the other, a (mere) privation' (*Metaphysics* 1011b 18f). A modern rite of passage that symbolically marks a child's entry, via the mediating force of the Oedipus complex, into the domain of law, order and language, presents an illustration of this binary inequity. The symbolic movement from the world of the mother and the imaginary into the world of the father, a movement which is more problematic and less rewarding for girls than boys, signifies a cultural rebirth, a transition from female to male that privileges phallocentricism and excludes the female. In the woman-centred territory and patterning of Sappho's lyrics, such oppositions are destabilised. It is not women but men and the masculine symbols that are associated with male bodies, value systems, consciousness and activities, which appear as 'other'.

Accessible mainly through the fragmentary songs of Sappho and other (male) poets, the links between this environment and some non-discursive 'reality' are necessarily decentred and arbitrary, as are the links between these poets, their world and their constructions and commentators of the twentieth century. Psychoanalytic theory makes a claim for universality, for some ahistorical, temporally non-specific space inhabited by the unconscious. It fails. Psychoanalysis, like any other discipline or practice is historically determined, as is its attitude towards women. The symbolic world constructed by Lacan is historically, culturally specific and within the structures and strategies relevant to that particular culture it reflects/reconstructs the phallocentric attitudes of one specific group, of this moment in time. Sappho's symbolic world is equally historically, culturally and temporally specific. These disparate – poetic and psychoanalytic – constructs emanate from different worlds, from distinctive voices and differently sexed bodies. A comparison of Sappho's lyrics with the lyrics of the other poets of her own time and space is also productive of difference. It produces a catalogue of differences that should, ideally, as Irigaray proposes, 'be linked (both at once) in a kind of creative and fertile partnership' . . . so that in a 'double gesture, neither would be elevated over the other, and interpretation would embody the symbolic possibilities of sexual difference' (Whitford 1991: 25).

As a twentieth-century philosopher, Irigaray makes some claims about a form of discourse that could be potentially capable of articulating a woman's thoughts, imaginary worlds and her sexuality: its style is diffusive, but unified. Fluid and with an aspect of simultaneity, it resists and explodes established concepts, forms and figures. Arguably, Sappho's discourse is diffusive, but unified, and it possesses a quality of simultaneity. In her own form of the 'double gesture', the conflation of binary concepts such as pain/pleasure, sweet/bitter, these constructs are combined and destabilised. Despite a proliferation of multi-meanings and moments of erotic *jouissance* or excess however, it does not explode every 'form, figure, idea or concept' (Irigaray 1985: 79). Remaining within the conventions of lyric poetry, within the hegemonic discourse of Sappho's culture, it appears nevertheless to be distinctive and to differ substantially from the lyric configurations of male poets. From within a private circle that itself symbolises a circle of women gathered around a central singer/musician, Sappho constructed a somewhat utopian symbolic universe. In lyrics that were, if the construction of Sappho 1 can be assumed to have been reproduced in other more fragmentary songs, also circular. These lyrics combine to provide an example of a symbolic territory constructed by a woman at a time when attitudes to women were differently constructed. Throughout the course of western culture poets and lovers have looked with desire and wonder at these imaginative and musical songs, gazing at the representation of a distinctive, archaic and female specificity, listening to a woman's voice singing of a woman-made world.

Notes

INTRODUCTION

1 Our sources, like the fragments of Sappho's songs, are sadly worn by time. It seems however, that other women poets could have flourished contemporaneously with – as suggested by frr. 55 and 71 – or prior to, Sappho.
2 Conventionally, a distinction is most commonly made between songs which were sung and accompanied by music (i.e. lyric songs accompanied by the lyre), and poems or blank verse which were spoken and unaccompanied. The lyric compositions of Sappho and her contemporaries were, it appears, originally sung/accompanied and should therefore be categorised as songs, even though we often apprehend them as poems which we read from a page.
3 While definitions of what types of ancient Greek poetry the term 'lyric' actually embraces do vary, in accordance with Lattimore (1971: preface iv), and Campbell (1982b: intro. xiv), I include monody, choral and iambic poetry and elegiac couplets.
4 Discussing the problematic split between 'biological sex' and the cultural markers of difference that come under a heading of 'gender', Laqueur (1990: 11–12) attempts to demonstrate that 'on the basis of historical evidence . . . almost everything one wants to *say* about sex – however sex is understood – already has in it a claim about gender'. Both sex and gender are, in this analysis, politically, historically and culturally specific and 'the body . . . is so hopelessly bound to its cultural meanings as to elude unmediated access'.
5 Rhode (1990: 3–5) considers that late twentieth-century western culture is based upon, and grows out of, 'a historical tradition that ascribed overriding importance to biological explanations for differences in the sexes' social roles and status'.
6 Some pertinent examples are: 'Identity, in which A = A, is the most basic axiom in Aristotelian logic . . . In opposing a logic of identity, a logic of Being, and in advocating a "logic" of difference or becoming, Nietzsche initiated a major critical trajectory in contemporary theory.' 'Saussure demonstrated that such a "logic" of difference is necessary to explain the complexity and functioning of language, and

representation more generally.' 'The concept of difference in the context of Saussurian linguistics refers to the fact that no sign has any positive characteristics in and of itself. Each sign can only be defined in terms of what it is not' (Grosz 1989: preface ix–xvii). Derrida's concept of différance combines 'the coincidence of meanings in the verb différer: to differ (in space) and to defer (to put off in time, to postpone presence) . . . and plays on both meanings at once' (Derrida 1978: intro. xvi).

7 By Havelock (1986: 24–7), who poses the question of whether 'an oral consciousness is quite different from a literate state of mind'.

8 A language which was sufficiently accessible, flexible and multi-vocal to allow the participation of women in an oral poetic tradition. Skinner (1993: 131–5) who, in a search for a female voice, examines some of Sappho's songs and discusses their orally oriented mode of construction, positions these songs within a culture in which alternative frameworks could coexist.

9 Not without some dissension. See Davison (1968: intro. xxi), Cairns (1971: 70), and Kirkwood (1974: 10–11) for some variant opinions on this subject.

10 The split between these two worlds is not as extreme as may appear. Winkler (1981: 65) contends that Sappho's world was also public, albeit in a different manner. The personal sentiments she articulates were 'in some measure formulaic', and her songs were also shared, even if it was more often 'outside the public world of men' and between 'other "private" persons'.

11 See Gatens (1983: 145).

12 Laqueur (1990: 11) asserts that 'everything one wants to *say* about sex – however sex is understood – already has in it a claim about gender'.

13 Such as Iphigenia's statement that 'We are women; as a race, we think kindly of each other; we can count on each other to protect our common aims' (Euripides, *Iphigenia in Tauris:* 1058–60).

14 'Dichotomous categories of thought can be traced to the beginnings of philosophy in ancient Greece . . . Even in the modern period, in the work of Descartes, for example, dichotomies dominate philosophical reflections on the world, human knowledge and human nature' (Gatens 1991: 92).

15 Juliet Mitchell emphasises this point strongly, stressing the conceptual split instituted between the sexes by Freud and Lacan. For them: 'no human being can become a subject outside the division into two sexes' (Mitchell and Rose 1982: 6–7).

16 McMillan (1982: 11) discusses this philosophical tendency in greater detail.

17 Gatens (1991: 4) suggests that 'this problematic is one which has been constructed around the dichotomies which have dominated modern philosophy: mind/body, reason/passion and nature/culture. Undoubtedly, these dichotomies interact with the male/female dichotomy in extremely complex and prejudicial ways.'

18 'It can be said that this signifier is chosen because it is the most

tangible (*le plus saillant*) element in the real of sexual copulation, and also the most symbolic in the literal (typographical) sense of the term, since it is equivalent here to the (logical) copula' (Lacan 1977: 287).

19 Lacan's (1975: 68) theory is taken to be an explanation of women's oppression. Women are constructed in the domain of a male sign, and therefore they are, as Lacan put it, 'excluded by the nature of things, which is the nature of words'.

20 Beye (1975: 80) also remarks on Sappho's idiosyncratic use of language, the way she deliberately breaks the epic linguistic patterns, employing techniques which successfully 'fracture and recast traditional language'.

21 In his exploration of psychoanalytic theory and its place in classical analysis Caldwell (1989: 51) develops this idea more fully.

22 Throughout my discussion I shall use the term 'feminine' to refer to the traditional and/or stereotypical set of characteristics employed to categorise women of later western culture.

23 Sartre (1974: 67) recognised that the look is the domain of domination and mastery; it can provide access to its subject without establishing physical contact with it.

24 For further discussion see Grosz (1989: 31–2).

25 Halperin,Winkler and Zeitlin (1990: intro. 5).

26 For Irigaray, as she is interpreted by Meagan Morris (1982: 88), 'women's speaking MAY BE: it has no triumphal, concrete existence, and everything is yet to be fought for'.

27 'A word with *simultaneously* sexual, political and economic overtones' (Cixous and Clement 1986: Glossary 165).

28 Therefore defying what Derrida (1978: intro. xvi) considers to be philosophical totalitarianism: structuralist attempts 'to account for the totality of a phenomenon by reduction of it to a formula that governs it totally'.

1 APHRODITE

1 Gentili (1988: 84–5) is one of the commentators who supports the idea of religious cult which he and others (Parker [1993: 339] provides a comprehensive list), call a *thiasos*. Alternatively, Parker asserts that the term *thiasos* 'is never used anywhere in any of the poems of Sappho . . . nor is it ever used anywhere in any ancient source about her'. 'And its primary purpose is to isolate Sappho from all other lyric poets' (Parker 1993: 338–9).

2 A number of commentators, e.g. Hawkes (1968), Gimbutas (1974), Briffault (1927), Friedrich (1978) and Stone (1976), posit, on the evidence of a predominant number of female representations dating from 7,000 to 3,000 BC, the existence of religious/cultural systems in which the status of women was pre-eminent. As Hawkes (1968: 25) states: 'All over South-West Asia early farming communities seem to have focused their worship upon fertility and the life-creating forces expressed through a maternal figure in human form.'

3 In his search for the origins of Aphrodite, Friedrich (1978: 6–22) attempts to trace these mythic figures and their symbols and imagery syncretically, 'through a network of significant dimensions of meaning, to produce "a partial synthesis" in the shape of the Greek Aphrodite'.
4 See Winkler's (1990: 166–7) discussion of the alternative readings of *poikilothron* (variegated, changeful) or *poikilophron* (mental subtlety).
5 In her depiction of 'the clash and mingling of northern Indo-European and Mediterranean traditions' Hawkes (1968: 30) describes 'the father-figure Zeus – who did not care for the dark, slow earth but ruled the sky with lightning in his hand'.
6 According to Winkler (1981: 67) Homer 'identifies Aphrodite as a "feminine" goddess, weak (*analkis*), unsuited to take part in male warfare . . . Her appropriate sphere, says Diomedes exulting in his victory over her, is to seduce weak (*analkides*) women (*Iliad* 5. 348ff.)'.
7 Birds, like snakes and double-axes, were symbols associated with goddess figures which later 'became the emblem of the goddesses of human beauty, love and fertility – Aphrodite and Venus' (Hawkes 1968: 138).
8 'A complex word like *deute* can create a complex tone. *De* places you in time and emphasises that placement: *now*. *Aute* intercepts "now" and binds it into a history of "thens"' (Carson 1986: 119).
9 Such as relationships defined by de Beauvoir (1975: 465), in which 'separateness is abolished, there is no struggle, no victory, no defeat; in exact reciprocity each is at once subject and object, sovereign and slave; duality becomes mutuality'.
10 Although perhaps as Gatens (1991: 137) suggests, 'it is not so much that women are explicitly conceptualised as irrational but rather that rationality itself is defined against the "womanly".'
11 'The reference is to St Elmo's fire, the electrical discharge which creates a glow about the mast-head and rigging of ships' (Campbell 1982a: 247).
12 See discussion in Stehle (1990: 88–112).

2 SONGS OF LOVE

1 In my discussions of single-sex relationships in Sappho's songs I prefer to use the term 'homoerotic' rather than 'homosexual' since the songs focus not on sexual/genital interaction but on the representation of love between women.
2 Apart from the awareness that 'overt and unrepressed homosexuality' was a conspicuous feature of Greek life, Dover (1978: 1–2) considers that 'we are sadly short of evidence' of the details of male homoerotic relationships and as far as female homoeroticism is concerned the evidence is 'exiguous by comparison'.
3 'We now live, so the argument goes, with a model of personality centred on sex' (Halperin, Winkler and Zeitlin 1990: intro. 5).

4 'The issue of homosexuality intrudes on, if it does not dominate, almost every discussion of Sappho in a way that does not happen with male poets' (Stigers 1979: 465).
5 'Desire in the lacanian emphasis, libido in the freudian emphasis, is disinterested . . . has no interest in, no cognitive understanding of, the objects of its desire' (Kappeler 1986: 196–7).
6 Campbell (1982b: 292) questions Alcaeus' choice of Thetis, who 'was not a model wife . . . nor was she a happy mother'.
7 Winkler (1990: 162–3) provides an example: 'Because Lobel and Page assumed the validity of Victorian no-no's they were (it now seems to us) deaf to much of what Sappho was saying, tone-deaf to her deeper melodies.'
8 Page (1955: 32–3) cites Tietze, Snell and Wilamowitz as three proponents of this theory.
9 Another Homeric echo comparable to *Odyssey* 22.294 and *Iliad* 14.294. See Marcovich (1972: 26).
10 There are some textual ambiguities in this song, at this point there is a choice of ψυχή or ψυχρός, and considering the previous reference to 'ψυχρα φλογ . . .' (123.6), cold rather than soul seems the most viable interpretation.
11 As usual, Sappho 'is not recording the history of a love affair but the instant of desire. One moment staggers under pressure of eros; one mental state splits. A simultaneity of pleasure and pain is at issue' (Carson 1986: 4).
12 'As far as we know the idea [of sweet-bitter love] is expressed first here' (Campbell 1983: 18).

3 A WOMAN'S DESIRE

1 Sexuality 'has become a new category – central and centralised; universally organised as a tool for understanding, placing, and controlling individuals' (Halperin, Winkler and Zeitlin 1990: 6).
2 'Plato . . . changes the course of ideology, intervening in it in a new way both to reaffirm old patterns of dominance and to establish through new rationalization certain objects of knowledge, certain forms of power' (duBois 1988: 2).
3 This attitude is foregrounded by Lardinois (1989: 18) in his commentary, while DeJean's (1989: 201–20) discussion charts a history of pederastic inferences. Parker (1993: 322) is justifiably suspicious about 'this reinscription of Sappho along the lines of male power relations'.
4 'One might be tempted to say: Freud, like those who follow him here [i.e., Lacan], does nothing else but *describe* the necessity of phallogocentricism, explain its effects which are just as obvious as they are massive' (Derrida 1975: 97).
5 Van Gennep (1960: intro. xvi) deplores the individualistic trend in psychoanalytic literature and considers that 'there is practically nothing about the relation of these to rites of passage'. But despite

the absence of communal interaction, perhaps the Freudian Oedipal stage can be compared to other constructed entrances into the world of sexuality and sexual difference.

6 A list of these physical/erotic phenomena demonstrates their comprehensive physicality: sweet voice, lovely laughter - 'ἆδυ φωνείσας', 'γελαίσας ἰμέροεν', 31.3–5; heart in breast - 'καρδίαν ἐν στήθεσιν', 31.6; tongue, ' γλῶσσα', 31.9; flesh, 'χρῷ', 31.10; sight, 'ὄρημμ', 31.11; hearing, 'ἄκουαι', 31.12; sweat, 'ἴδρως κακχέεσαι', 31.13; trembling 'τρόμος', 31.13; pallor, 'χλωροτέρα', 31.14; death, 'τεθνάκην', 31.15.

7 'The ordinary ancient concern with fertility, health and bodily function generated a large family of natural metaphors for human sexuality . . . A high degree of personal modesty and decorum is in no way compromised by a daily language which names the world according to genital analogies . . .' (Winkler 1981: 77).

8 'The sensitivity of these objects to pressure is one of the bases for the analogy; I will quote just one. And what is called a *mêlon* is a form of fleshy bump (*staphyloma*, grape-like or uvular swelling, big enough to raise eyelids, and when it is rubbed it bothers the entire lid-surface' (Winkler 1981: 79).

9 'Freud's argument, flying as it does in the face of centuries of anatomical knowledge, is a testament to the freedom with which the authority of nature can be rhetorically appropriated to legitimize the creations of culture' (Laqueur 1990: 241).

10 'Sexual difference is encoded in ancient Greece in terms not of castration, of the presence or absence of the penis or phallus, but rather in terms that are analogous to those used of agricultural production . . . The female body is seen not as castrated but as full and self-sufficient' (duBois 1988: 28).

11 In the context of the male reworking of this particular metaphor, the earth/woman's body, in accordance with 'the demands and needs of culture', duBois (1988: 63) emphasises 'the contestation, the challenging and putting into question of cultural "sets"'. Solon, on the basis of a mythical female body, constructs a very male political argument, using ancient models, such as 'the myths of autochthony that name all Athenian citizens as children of Earth' and transforms the concept of female parthenogenesis which Sappho employs in fr. 96.

12 'The goal of the Greek male is to dominate the female and her body, to control its potentiality, to subdue it to his interests. This is done through elaborate ideological mechanisms' (duBois 1988: 147).

13 Semonides uses Hesiod's creation of the woman 'Hephaestos had used earth mixed with water to create' (Campbell 1983: 142).

14 'Ancient tradition insisted that Neobule, the faithless beloved, had broken her word to Archilochus and had been hounded by his retaliatory verses until she hanged herself, along with her sister(s) and their father Lycambes' (Burnett 1983: 89).

15 'Each confrontation with the fresh girl makes the Neobule figure filthier, and in this way each comparison serves the abusive function of the song' (Burnett 1983: 94).

16 Belsey (1985: 45) applies her remarks to the classic realist fiction of the nineteenth and twentieth century, but it seems that Sappho's creations, constructed in the dominant form of the seventh century BC – poetic discourse – also interpolate the reader/listener, addressing themselves 'to him or her directly, offering the reader a position from which the text is most "obviously" intelligible, the position of the *subject* in (and of) ideology'.

17 Jones (1985: 96) certainly feels that the concept is problematic: 'Can the body be the source of a new discourse? Is it possible, assuming an unmediated and *jouissant* (or more likely, a positively reconstructed) sense of one's body, to move from that state of unconscious excitation directly to a written female text?'

18 'The transformation of the fertile earth, the naming of the woman as furrow, is an important reinscription of the inherited paradigm, a reduction of her potential, a mastering of her fertility' (duBois 1988: 72).

19 'There is no woman but excluded from the nature of things which is the nature of words' (Lacan 1975: 68).

4 'VIRGINITY'

1 Terminology is clearly a problem here, so when I refer to 'virginity' it will be in the twentieth-century sense of the word.

2 The authorship of fr. 44a has been the subject of some controversy. In agreement with Treu, Kirkwood and Campbell, however, I have assigned the fragment to Sappho. See Campbell (1982a: 91).

3 'This pattern of longing for the ever uncapturable essence of Eros and excitement at discovering its momentary embodiment in a vulnerable, innocent figure, is the poetic rhythm of the male lyric poets' (Stigers 1981: 49).

4 'Marriage is the means, in the Greek view, whereby man can control the wild *eros* of women and so impose civilized order on the chaos of nature' (Carson 1990: 143).

5 Artemis' geographical detachment seems symbolic, to represent an analogue for her physical sexual state; as Sissa (1990b: 34) states: 'sexual 'virginity' is the primordial condition of distance, of detachment from all that is exterior'.

6 The 'female nature lacks the *sôphrosyne* ("soundness of mind" or "sobriety and self-control") by which men subject desires to rational mastery from within' (Carson 1990: 142).

7 'The stable, ahistorical, sexed body – is understood to be the epistemic foundation for prescriptive claims about the social order' (Laqueur 1990: 6).

8 Hippolytos' 'virginity' (sexual purity) is also foregrounded in this play, but his fate, as represented by Euripides, suggests that male 'virginity' is not approbated in the public world.

9 Hunting is a masculine pursuit that is frequently associated with sexuality (see discussion in Dover 1978: 87). References to more sexual

versions of the chase are found in the songs of the male poets (e.g. Anacreon fr. 408).

10 Solon is said to have levelled sexual inequity in Athens by stationing 'women in various public locations, equipped and fitted out as common possessions for all'. 'In this way, by insuring that there would always be a category of persons for every citizen to dominate, both socially and sexually, Solon underwrote the manhood of the Athenian citizen body' (Halperin 1990a: 100).

11 In what sounds like a similar ritual sequence Pollux informs us that on the day before the wedding, 'the bride performed preliminary rites (προαύλια or προτέλεια) in which she said farewell to her girlhood and consecrated her toys to Artemis' (Carson 1990: 151).

12 'Each line launches an impression that is at once modified, then launched again . . . This motion is corroborated in the rhythm of the verse: dactyls (in lines 1 and 2) slow and elongate to spondees (in line 3) as the apple begins to look farther and farther away' (Carson 1986: 27).

13 The mythical connection with the beautiful young boy Hyakinthos who died as a result of the passion of two gods and whose spilt blood is immortalised by the colour and shape of the hyacinth seems to provide an appropriate image.

5 GAZING AT BEAUTY

1 Any discussion of beauty in ancient Greece must take into consideration the fact that whereas authors of the twentieth century are likely to distinguish between beautiful women and handsome men, in Greek, beauty is defined by the correct grammatical version of the same word: 'καλός'. See Dover (1978: 15–16).

2 'The convention of perspective, which is unique to European art . . . centres everything on the eye of the beholder . . . Perspective makes the single eye the centre of the visible world' (Berger 1978: 16).

3 According to Kaplan (1983: 311), men, or at least the male subjects of modern signifying practices, 'do not simply look; their gaze carries with it the power of action and of possession that is lacking in the female gaze. Women receive and return a gaze, but cannot act on it.'

4 See Kaplan (1983: 319) for further discussion.

5 In the words of Adrienne Rich (1989: 107): 'two women, eye to eye, measuring each other's spirit, each other's limitless desire / . . . Vision begins to happen in such a life.'

6 Certainly it seems to accord with Kaplan's (1983: 310) description of voyeurism: 'i.e., the male pleasure in his own sexual organ transferred to pleasure in watching other people having sex'.

7 'The sexualisation and objectification of women is not simply for the purposes of eroticism; from a psychoanalytic point of view, it is designed to annihilate the threat that woman (as castrated, and possessing a sinister genital organ) poses. Karen Horney goes to literature to show that "men have never tired of fashioning expressions

for the violent force by which man feels himself drawn to the woman, and side by side with this longing, the dread that through her he might die and be undone"' (Kaplan 1983: 311).

8 'It is important to underline that the contrast of *physis* and *nomos*, of nature and culture, is itself a cultural item, a habit of thought once discovered, promoted, and eventually adopted as a convention' (Winkler 1981: 172).

9 'It is women who have been so frequently associated with nature and described as prone to the passions which stem from their disorderly bodies . . . The historical associations between women, nature, passion and the body are surprisingly influential in contemporary thought' (Gatens 1991: 5).

10 Carson (1990: 140) suggests that 'as the poem shifts delicately from weather to sexuality, it becomes clear that the focus of male concern (and perhaps resentment) here is not a summer heat wave but the unwitherable appetite and capacity of the female sex'.

11 'Male halcyons are called ceryli. When they become weak from old age and are no longer able to fly, the females carry them, taking them on their wings' (Antig. Caryst. *Mir.* 23 (27) (8 Keller)).

12 Bacchylides was called the honey-tongued nightingale of Ceos.

13 As producer of this beautiful, flowery bounty the Earth assumes a maternal persona and it appears that mythically she has often been labelled as female, as Mother Earth. For further discussion, see Stone (1976): 18.

14 See McEvilley (1973: 266).

15 See Irigaray (1985: 79).

16 See Gatens (1991: 5).

6 CIRCLES OF WOMEN

1 Burnett (1983: 211) is one of the commentators who refers to this group as Sappho's circle and suggests that it 'had a place within the public order as a discrete social organism where society's usual rules for a time did not prevail'.

2 Calame (1977a: 50 and 56), who analyses the choral poetry of a contemporary of Sappho's, Alcman of Sparta, but relates this lyric environment to Sappho's circle, states that: 'Le choeur lyrique grec est fondamentalement composé d'un certain nombre de danseurs ou de danseuses, appelés *choreutes* (Les chiffres de dix et onze, qui correspondent à ceux indiqués dans le fragment cité d'Alcman sont bien attestés.), et d'une personne qui les dirige, le ou la *chorège*.'

3 'Les femmes groupées en choeur sont très fréquemment désignées d'un nom collectif' (Calame 1977a: 70).

4 'The change in discourse that Irigaray envisages only takes place when one's deep unconscious feelings are mobilized . . . in the relationship between lovers and, perhaps most crucially, in the love between women – as actual or spiritual mothers and daughters or sisters – in subject-to-subject relationships' (Whitford 1991: 48).

5 Parker (1993: 325–6) , states that 'archaic Lesbos and archaic Sparta share only a single factor: expressions of desire by women for women'.

6 'Premièrement, cette personne n'est en général pas identifiable avec le poète qui a composé le chant choral, mais avec le choeur qui l'interprète; . . . En outre, même si le *je* lyrique est souvent grammaticalement au singulier, il se réfère en général à l'ensemble des choreutes qui exécutent le poème' (Calame 1977a: 436).

7 'Le moment même de l'agrégation à cet ordre est très souvent marqué par un grand banquet collectif qui consacre l'union des nouveaux initiés et des membres de la tribu' (Calame 1977a: 37).

8 Calame (1977a: 369–70) cites an illustration from the Palatine Anthology which describes a similar situation: 'Ces jeunes filles, précise Philostrate, sont conduites (ἄγει) par une chorège (διδάσκαλος) encore jeune qui frappe la mesure pendant que les adolescentes (παῖδες) chantent la déesse; en marquant le rythme, la chorège permet aux jeunes filles d'entonner le chant au moment voulu.'

9 'Cette étude a une double finalité: premièrement la détermination d'une éventuelle spécificité des cultes dans lesquels une part du rituel est constituée par une interprétation chorale féminine, secondement, la définition de la figure des divinités auxquelles ces rituels choraux sont consacrés' (Calame 1977a: 25).

10 As a term that defines states of release, freedom, relief or relaxation, the use of λῦσ . . . appears to imply a state, in both Alcman's and Sappho's lyrics, that is not unpleasant.

11 Calame (1977a: 436–7) considers that this is not woman-to-woman interaction but women-to-woman: 'si le *je* lyrique est souvent grammaticalement au singulier, il se réfère en général à l'ensemble des choreutes qui exécutent le poème. Ainsi, il est parfaitement possible que des jeunes filles puissent exprimer à une autre jeune fille ou femme des sentiments de nature pour nous purement individuelle dans des vers composé par une tierce personne.'

12 Since these are references which 'come from the area of male interest in breeding and racing horses' (Stigers 1979: 469).

13 See discussion in Campbell (1988: 367). Calame (1977b: 89) also takes time to examine 'une contexte érotique'.

14 Calame (1977a: 369) considers that the musical, institutional character of the Sapphic circle, as well as the interactions between poet and choristers, and the links of loving friendship 'font apparaître pour le cercle de Lesbos des structures analogues à celles que nous avons définies comme caractéristiques du choeur lyrique féminin: des jeunes filles, unies àcelle qui les dirige par des liens que définit le terme de *hétaira*, s'exercent ensemble à la danse et au chant'.

15 The erotic sequence is not dissimilar to the action represented in Alcman 3.79–81.

16 These expressions seem to come directly from Hesiod's *Theogony* where Eros is described as λυσιμελής, limb-loosening (120–2) and it

is stated that from the Graces' 'eyes as they glanced love dripped down, loosener of limbs'.

17 As in fr. 1 Sappho is named within the song.

18 'A passage of nine consecutive verses is preserved, followed by twenty very fragmentary verses. The beginning is lost and there is no way of knowing how much preceded' (Kirkwood 1974: 133).

19 See Page (1955: 76–7) and Burnett (1983: 295).

7 A CHAIN OF REMEMBRANCE

1 'This pattern of longing for the ever uncapturable essence of Eros and excitement at discovering its momentary embodiment in a vulnerable, innocent figure, is the poetic rhythm of the male lyric poets' (Stigers 1981: 49).

2 'Memory is a very complicated function which is related to important psychological categories such as time and identity. It brings into play a whole collection of complex mental operations with all the effort, training, and exercise that are needed to master them . . . The consecration of Mnemosune indicates the value that is set upon it' (Vernant 1983: 76).

3 'A single word which itself presents, in microcosm, the temporal dilemma of eros. It is the adverb *deute* . . . The particle *de* signifies vividly and dramatically that something is taking place at the moment . . . The adverb *aute* means 'again, once again, over again' (Carson 1986: 118).

4 See discussion in Grosz (1990: 64).

5 The word 'γυναίκεσσιν' (96.6), is used to describe her Lydian companions.

6 See Vernant (1983: 89).

7 While they lived in the circle 'they had the daily experience of hearing themselves transposed into music, and by taking her songs with them when they left, they took a poetic vision of their life along' (Burnett 1983: 224–5).

8 Stigers (1979: 470) considers that 'Sappho consciously wished to connect woman with the mysterious rhythms of the moon as separate from the sharp, bright images of sun and stars.' It seems that the male poets are more attracted not only to the 'sharp, bright images of sun' but also to the schemes of hours and days that relate to this powerful planet/divinity.

9 'The only season is the growing season of young girls; it is like spring because they are like flowers, but it lasts all year because their growing season is not measured in months' (McEvilley 1973: 270).

10 'At some point, Alexander Marshak considers, someone may have noticed the similarity of the female and lunar cycles, or projected one from the other. The moon, after all, is visible in the sky for a period of twenty-seven or twenty-eight days' (Vlahos 1979: 151).

11 Sappho shows 'that the artful wish for death was a poetic practice that she allowed herself' (Burnett 1983: 294).

8 EPITHALAMIA

1 Halperin (1990a: 17–18) discusses 'the comparatively recent genesis of heterosexuality', as a term which designates 'the mode of sexual behaviour favoured by the vast majority of people in our culture'. I will use this word to denote interaction between 'others', between female and male participants.
2 See Carson (1990: 161).
3 Sissa (1990b: 98) suggests that a dramatic representation of a wedding by Menander proffers a reason for these songs: 'Later, to cover the cry that she [the bride] will emit in the midst of her first embrace, the epithalamium will be sung.'
4 See Athenaeus (1969: iii 110f, 111).
5 'Woman is a mobile unit in a society that practises patrilocal marriage (which Greek society is generally agreed to have done), and man is not' (Carson 1990: 136).
6 See Winkler (1981: 77–84) and Bagg (1964: 54).
7 'Already in antiquity the range of conjecture was vast, as Muth has observed. Despite the apparent and plausible proximity, the relation between the hymeneal song and the hymen of histology remains "obscure"' (Sissa 1990b: 109).
8 'Not only did the veil cover the *nymphê*; the marriage bed was veiled by curtains: Pollux explicitly draws the analogy. Discreetly yet by virtue of a precise correspondence the bridal veil suggested the canopy of the bed. Like the *nymphê's* body, the place where the marriage was consummated was shielded from view' (Sissa 1990b: 96). Winkler's (1981: 78) discussion of 'the outer part of the female genital system which . . . has the name "wings" (*pteryges*)' seems to add yet another dimension to the secrets of veils and symbolic barriers.
9 'At the moment of unveiling, for the first time, the intact boundary of her person is violated by contact: the contact of vision' (Carson 1990: 163).
10 Since Hermes is the god who leads mortals into the underworld, his inclusion again implies the possibility of some link between weddings and death.
11 Perhaps 'the archaic poets, like the Hellenistic writers at a later time, could vary their metrical and prosodic techniques to achieve a variety of aesthetic effects' (Halporn, Ostwald and Rosenmeyer 1963: 6).
12 Thalmann's (1984: 4) definition of parataxis provides an apt description of Sappho's technique: 'whereby clauses in a sentence are not subordinated one to the other according to their logical relations but are strung together as coordinate and thus equal in value and importance'.
13 Perhaps with the varied derivation of these precious objects, there is also an attempt to represent a geographic inclusiveness, to take in 'τ' ἄλλας 'Ασίασ'.
14 'Significantly, the only writer of the archaic and classical periods who delights in the details of marriage rites for their own sake, and who in fact regards the marital union as an important and equal source of pleasure to bridegroom as well as bride, is Sappho' (Hallett 1979: 456).

15 'The social practice of the Greeks led to the segregation of young women . . . Traded from one family to another to establish lines of connection between families, they insured the perpetuation of one family line in the *polis*' (duBois 1982: 115).

9 IMMORTALITY

1 'It is clear that for many centuries after her death, Sappho enjoyed immense popularity for the sheer beauty of her language and the directness and power of her expression' (Snyder 1989: 7).
2 Davison (1968: 227) cites Horace (*Epp.* i 19.28) as the initiator of this thought.
3 'The Muses . . . can deliberately mislead a poet by presenting him with a false version which he transmits in the belief that it is true' (Campbell 1983: 253).
4 Allen and Young (1989: intro. 1).
5 Whitford (1991: 45) in relation to Irigaray (1984: 122 and 143).
6 'The images do more than add richness and excitement to the songs: they constantly draw attention to the lofty view which Pindar takes of his god-given art' (Campbell 1983: 283).
7 'The formal, rhythmic and ritual effects of the song are felt to be capable of working real magic on the body and soul of the hearer, whether for healing or for pleasure' (Segal 1974: 144).
8 This written, alphabeticised version of oral language was 'a script which could fluently and unambiguously transcribe the full gamut of orally preserved speech' (Havelock 1986: 90).
9 Beye (1975: 79) suggests that Sappho's 'sensuality is matched by the wide range of meters she uses, far more sensual themselves than the conventional meters of her poetic colleagues'.
10 'Rational thought has, as it were, its personal credentials in order: its date and place of birth are known. It was in the sixth century BC, in the Greek cities of Asia Minor, that a new positivist type of thought about nature emerged' (Vernant 1983: 343).
11 As is suggested in McMillan (1982: 11).

10 HONOUR

1 '*Time* carries a very high emotive charge, and it is not surprising that to defend one's own *time*, if possible to acquire more, and at all events not to lose any of what one has, is the principal motivation of Homeric man' (Adkins 1972: 15).
2 As Adkins (1972: 31) reminds us, in the agonistic world of archaic Greece the resources, prowess and courage of the individual are valued by the group since 'it is by success, not by good intentions, that the group continues to exist'.
3 There is a tale about Solon, who having heard a song of Sappho's at a drinking party, asked his nephew to teach it to him 'so that I may learn it and die' (Aelian [quoted by Strobaeus, *Anthology*]).

4 Winkler (1990: 182) considers that 'the biographical tradition which regards Kleis as the name of Sappho's daughter and mother may be (as so often) based on a fact-hungry reading of her poems'.
5 'A beloved who refuses to take the *charis* that is offered breaks the law of love, spoiling the proper balance that is *dike*, and thus becoming guilty of injustice, or *adika*' (Burnett 1983: 256).
6 'The cultural understanding of competition was not simply that winners gained rewards and honour, but that losers were stigmatised with shame and penalties in proportionate amounts, or, to put it another way, winners won at the direct expense of losers' (Winkler 1990: 178).
7 An older contemporary of Tyrtaeus, Callinus of Ephesus also composed poetry in this style, spurring the Ephesians into battle.
8 'The nobles of Mytilene . . . were united by habits of honour and rites of honour . . . this fierce sense of clan was reinforced by a system of *hetaireiai* – clubs that associated cousins, brothers and more distant kin in one another's constant society' (Burnett 1983: 110).

11 SYMBOLIC REALMS

1 'We lack, we women with a sex of our own, a God in which to share, a word/language to share and to become' (Irigaray 1987: 83).
2 'Memories of a symbiotic paradise lost in the past underlie Hesiod's myth of a "golden race" (*Works and Days* 110–27), and the impossible wish to regain this paradise appears in afterlife myths of the "islands of the blessed" (*Works and Days* 170), the "Elysian field" (Homer, *Odyssey* 4.564)' (Caldwell 1990: 359).
3 Mythologically (e.g. *Iliad* 16.672 and Hesiod *Th.* 211–2), Death, *Thanatos*, and Sleep, *Hupnos*, are represented as twin brothers.
4 Simonides, Mimnermus and Semonides are three examples.
5 'Irigaray argues that we have to go back to Greek mythology to find available, culturally embodied representations of the mother–daughter relationship' (Whitford 1991: 75–7).
6 'It is not masculinity *per se* that is valorised in our culture but the *masculine male*' (Gatens 1983: 154).
7 'The transformation of the fertile earth, the naming of woman as furrow, is an important reinscription of the inherited paradigm, a reduction of her potential, a mastering of her fertility' (duBois 1988: 72).
8 'The warrior male insulates himself from the threat of dissolution . . . by turning his body into an armoured surface that both repels the femininity on the outside and contains the "primitive", feminised flesh of his own interior' (Nead 1992: 17).
9 According to Irigaray's definition of sexual pleasure, it 'is not singular, unified, hierarchically subordinated to a single organ, definable or locatable according to the logic of identity' (Grosz 1989: 115).
10 'When Juliet Mitchell was asked . . . at a talk she gave at Melbourne University, by a male member of the audience: "What Do Women

Want?", she replied, "I think that women simply want to be allowed to want"' (Creed 1981–3: 87).

11 Irigaray, quoted in Whitford (1991: 43).

12 See discussion in Whitford (1991: 57–8).

Bibliography

PRIMARY SOURCES

The numbers of the songs and fragments are those used in the following editions:

Campbell, D.A. (1982a; 1988; 1991 and 1992) *Greek Lyric*, 4 vols, Loeb Classical Library, London: Heinemann. [For Campbell 1982b, *see under* Secondary Texts.]

Hubert, J. (1959) *Homère Hymnes,* Paris: Société d'Edition Les Belles Lettres.

Sandys, Sir J. (1946) *The Odes of Pindar,* Loeb Classical Library, London: Heinemann.

West, M.L. (1971) *Iambi et Elegi Graeci*, 2 vols, London: Oxford University Press.

Young, D. (1961) *Theognis,* Leipzig: Teubner.

Other editions consulted:

Diehl, E. (1936-42) *Anthologia Lyrica Graeca*, 2 vols and supplement, Leipzig: Teubner.

Edmonds, J.M. (1968) *Elegy and Iambus with the Anacreontea*, 2 vols, Loeb Classical Library, London: Heinemann.

Frazer, B.M. (trans.) (1983) *The Poems of Hesiod,* Norman: University of Oklahoma Press.

Gulick, C.B. (trans.) (1969) *Athenaeus: Deipnosophists,* 2 vols, Cambridge: Harvard University Press.

Lattimore, R. (trans.) (1961) *The Iliad of Homer,* Chicago and London: Chicago University Press.

Lattimore, R. (trans.) (1967) *The Odyssey of Homer,* New York: Harper & Row.

Lobel, E. and Page, D.L. (1963) *Poetarum Lesbiorum Fragmenta,* London: Oxford University Press.

Page, D.L. (1962) *Poetae Melici Graeci*, Oxford: Oxford University Press.

—— (1974) *Supplementum Lyricis Graecis*, Oxford: Oxford University Press.

Page, T.E. (ed.) (1960) *Aristotle, The Poetics, 'Longinus', On The Sublime, Demetrius, On Style*, London: Heinemann.
Peck, A.L. (trans.) (1963) *Aristotle: Generation of Animals*, Cambridge: Harvard University Press.
Tredennick, H. (trans.) (1961) *Aristotle: The Metaphysics, Books I–IX*, Cambridge: Harvard University Press.
Usener, H. and Radermacher, L. (eds) (1965) *Dionysius Halicarnasseus*, Stuttgart: Teubner.
Welldon, J.E.C. (trans.) (1886) *The Rhetoric of Aristotle*, London: Macmillan.

ABBREVIATIONS FOR CLASSICAL WORKS

Antig. Caryst. *Mir.* Antigonus of Carystus (Keller)

Aristoph. *Plut.* Aristophanes *Plutus*

Demetrius *Eloc.*

Horace *Epp.* *Epodes*

Pind. *Isthm.* Pindar *Isthmian Odes*
Nem. *Nemean Odes*
Olympian *Olympian Odes*

SLG Supplementum Lyricis Graecis (Page 1974)

SECONDARY TEXTS AND OTHER WORKS

Abel, E. (ed.) (1982) *Writing and Sexual Difference*, Sussex: Harvester.
Abel, E. and E.K. (eds) (1983) *The Signs Reader*, Chicago and London: University of Chicago Press.
Adkins, A.W.H. (1972) *Moral Values and Political Behaviour in Ancient Greece*, London: Chatto & Windus.
—— (1985) *Poetic Craft in the Early Greek Elegists*, Chicago: University of Chicago Press.
Allen, J. and Young, I.M. (eds) (1989) *The Thinking Muse: Feminism and Modern French Philosophy*, Bloomington and Indianapolis: Indiana University Press.
Allen, W. Sidney (1973) *Accent and Rhythm*, Cambridge: Cambridge University Press.
Althusser, L. (1972) *Lenin and Philosophy and Other Essays*, trans. B. Brewster, New York: Monthly Review.
Arthur, M.B. (1984) 'Early Greece: The Origins of the Western Attitude Toward Women', in *Women in the Ancient World: The Arethusa Papers*, eds J. Peradotto and J.P. Sullivan, Albany: State University of New York Press: 7–58.
Bagg, R. (1964) 'Love, Ceremony and Daydream in Sappho's Lyrics' *Arion*, 3: 44–81.

Baldrick, C. (1992) *The Concise Oxford Dictionary of Literary Terms*, Oxford and London: Oxford University Press.

Balmer, J. (trans.) (1984) *Sappho, Poems and Fragments*, London: Brilliance Books.

Barrett, M. (1985) 'Ideology and the cultural production of gender', in *Feminist Criticism and Social Change*, eds J. Newton and D. Rosenfelt, New York and London: Methuen: 65–85.

—— (1989) 'Some different meanings of the concept of "difference"', in *The Difference Within*, eds E. Meese and A. Parker, Philadelphia: John Benjamins Publishing: 37–48.

Belsey, C. (1985) 'Constructing the subject: deconstructing the text', in *Feminist Criticism and Social Change*, eds J. Newton and D. Rosenfelt, London and New York: Routledge: 45–64.

Berger, J. (1978) *Ways of Seeing*, London: BBC and Penguin.

Bernikow, L. (ed.) (1984) *The World's Split Open: Women Poets 1552–1950*, London: Women's Press.

Beye, C.R. (1975) *Ancient Greek Literature and Society*, New York: Anchor Press.

Blok, J. and Mason, P. (eds) (1987) *Sexual Asymmetry*, Amsterdam: J. Gieben.

Boedeker, D. (1984) *Descent From Heaven: Images of Dew in Greek Poetry and Religion*, Chiko, California: Scholars Press.

Bold, A. (ed.) (1983) *The Sexual Dimension in Literature*, London: Vision, Barnes & Noble.

Bowra, C.M. (1938) *Early Greek Elegists*, Cambridge: Harvard University Press.

—— (1961) *Greek Lyric Poetry*, Oxford: Clarendon Press.

Bremmer, J. (ed.) (1989) *From Sappho to de Sade: Moments in the History of Sexuality*, London and New York: Routledge.

Briffault, R. (1927) *The Mothers*, London: Cambridge University Press.

Burn, A.R. (1960) *The Lyric Age of Greece*, London: Edward Arnold.

Burnett, A.P. (1983) *Three Archaic Poets: Archilochus, Alcaeus, Sappho*, Cambridge: Harvard University Press.

—— (1985) *The Art of Bacchylides*, Cambridge: Harvard University Press.

Cairns, F. (1971) *Generic Composition in Greek and Roman Poetry*, Edinburgh: Edinburgh University Press.

Calame, C. (1977a and b), *Les Choeurs de Jeunes filles en Grèce archaïque*, 2 vols, Rome: Edizioni dell'Ateneo & Bizzarri.

Caldwell, R. (1989) *The Origin of the Gods*, New York: Oxford University Press.

—— (1990) 'The Psychoanalytic Interpretation of Greek Myth', in *Approaches to Greek Myth*, ed. L. Edmonds, Baltimore: Johns Hopkins University Press: 342–92.

Cameron, D. (1985) *Feminism and Linguistic Theory*, London: Macmillan.

Cambell D.A. (1982a) *See under* Primary Sources.

Campbell, D.A. (1982b) *Greek Lyric Poetry: A Selection of Early Greek Lyric, Elegiac and Iambic Poetry*, Bristol: Bristol Classical Press.

—— (1983) *The Golden Lyre: The Themes of the Greek Lyric Poets*, London: Duckworth.

Cantarella, E. (1987) *Pandora's Daughters: The Role and Status of Women in Greek and Roman Antiquity*, trans. M.B. Fant, Baltimore: Johns Hopkins University Press.

Carey, C. (1978) 'Sappho Fr. 96 LP', *Classical Quarterly* 28: 366–71.

Carson, A. (1986) *Eros the Bittersweet: An Essay*, Princeton: Princeton University Press.

—— (1990) 'Putting Her in Her Place: Woman, Dirt, and Desire', in *Before Sexuality: The Construction of Erotic Experience in the Ancient Greek World*, eds D.M. Halperin, J.J. Winkler and F.I. Zeitlin, Princeton, New Jersey: Princeton University Press: 135–70.

Case, S.-E. (1988) 'Traditional History: A Feminist Deconstruction', in *Feminism and Theatre*, Hampshire: Macmillan: 5–42.

Cixous, H. (1981) 'Sorties', in *New French Feminisms*, eds E. Marks and I. de Courtivron, Brighton: Harvester Press: 90–8.

—— (1988) 'Extreme Fidelity', in *Writing Differences: Readings from Hélène Cixous*, ed. S. Sellers, Oxford: Alden Press: 14–25.

Cixous, H. and Clément C. (1986) *The Newly Born Woman*, trans. B. Wing, Minneapolis: University of Minnesota Press.

Cornford, F.M. (1957) *From Religion to Philosophy: A Study in the Origins of Western Speculation*, New York: Harper and Row.

Cranny-Francis, A. (1992) *Engendered Fiction: Analysing Gender in the Production and Reception of Texts,* Kensington: New South Wales University Press.

Creed, B. (1981–3) 'Pornography and Pleasure: The Female Spectator', *Australian Journal of Screen Theory*, 9-16, Issue 15/16: 67–88.

Daly, M. (1978) *Gyn/Ecology: The Metaethics of Radical Feminism*, Boston: Beacon Press.

Davenport, G. (1980) *Archilochus, Sappho, Alcman: Three Lyric Poets of the Late Greek Bronze Age*, Berkeley and Los Angeles: University of California Press.

Davison, J.A. (1968) *From Archilochus to Pindar*, London: Macmillan.

Dean-Jones, L. (1991) 'The Cultural Construct of the Female Body in Classical Greek Science', in *Women's History and Ancient History*, ed. S.B. Pomeroy, Chapel Hill: University of North Carolina Press: 111–37.

de Beauvoir, S. (1975) *The Second Sex*, trans. H.M. Parshley, Harmondsworth: Penguin.

DeJean, J. (1989) *Fictions of Sappho 1546–1937*, Chicago and London: University of Chicago Press.

de Lauretis, T. (ed.) (1987) *Technologies of Gender: Essays on Theory, Film, and Fiction*, Hampshire and London: Macmillan.

Derrida, J. (1975) 'The Purveyor of Truth', trans. W. Domingo, J. Hulbert, M. Ron and M.-R. Logan, *Yale French Studies* 52: 92–108.

—— (1978) *Writing and Difference*, trans. A. Bass, Chicago: University of Chicago Press.

Detienne, M. (1977) *The Gardens of Adonis: Spices in Greek Mythology*, Sussex: Harvester Press.

Devereux, G. (1970) 'The Nature of Sappho's Seizure in Fr. 31 LP as Evidence of Her Inversion', *Classical Quarterly* 20: 17–31.

Diehl, J.F. (1978) '"Come Slowly – Eden": An Exploration of Women Poets and Their Muse', *Signs* 3, Vol. 3: 572–87.

Dover, K.J. (1976) *Greek Popular Morality*, Oxford: Blackwell.

—— (1978) *Greek Homosexuality*, London: Duckworth.

Dowden, K. (1989) *Death and the Maiden: Girls' Initiation Rites in Greek Mythology*, London and New York: Routledge.

Duban, J.M. (1983) *Ancient and Modern Images of Sappho*, Lanham: University Press of America.

duBois, P. (1982) *Centaurs and Amazons: Women and the pre-history of the great chain*, Ann Arbor, Michigan: University of Michigan Press.

—— (1984) 'Sappho and Helen', in *Women in the Ancient World: The Arethusa Papers*, Albany: State University of New York Press: 95–106.

—— (1988) *Sowing the Body: Psychoanalysis and Ancient Representations of Women*, Chicago: University of Chicago Press.

—— (1991) *Torture and Truth*, New York: Routledge.

Dudley, M.I. and Edwards, M.I. (eds) (1986) *The Cross-Cultural Study of Women*, New York: Feminist Press.

Eagleton, M. (ed.) (1986) *Feminist Literary Theory: A Reader*, Oxford: Blackwell.

Eagleton, T. (1983) *Literary Theory: An Introduction*, Minneapolis: University of Minnesota Press.

—— (1986) *Criticism and Ideology*, London: Verso, Thetford Press.

Edmonds, L. (ed.) (1990) *Approaches to Greek Myth*, Baltimore: Johns Hopkins University Press.

Figueira, T.J. & Nagy, G. (1985) *Theognis of Megara: Poetry and the Polis*, Baltimore: Johns Hopkins University Press.

Finnegan, R. (ed.) (1978) *The Penguin Book of Oral Poetry*, Harmondsworth: Penguin.

Foley, H.P. (ed.) (1981) *Reflections of Women in Antiquity*, New York: Gordon & Breach.

Foster, H. (ed.) (1983) *The Anti-aesthetic: Essays on PostModern Culture*, Washington: Bay Press.

Foucault, M. (1972) *The Archaeology of Knowledge*, trans. A. Sheridan Smith, New York: Harper Torchbooks.

—— (1987) *The History of Sexuality, Volume II, The Use of Pleasure*, trans. R. Hurley, Harmondsworth: Penguin.

Fowler, A. (1982) *Kinds of Literature*, Cambridge: Harvard University Press.

Fowler, R.L. (1987) *The Nature of Early Greek Lyric: Three Preliminary Studies*, Toronto: University of Toronto Press.

Freud, S. (1900) *Standard Edition of the Complete Psychological Works*, trans. J. Strachey, London: Hogarth Press.

Friedrich, P. (1978) *The Meaning of Aphrodite*, Chicago: University of Chicago Press.

Gardiner, J.K. (1983) 'On Female Identity and Writing by Women', in *The Signs Reader*, eds E. and E.K. Abel, Chicago and London: University of Chicago Press: 177–92.

Garner, S.N., Kahane, C. and Sprengnether, M. (eds) (1985) *The (M)other Tongue*, Ithaca and London: Cornell University Press.

Gaters, M. *Feminism and Philosophy: Perspectives on Difference and Equality*, Bloomington and Indianapolis: Indiana University Press.
—— (1983) 'A Critique of the Sex-Gender Distinction', in *Beyond Marxism*, eds. J. Allen and B. Patton, Sydney: Intervention: 142–60.
Gentili, B. (1988) *Poetry and its Public in Ancient Greece: From Homer to the Fifth Century*, trans. A. T. Cole, Baltimore: Johns Hopkins University Press.
Gerber, D.E. (1970) *Euterpe: An Anthology of Early Greek Lyric, Elegiac and Iambic Poetry*, Amsterdam: Hakkert.
—— (1982) *Pindar's Olympian One: A Commentary*, Toronto: University of Toronto Press.
—— (1984) *Greek Poetry and Philosophy*, Chico, California: Scholars Press.
Gimbutas, M. (1974) *The Goddesses and Gods of Old Europe*, London: Thames and Hudson.
Gold, B.K. (1987) *Literary Patronage in Greece & Rome*, Chapel Hill: University of North Carolina Press.
Greer, G. (ed.) (1988) *Kissing the Rod: An anthology of seventeenth-century women's verse*, London: Virago.
Grosz, E. (1989) *Sexual Subversions: Three French Feminists*, Sydney: Allen & Unwin.
—— (1990) *Jacques Lacan: A Feminist Introduction*, Sydney: Allen & Unwin.
—— (1994) *Volatile Bodies: Towards a Corporeal Feminism*, Sydney: Allen & Unwin.
Guillen, C. (1971) *Literature as a System,* Princeton: Princeton University Press.
Guthrie, W.K.C. (1969) *A History of Greek Philosophy*, 3 vols, Cambridge: Harvard University Press.
—— (1978) *The Greek Philosophers: from Thales to Aristotle*, London: Methuen.
Hallett, J.P. (1979) 'Sappho and Her Social Context: Sense and Sensuality', *Signs* 3, Vol.4: 447–67.
Halperin, D.M. (1990a) *One Hundred Years of Homosexuality*, New York and London: Routledge.
—— (1990b) 'Why Is Diotima a Woman? Platonic *Eros* and the Figuration of Gender', in *Before Sexuality*: 257–308.
Halperin, D.M., Winkler, J.J. and Zeitlin F.I. (eds) (1990) *Before Sexuality: The Construction of the Erotic Experience in the Ancient Greek World*, Princeton, New Jersey: Princeton University Press.
Halporn, J.W., Ostwald, M. and Rosenmeyer, T.G. (eds) (1963) *The Meters of Greek and Latin Poetry*, London: Methuen.
Harland, R. (1987) *Superstructuralism*, London: Methuen.
Havelock, E.A. (1963) *Preface to Plato*, Cambridge: Harvard University Press.
—— (1986) *The Muse Learns to Write*, New Haven: Yale University Press.
Hawkes, J. (1968) *The Dawn of the Gods*, London: Chatto & Windus.

Hawkes, T. (1986) *Structuralism and Semiotics*, London: Methuen.
Heath, S. (1978) 'Difference', *Screen* 19: 50–112.
Heidegger, M. (1971) *Poetry, Language, Thought*, trans. A. Hofstadter, New York: Harper & Row.
Henderson, J. (1988) 'Greek Attitudes to Sex', in *Civilisation of the Ancient Mediterranean: Greece and Rome*, eds. M. Grant and R. Kitzinger, New York.
Hernaldi, P. (1972) *Beyond Genre*, London: Cornell University Press.
Hess, B.B. and Ferree, M.M. (eds) (1987) *Analysing Gender*, California: Sage Publications.
Higginbotham, J. (ed.) (1969) *Greek and Latin Literature*, London: Methuen.
Hine, D. (trans.) (1972) *The Homeric Hymns*, New York: Athenaeum.
Hooker, J.T. (1977) *The Language and Text of the Lesbian Poets*, Innsbruck: Beiträge zur Sprachwissenschaft.
Hunter, D. (ed.) (1989) *Seduction and Theory: Readings of Gender, Representation and Rhetoric*, Urbana and Chicago: University of Illinois Press.
Irigaray, L. (1977) 'Women's Exile', in *Ideology and Consciousness* No.1: 62–76.
—— (1978) Interview, *Les femmes, la pornographie, l'érotisme*, eds M.-F. Hans and G. Lapouge, Paris: Seuil: 43-58 and 302–4.
—— (1984) *Éthique de la différence sexuelle*, Paris: Minuit.
—— (1986) *This Sex Which Is Not One*, trans. C. Porter with C. Burke, Ithaca and New York: Cornell University Press.
—— (1987) *Sexes et parentés*, Paris: Minuit.
Jacobus, M. (ed.) (1979a) *Women Writing and Writing About Women*, London: Croom Helm.
—— (ed.) (1979b) 'The Difference of View', in *Women Writing and Writing about Women*: 10–21.
Jameson, F. (1983) 'Postmodernism and Consumer Society', in *The Anti-Aesthetic: Essays on Postmodern Culture*: 111–25.
Jardine, A.A. (1985) *Gynesis: Configurations of Woman and Modernity*, Ithaca and London: Cornell University Press.
Jay, N. (1981) 'Gender and dichotomy', *Feminist Studies*, 7, 1: 38–56.
Jenkins, R. (1982) *Three Classical Poets: Sappho, Catullus, and Juvenal*, London: Duckworth.
Johnson, W.R. (1982) *The Idea of Lyric*, Berkeley and Los Angeles: University of California Press.
Jones, A.R. (1985) 'Writing the Body: toward an understanding of l'écriture féminine', in *Feminist Criticism and Social Change*, eds J. Newton and D. Rosenfelt, New York and London: Routledge: 86–101.
Jung, C.G. (ed.) (1968) *Man and His Symbols*, London: Aldus Books.
Kaplan, E. Ann (1983) 'Is the Gaze Male?', in *Powers of Desire: The Politics of Sexuality*, eds A. Snitow, C. Stansell and S. Thomson, New York: Monthly Review Press: 309–27.
—— (ed.) (1988) *Postmodernism and its Discontents*, London and New York: Routledge.
—— (1990) *Psychoanalysis and Cinema*, New York: Routledge.

Kappeler, S. (1986) *The Pornography of Representation*, Cambridge: Polity Press.

Kauffman, L.S. (1986) *Discourses of Desire: Gender, Genre, and Epistolary Fictions*, Ithaca: Cornell University Press.

Kelly, J. (1984) *Women, History & Theory: The Essays of Joan Kelly*, Chicago and London: University of Chicago Press.

Kinnear, M. (1982) *Daughters Of Time*, Michigan: University of Michigan Press.

Kirk, G.S. (1963) 'A Fragment of Sappho Reinterpreted', *Classical Quarterly* 13: 51–52.

Kirk, G.S., Raven, J.E. and Schofield, M. (1983) *The Presocratic Philosophers: A Critical History with a Selection of Texts*, Cambridge: Cambridge University Press.

Kirkwood, G.M. (1974) *Early Greek Monody: The History of a Poetic Type*, Ithaca: Cornell University Press.

Klein, M. (1975) *The Psycho-analysis of Children, Volume II*, trans. A. Strachey, revised by H.A. Thorner, New York: The Free Press.

Klintz, L. (1989) 'In-different Criticism, the Deconstructive "Parole"', in *The Thinking Muse*, eds J. Allen and I.M. Young, Bloomington and Indianapolis: Indiana University Press: 113–35.

Kolodny, A. (1985a) 'A Map for Rereading: Gender and the Interpretation of Literary Texts', in *The New Feminist Criticism,* ed. E. Showalter, New York: Pantheon Books: 46–63.

—— (1985b) 'Dancing Through the Minefield: Some Observations on the Theory, Practice and Politics of a Feminist Literary Criticism', in *The New Feminist Criticism*, ed. E. Showalter, New York: Pantheon Books: 144–67.

Konstan, D. (1994) *Sexual Symmetry: Love in the Ancient Novel and Related Genres*, Princeton, New Jersey: Princeton University Press.

Kristeva, J. (1976) 'Signifying Practice and Mode of Production', *Edinburgh Review* 1.

—— (1981) 'Oscillation between Power and Denial', in *New French Feminisms: an anthology*, eds E. Marks and I. de Courtivron, Brighton: Harvester Press: 165–7.

—— (1984) *The Revolution in Poetic Language*, trans. M. Waller, New York: Columbia University Press.

—— (1986) 'Women's Time', in *The Kristeva Reader*, T. Moi (ed.), trans. A. Jardine and H. Blake, London: Blackwell: 187–213.

Lacan, J. (1975) *Encore: Le séminaire XX*, Paris: Seuil.

—— (1977) *Écrits: A Selection,* trans. A. Sheridan, London: Tavistock.

Lang, A. (trans.) (1972) *The Homeric Hymns*, New York: Books For Libraries Press.

Laqueur, T. (1990) *Making Sex: Body and Gender from the Greeks to Freud*, Cambridge and London: Harvard University Press.

Lardinois, A. (1989) 'Lesbian Sappho and Sappho of Lesbos', in *From Sappho to de Sade*, ed. J. Bremmer, London and New York: Routledge: 15–35.

Lattimore, R. (trans.) (1971) *Greek Lyrics*, Chicago and London: University of Chicago Press.

—— (trans.) (1976) *The Odes of Pindar*, Chicago: University of Chicago Press.

Lefkowitz, M.R. (1973) 'Critical Stereotypes and the Poetry of Sappho', *Greek, Roman and Byzantine Studies* 14: 113–23.

—— (1976) *The Victory Odes: An Introduction*, New Jersey: Noyes Press.

—— (1981a) *The Lives of the Greek Poets*, Baltimore: Johns Hopkins University Press.

—— (1981b) *Heroines and Hysterics*, London: Duckworth.

—— (1986) *Women in Greek Myth*, London: Duckworth.

Lesky, A. (1966) *A History of Greek Literature*, London: Methuen.

Levi, P. (1985) *The Pelican History of Greek Literature*, Harmondsworth: Penguin.

Levinas, E. (1986) *Face-to-Face with Levinas*, New York: State University of New York Press.

Lloyd, G. (1984) *The Man of Reason: 'Male' and 'Female' in Western Philosophy*, London: Methuen.

Lloyd, G.E.R. (1966) *Polarity and Analogy: Two Types of Argumentation in Greek Thought*, Cambridge: Cambridge University Press.

Lloyd-Jones, H. (1975) *Females of the Species: Semonides on Women*, London: Duckworth.

Loraux, N. (1987) *Tragic Ways of Killing a Woman*, trans. A. Forster, Cambridge and London: Harvard University Press.

McConnell-Ginet, S., Barker, R. and Furman, N. (eds) (1980) *Women and Language in Literature and Society*, New York: Praeger Publishers.

McEvilley, T. (1971) 'Sappho, Fragment Ninety-four', *Phoenix*, Vol. 25: 1–11.

—— (1972) 'Sappho, Fragment Two', *Phoenix*, Vol. 26: 23–33.

—— (1973) 'Sapphic Imagery and Fragment 96', *Hermes* 101: 257–78.

McMillan, C. (1982) *Women, Reason and Nature: Some Philosophical Problems with Feminism*, Princeton, New Jersey: Princeton University Press.

Marcovich, M. (1972) 'Sappho Fr. 31: Anxiety Attack or Love Declaration', *Classical Quarterly* 22: 19–32.

Marks, E. and de Courtivron, I., (eds) (1981) *New French Feminisms: an anthology*, Brighton: Harvester Press.

Meese, E. and Parker, A. (eds) (1989) *The Difference Within: Feminism and Critical Theory*, Philadelphia: John Benjamins Publishing.

Miller, J.A. (ed.) (1988) *The Seminar of Jacques Lacan*, Volumes I and II, New York: Norton.

Mitchell, J, and Rose, J. (eds) (1982) *Feminine Sexuality: Jacques Lacan and the École Freudienne*, London: Macmillan.

Moi, T. (ed.) (1985) *Sexual/Textual Politics: Feminist Literary Theory*, London: Methuen.

—— (1986) *The Kristeva Reader*, Oxford: Blackwell.

Morris, M. (1982) 'A-mazing Grace: Notes on Mary Daly's Poetics', *Intervention* 16: 70–92.

Mulvey, L. (1975) 'Visual Pleasure and Narrative Cinema', *Screen* 16: 6–18.

—— (1989) *Visual and Other Pleasures*, London: Macmillan.

Nead, L. (1992) *The Female Nude*, London and New York: Routledge.

Newton, J. and Rosenfelt, D. (eds) (1985) *Feminist Criticism and Social Change*, New York and London: Methuen.

Norris, C. (1982) *Deconstruction Theory and Practice*, London: Methuen.

—— (1986) *Deconstruction: Theory and Practice*, London and New York: Methuen.

Nye, A. (1988) *Feminist Theory and The Philosophies of Man*, New York: Croom Helm.

Ortner, S.B. (1973) 'Is Female to Nature as Nature Is to Culture?', in *Women, Culture and Society*, eds M.Z. Rosaldo and L. Lamphere, Stanford: Stanford University Press: 65–87.

Owens, C. (1983) 'The Discourse of Others: Feminists and Postmodernism', in *The Anti-aesthetic: Essays on Postmodern Culture*: 57–82.

Pack, R.A. (1965) *The Greek and Latin Literary Texts from Greco-Egypt*, Ann Arbor, Michigan: University of Michigan Press.

Page, D.L. (1950) *Select Papyri*, Cambridge: Harvard University Press.

—— (1955) *Sappho and Alcaeus*, London: Oxford University Press.

—— (1979) *Alcman: The Partheneion*, New York: Arno Press.

Parker, H.N. (1993) 'Sappho Schoolmistress', *Transactions of the American Philogical Association* 123: 309–51.

Peradotto, J. and Sullivan, J.P. (eds) (1984) *Women in the Ancient World: The Arethusa Papers*, Albany: State University of New York Press.

Podlecki, A. (1984) *The Early Greek Poets and Their Times*, Vancouver: University of British Columbia Press.

Pollitt, J.J. (1972) *Art and Experience in Classical Greece*, Cambridge: Harvard University Press.

Pomeroy, S.B. (1975) *Goddesses, Whores, Wives, and Slaves: Women in Classical Antiquity*, New York: Schocken Books.

—— (ed.) (1991) *Women's History and Ancient History*, Chapel Hill and London: The University of North Carolina Press.

Prato, C. (1968) *Tyrtaeus*, Rome: Edizioni Dell'Ateneo.

Preminger, A.W.H. (1965) *Encyclopedia of Poetry and Poetics*, Princeton, New Jersey: Princeton University Press.

Rabinowitz, N.S. and Richlin, A. (eds) (1993) *Feminist Theory and the Classics*, New York and London: Routledge.

Redfield, J. (1978) 'The Women of Sparta', *Classical Journal* 73: 146–61.

—— (1990) 'From Sex to Politics: The Rites of Artemis Triklaria and Dionysos Aisymnetes at Patras', in *Before Sexuality*: 115–34.

Rhode, D.L. (ed.) (1984) *Theoretical Perspectives on Sexual Difference*, New Haven and London: Yale University Press.

Rich, A. (1978) *The Dream of a Common Language*, New York: Norton.

—— (1983) 'Compulsory Heterosexuality and Lesbian Experience', in *The Signs Reader*: 139–68.

Rogers, W.E. (1983) *The Three Genres and The Interpretation of Lyric*, Princeton, New Jersey: Princeton University Press.

Rose, H.J. (1959) *A Handbook of Greek Mythology*, New York: Dutton.

Rosmarin, A. (1985) *The Power of Genre*, Minneapolis: University of Minnesota Press.

Rossi, A. (1976) 'Children and Work in the Lives of Women' (paper delivered at the University of Arizona, Tucson), in *The Signs Reader*: 139.

Rousselle, A. (1988) *Porneia: on desire and the body in antiquity*, Oxford: Blackwell.

Russo, J. (1974) 'Reading the Greek Lyric Poets (Monodists)', *Arion*, Vol. 1: 707–30.

Sartre, J.-P. (1976) *Being and Nothingness: An Essay on Phenomenological Ontology*, trans. H.E. Barnes, London: Methuen.

Segal, C. (1974) 'Eros and Incantation: Sappho and Oral Poetry', *Arethusa*, Vol. 7: 139–60.

Segal, L. (1988) *Is the Future Female? Troubled Thoughts on Contemorary Feminism*, London: Virago.

Selden, R. (1986) *A Reader's Guide to Contemporary Literary Theory*, Sussex: Harvester Press.

Sellers, S. (ed.) (1988) *Writing Differences: Readings From Hélène Cixous*, Oxford: Alden Press.

Shaktini, N. (1989) 'Displacing the Phallic Subject', in *The Thinking Muse*: 195–210.

Sissa, G. (1990a) 'Maidenhood without Maidenhead: The Female Body in Ancient Greece', in *Before Sexuality*: 339–64.

—— (1990b) *Greek Virginity*, trans. A. Goldhamer, Cambridge: Harvard University Press.

Skinner, M. (1993) 'Woman and Language in Archaic Greece, or, Why Is Sappho a Woman?', in *Feminist Theory and the Classics*: 125–44.

Smith-Rosenberg, C. (1983) 'The Female World of Love and Ritual: Relations between Women in Nineteenth-Century America', in *The Signs Reader*: 27–56.

Snell, B. (1953) *Discovery of the Mind*, trans. T. G. Rosenmeyer, Oxford: Blackwell.

—— (1981) *Poetry and Society*, Bloomington: Indiana University Press.

Snitow, A., Stansell, C. and Thomson, S. (eds) (1983) *Powers of Desire*, New York: Monthly Review Press.

Snyder, J.M. (1989) *The Woman and the Lyre: Women Writers in Classical Greece and Rome*, Bristol: Bristol Classical Press.

—— (1991) 'Public Occasion and Private Passion in the Lyrics of Sappho of Lesbos', in *Women's History and Ancient History*: 1–19.

—— (1994) 'The Configuration of Desire in Sappho Fr. 22 L.P., *Helios* 1: 3–8.

Spacks, P.A.M. (1975) *The Female Imagination*, New York: Alfred A. Knopf.

Spender, D. (1980) *Man Made Language*, London: Routledge.

—— (1982) *Women of Ideas and What Men Have Done to Them*, London: Routledge.

Spivak, G.C. (1987) *In Other Worlds: essays in cultural politics*, New York: Methuen.

Stanley, K. (1976) 'The Role of Aphrodite in Sappho Fr. 1', *Greek, Roman and Byzantine Studies* Vol. XVII: 305–21.

Stehle, E.S. (1990) 'Sappho's Gaze: Fantasies of a Goddess and Young Man', *Differences* 2: 88–125.

Stigers, E.S. (1977) 'Retreat from the Male: Catullus 62 and Sappho's Erotic Flowers', *Ramus*, Vol.6: 83–103.

—— (1979) 'Romantic Sensuality, Poetic Sense: A Response to Hallett on Sappho', *Signs* 3, Spring 1979: 465–71.

—— (1981) 'Sappho's Private World', in *Reflections of Women in Antiquity*: 45–61.

Stone, M. (1976) *The Paradise Papers: The Suppression of Women's Rites*, London: Virago, in association with Quartet Books.

Strelka, J.P (ed.) (1978) *Theories of Literary Genre*, Pennsylvania: The State University Press.

Suleiman, S.R. (1986) *The Female Body in Western Culture*, Cambridge: Harvard University Press.

Talalay, L.E. (1994) 'A Feminist Boomerang: The Great Goddess of Greek Prehistory', *Gender & History* Vol. 6, No. 2: 165–83.

Thalmann, W.G. (1984) *Conventions of Form and Thought in Early Greek Epic Poetry*, Baltimore: Johns Hopkins University Press.

Thomson, G. (1929) *Greek Lyric Metre*, Cambridge: Cambridge University Press.

Threadgold, T. and Cranny-Francis, A. (eds) (1990) *Feminine/Masculine and Representation*, Sydney: Allen & Unwin.

Todorov, T. (1973) *The Fantastic*, trans. R. Howard, Cleveland: The Press of Case Western Reserve University.

Trypanis, C.A. (1981) *Greek Poetry From Homer to Seferis*, London: Faber & Faber.

Tsagarakis, O. (1977) *Self-Expression in Early Greek Lyric, Elegiac and Iambic Poetry*, Wiesbaden: Franz Steiner.

Turner, E.G. (1980) *Greek Papyri*, Oxford: Clarendon Press.

Van Gennep, A. (1960) *The Rites of Passage*, trans. M.B. Vizendom and G.L. Caffee, London: Routledge.

Vernant, J.-P. (1983) *Myth and Thought among the Greeks*, London and Boston: Routledge.

—— (1989) 'Dim Body, Dazzling Body', in *Fragments for a History of the Human Body, Part One*, eds M. Feher, R. Naddaff and N. Tazi, New York: Urzone: 19–47.

—— (1990) 'One . . . Two . . . Three: *Eros*', in *Before Sexuality*: 465–78.

Vlahos, O. (1979) *Body the Ultimate Symbol: Meanings of the human body through time and place*, New York: Lippincott.

Wedeck, T.E. (1969) *Late Latin Writers and Their Greek Sources*, Cambridge: Harvard University Press.

Welleck, R. and Warren, A. (eds) (1980) *Theory of Literature*, Harmondsworth: Pelican Books.

West, M.L. (1974) *Studies in Greek Elegy*, Berlin: Walter de Gruyter.

—— (1980) *Delectus ex Iambis et Elegis*, London: Oxford University Press.

—— (1982) *Greek Metre*, Oxford: Oxford University Press.

—— (1987) *An Introduction to Greek Metre*, Oxford: Clarendon Press.

White, H. (1978) *Tropics of Discourse: Essays in Cultural Criticism*, Baltimore and London: Johns Hopkins University Press.

Whitford, M. (1991) *Luce Irigaray: Philosophy in the Feminine*, London and New York: Routledge.
Whitmont, E.C. (1987) *Return of the Goddess*, London: Arkana.
Wills, G. (1967) 'Sappho 31 and Catullus 51', *Greek, Roman and Byzantine Studies*, Vol. 8: 167–97.
Winkler, J.J. (1981) 'Gardens of Nymphs: Public and private in Sappho's lyrics', in *Reflections of Women in Antiquity*: 63–89.
—— (1990) *Constraints of Desire: The Anthropology of Sex and Gender in Ancient Greece*, New York: Routledge.
Winkler, J.J. and Zeitlin, F.I. (eds) (1990) *Nothing to Do with Dionysus: Athenian Drama in Its Social Context*, Princeton, New Jersey: Princeton University Press.
Wittig, M. (1992) *The Straight Mind and Other Essays*, Boston: Beacon Press.
Wolff, J. (1990) *Feminine Sentences: Essays on Women and Culture*, Cambridge: Polity Press.
Worthington, I. (ed.) (1994) *Persuasion: Greek Rhetoric in Action*, London and New York: Routledge.
Zeitlin, F.I. (1981) 'Travesties of Gender and Genre', in *Reflections of Women in Antiquity*: 169–213.
—— (1982) 'Cultic Models of the Female: Rites of Dionysos and Demeter', *Arethusa*, Vol. 15, 2: 129–57.

Index